BORGES

The Passion of an Endless Quotation

Lisa Block de Behar

*Translated
and with an introduction by
William Egginton*

STATE UNIVERSITY OF NEW YORK PRESS

Published by
State University of New York Press, Albany

© 2003 State University of New York

For information, address State University of New York Press,
90 State Street, Suite 700, Albany, NY, 12207

Production by Diane Ganeles
Marketing by Patrick Durocher

Library of Congress Cataloging in Publication Data

Block de Behar, Lisa
  [Borges, la pasión de una cita sin fin. English]
  Borges, the passion of an endless quotation / Lisa Block de Behar ; translated
and with an introduction by William Egginton.
    p. cm. — (SUNY series in Latin American and Iberian thought and culture)
  Includes bibliographical references and index.
  ISBN 0-7914-5555-6 (hb.: alk. paper) — ISBN 0-7914-5556-4 (pbk.: alk
paper)
    1. Borges, Jorge Luis, 1899—Criticism and Interpretation. 2. Quotation in
literature. I. Title. II. Series.

PQ7797.B635 Z6344213 2002
868'.6209—dc21   2002017575

10 9 8 7 6 5 4 3 2 1

Contents

Acknowledgments

I would like to thank the following people for the time and expertise they generously provided: Rosemary Geisdorfer Feal, Jorge Gracia, Michael Rinella, and Diane Ganeles for their enthusiastic response to my proposal; David Johnson for his invaluable criticism of earlier drafts; Bernadette Wegenstein for her comments on the introductory essay; Miguel Fernández Garrido for his input in the translation; Sepp Gumbrecht for having the idea of this collaboration; and above all Lisa Block de Behar, for her beautiful book and for her patient help and support at all stages of work on the translation.

The Interpretive Fix and the Fixations of Fiction

The *Ars Interpretans* of Lisa Block de Behar

William Egginton

B arthes once wrote that the only way to read a work of passion is with another work of passion. What was true for Barthes is equally true for Lisa Block de Behar, whose three or more decades of scholarly activity have produced an imposing body of scholarship on the work of Jorge Luis Borges, but more important and more urgently have resulted in the invention of a new way of thinking about the activity of reading, and the nature of meaning itself. If I may recur to a historical analogy, and one that is not without heuristic value for the case at hand, Block de Behar's relation to the texts of Borges is redolent of that of Heidegger to the poetry of Hölderlin. Having practiced fundamental ontology from the perspective of and in the language of philosophical discourse, albeit in a way that overturned the most basic presuppositions of that discourse, the Heidegger of the late thirties began to produce a kind of writing that refused to speak *about* Being, from the *outside*—as if one could have a vantage from which to see and speak that was itself not already *in* and *of* Being. Such a writing—one that would take seriously Heidegger's discovery that language does not report on beings but is rather the house of Being[1]—is exemplified not by philosophers and the history of their craft, but by the poets, and it was in the words of Hölderlin that Heidegger believed he could best listen to Being as it uttered the meanings of our most basic words.

By beginning with this analogy, I do not want to suggest that Block de Behar is a Heideggerian, or that she applies the thoughts of Heidegger to the works of Borges, in the now classic and utterly bankrupt application-paradigm of literary studies, in which the would-be critic sprinkles a dry literary text with a healthy dash of some spicy theory in order to serve it up fresh, and with newfound panache. Indeed, to say of her work that it applies a paradigm to the text of Borges is to miss one of the most fundamental of her insights, namely, that in his writing Borges anticipates the theoretical and philosophical currents of the late twentieth century, not merely in the sense of announcing their arrival *avant la lettre,* but more importantly by creating the very archetypes of thought that define our times. First comes poetry, then comes thought.

No, Block de Behar does not apply anything to Borges, but rather, like Heidegger did to Hölderlin, she listens to the poet, and hears in his writing the meanings of our most basic words. Rejecting the focus common to the scholarship around Borges—her work does not dwell on the plethora of metaphors associated with Borges's work, such as tigers or labyrinths or mirrors—what Block de Behar explores is the *originality* of Borges's imagination, one that finds its personal discourse in the propriety of words, in the fire of their minting. This, in fact, is the argument— if one can call it an argument, for Block de Behar seldom argues, choosing rather to read, to combine, to explore—of her 1994 book, *Una palabra propiamente dicha (A Word Properly Said),*[2] which proposes a reading style appropriate to the specificity of Borges's literary style. This would be a practice of comprehension entailing an activation of the primordial meanings of Borges's words, a peeling off the patina of everyday use and semantic localization, and a reaching for a transversal and plurilinguistic semantics that constitutes the core of Borges's originality, but also of his universality.

Primordiality, originality, universality—all of these concepts ring strangely out of tune in a zeitgeist dedicated to simulacra, difference, contemporaneity, to the belatedness of all attempts to establish a claim to originality. But Block de Behar does not read Borges as either a critique or a confirmation of this zeitgeist, but rather as having articulated the very conditions of its possibility. Originality as a key notion for understanding Borges—and this is the theme of her 1998 book, *Borges ou les gestes d'un voyant aveugle (Borges or the Gestures of a Blind Seer)*[3]—is neither a signifier of extravagance nor a designator of primacy, but denotes rather the poetic property and propriety of the revelation of that which disperses or disappears behind and among appearances, representations. And this thing, in the end, is not the thing in itself, a world stripped bare of the illusions of representation, but is rather the very intimacy of language and things that can never be dispersed, but only hidden by the certainties of positivism or the desperation of idealism. And is not this intimacy resonant with the linguistic horizons that make up the house of Being?

Much as her explorations of Borges's writing problematize the notion of a representational space separating words and things, Block de Behar's analysis of the reading practices suggested by Borges's work—and much of her contribution must be seen as a stylistics of reading, a poetics of the very production of meaning—deflate the categorical boundaries between production and reception. The theme of her first book on the subject of Borges—*Una retórica del silencio (A Rhetoric of Silence)*[4]—constituted a meditation on the figure of the reader and the reader's practice in the writings of Borges, and not merely as represented in those writings but, moreover, as presupposed by them. Pursuing this figure throughout Borges's oeuvre and especially in his "Pierre Menard, autor del Quijote," Block de Behar unearths a narrative whose protagonist is the inexistent author of a silent work, a narrative in which the hallowed boundaries between author and reader are blurred into nondistinction, merged into one and the same silence. But silence is not wordlessness. It is the suspension of the voice as a tacit verbal object, the guarantor of author's presence and hence authority, and thereby the jailer of unauthorized meaning. In the space of this suspension, then, a reader is constituted and reconstituted through the endless recombination of the written word. While this liberation of writing from the tyranny of voice is certainly the critical legacy of Derrida, we owe its poetic legacy in part to Borges, and to the careful reading of Block de Behar.

It is against the background of these and other rhetorical visions that Lisa Block de Behar has, in this book, turned her "readerly" attentions to the figure of the quotation. In many ways, it is in this figure that all of the themes that have characterized her work of reading to date are crystallized in their paradoxical plenitude, for is it not in the quotation that the issue of originality reaches its ultimate limit? As countless texts from Borges intimate, the search for originality must come up against the quotation as the figure of its own impossibility, and yet it is quoting itself—an act that merges reading and writing, in short, sense-making—that constitutes a break, a moment of *creatio ex nihilo* where something comes to be—a difference in pure repetition—where something was not before. Borges quotes innumerable authors in the pages making up his life's work, and innumerable authors have quoted and continue to quote him. More than a figure, then, the quotation is an integral part of the fabric of his writing, a fabric made anew by each reading and each re-citation it undergoes, in the never ending throes of a work in progress. Block de Behar makes of this reading a plea for the very art of communication, a practice that stakes community not in the totalized and totalizable soil of preestablished definitions or essences, but on the ineluctable repetitions that constitute language as such, and that guarantee the expansiveness—through etymological coincidences of meaning, through historical contagions, through translinguistic sharings of particular experiences—of a certain index of universality. Divergent times, places, spaces, scenes are brought suddenly and irreparably together in the ever-expanding library of Borges's words. "Words, words, words," Hamlet responds when Polonius asks him what he reads. Pressed on what the "matter" of those words might be, Hamlet replies, "Between who?" capturing in the inappropriateness of his answer that is also a question the interminable flight of the very meaning, or matter, Polonius seeks.[5] For is not that matter sought in words the very matter that disappears between two authors, two characters of Borges? Pierre Menard writes the very words written by Cervantes so many years ago, and in the immaterial difference between those same words a world of difference intervenes.[6] Words, words, words, when will they ever end? They will not; and it is this, and nothing else, that is the meaning of eternity.

In *Of Grammatology* Derrida writes, about the "tradition's" attitude toward writing:

> Writing is the dissimulation of the natural, primary, and immediate presence of sense to the soul within the logos. Its violence befalls the soul as unconsciousness. Deconstructing this tradition will therefore not consist of reversing it, of making writing innocent. Rather of showing why the violence of writing does not befall an innocent language. There is an originary violence of writing because language is first, in a sense I shall gradually reveal, writing. "Usurpation" has always already begun. The sense of the right side appears in a mythical effect of return.[7]

Of course, if language per se, language proper is, properly speaking, not innocent of the violence attributed to writing—its secondary nature, its perversion of intention, its homophonic, anagrammatic failures, and so on—then the question is begged of who or what is innocent, is innocence (is proper, per se, as such . . .). And lacking the primordiality of the innocent, the notion of violence itself seems curiously out of place. Indeed, for Block de Behar the engagement of writing and reading, as interlaced, mutually supporting and ultimately similar procedures, is an association that has lost the aggressivity of the initial assault on metaphysical presence. Hers is a poetics of creation that is at the same time a poetics of disappearance; a poetics of production that is equally a poetics of nothingness; a poetics of interpretation that is one with a poetics of *preterition*.

Preterition: the *Oxford English Dictionary*'s third definition, from rhetoric, runs thus: "A figure by which summary mention is made of a thing, in professing to omit it"; yet for Block de Behar, this figure becomes the paradoxical foundation of the production of meaning, and of interpretation itself. To negate a thing while at the same time affirming it; to affirm something while negating it. Preterition captures, for Block de Behar, the paradoxical core of how language works to produce meaning. The word names, and in naming takes away. It supplies an absence, which it has created, with a presence that leads to an absence, to the positive creation of another lack, which in turn produces a positivity. It will not be possible to categorize Block de Behar along with those Deleuze and Guattari christened as the priests of lack.[8] Her writing refuses to grant even negativity its privative power, since in the very instant of privation, in the very move itself, creation occurs, meaning is restored, albeit differently, anew. This movement is the very movement of human being itself: interpretation. In Block de Behar's world, *Homo ludens* becomes *homo interpretans*.

Thus *interpreterition* would seem to be the bastard child waiting to be born of these concepts, a construction not lacking a creative drive that occults, once again, a mutual origin, albeit one that defies etymological verification. The *pret* that is the root in common, the binding core between prefix and suffix, could claim a basic meaning in the Latin present preterite *praeterire*, to pass, to go by; the leaving behind while mentioning that presents us with the operative paradox of preterition; the passing through or, originally, translating—moving from one side to another—that the interpretive activity signified. But interpretation's root is the Sanskrit *prath*, signifying the action of spreading out, hence a spreading out between two or more in other places, in other circumstances, a spreading which would entail a passing through, and perhaps a passing by, a mentioning and invoking while negating and leaving behind, hence an *interpreterition*.

In its interpreteritional, and one might add original, manifestation, then, interpretation no longer connotes a search for an established or preexisting meaning, but rather a communicative (also in the sense of contagious) act of passage between—states, entities, times, spaces—and creation of—the same, which is at the same time the different. The root—and hence rational—*pret* of passing and spreading, passes and spreads between a pre*fix* of liminality, lability, and a suf*fix* of fixity, two fixes that mark the extremes of the movement of fixation, a movement that is itself that of interpretation, the movement from the labile to the fixed, and back again.

The rhetoric of preterition is thus also at work in the word *fix,* from the Latin, *figere,* originally meaning to fasten, to rivet one's eyes or attention on something, connoting the stoppage of a movement, or a tight place from which one needs to escape. Simultaneously, in current (North) American usage, it has come to denote the dosage of illicit drugs one needs, and hence is lacking, to regain a sense of fixity, stability, the homeostasis that Freud defined as the negation of pain.[9] Think of the psyche and the soma as interrelated, analogously comparable organic networks, living, changing networks of interconnected elements. The introduction of a narcotic like heroine into such a system produces an imbalance, a lability, which moves the organism to rewire itself and incorporate the new element into a newly established fixity. The disappearance of the narcosis provokes another change in the new fixity, a sensation of pain requiring the return of the lost element, the fix, in order to reestablish the new, albeit ultimately unstable, temporal, fixity. If the soma has a primal, primordial (perhaps imaginary) balance, the fix unfixes that balance, provokes a permanent flux between pleasure and pain. The psyche, because it is stratified, organized, is at a remove from the balanced soma (the plane of consistency, a body without organs, Deleuze and Guattari would call it), is always in flux; the psyche is a body on drugs. Its fix, however, is interpretive, a momentary fixation that, if were free ourselves from the self-imposed limits of etymological orthodoxy—the addition or subtraction of a letter, an *n,* almost a nothing, marks the difference between *figere* and *fingere,* to make believe— comes to us most often in the form of a fiction, one of those infinite possible worlds we hunger for in the delirium of our withdrawal from meaning.

We have mentioned Freud. Is not the "talking cure" in some sense the ultimate interpretive fix? The interpretation, especially in Lacanian practice, need not be an explanation, a putting into words of a symptom so as to make the symptom go away, as in the traditional, more hermeneutically inclined understanding of the practice. A Lacanian analyst enters into a theatrical relation with the analysand; roles are played, a fantasy formation is assumed; the analysand plays out in the transference, a verbal bridge between two subjects, the spectacle of his or her daily life, complete with deeply held convictions, emotions that graft to the skin of the ego. A hack, a cough, an interjection on the part of the analyst, and something breaks into the carefully constructed world of the transference: an interpretation, a moment of breakdown and reorganization, what Lacan calls presence.[10] The network is liminal again, and searches for a new fixity. The fix is experienced as meaning, as revelation, as truth, but this truth did not precede the event; it was generated by the fix.

Another recent book explores the interpretive fix through a sort of experiment in code building. In Christian Reder's (and in the spirit of Block de Behar we should remain attentive to the resonance of names, Reder, the one who speaks . . .[11]) latest book, *Words and Numbers, the Alphabet as Code,*[12] a simple, and plainly arbitrary—that is, unmotivated, as Saussure famously described the relation between words and their referents—encoding matrix is established: each letter in the Latin alphabet is assigned a number from one to twenty-six. The resulting schema becomes a sort of table of elements for the production of meaning, a meaning which is no less meaningful for the contrivance of its origins. What this artificial (*künstlich*) combinatory underscores is that the naturalness or artificiality of results tends to ride on the plausibility of correspondences between interpretation-formations and result-formations rather than on the correspondence to a preestablished truth, or reality,[13] an implicit understanding of thought that joins with the pragmatic philosophy of a Gilles Deleuze, a Richard Rorty[14] (both of whom are referred to in Reder's introduction), but also a Jacques Derrida and a Lisa Block de Behar, in their insistence on the primacy of creative activity over representative mirroring. As Deleuze and Guattari put it: "Concepts are not waiting for us ready-made, like heavenly bodies. There is no heaven for concepts. They must be invented, fabricated, or rather created and would be nothing without their creator's signature."[15]

What strikes us as unusual in our hyperskeptical, hypersecular present is the turn that this recentering of the interpretive activity makes toward unification, universalization, the resurrection of seemingly esoteric discourses, like that of Kabbalah,[16] and the seriousness of the attention paid to mere coincidence. Borges, Bioy Casares, Benjamin, and Blanqui are combined, truths are to be sought for in their combination because . . . because their names all begin with the letter *b*? Is this astrology masquerading as criticism? There is a revival of astrology going around under the name the Human Design System. Practitioners consult with their clients and offer them readings on the basis of a map constructed out of key temporal and spatial coordinates in their life. This interpretation refuses to be unmotivated in its self-presentation because its motivation, like astrology, is to be found in the influence of time and space, of astronomical events, on our genetic and emotional make up. The functioning is similar to a psychic "reading," where in this case the "chance" of the cards is replaced or occulted by the influence of spirits, or perhaps even to a psychoanalytic reading, where the chance of a combinatory of words is occulted by the truth of the unconscious, the "it speaks." The occultation, of course, is part of the combinatory; just as in psychoanalysis there can be no transference without a subject supposed to know, in every other interpretive fix, the act of interpretation requires a moment of occultation, and a moment of revelation. But in the open interpretive play of interpreterition, what lies beneath is not a fixity but another act of interpretation, beneath each reading lies another reading, beneath each book another book, beneath each word another word.

> We spoke of the anagrammatic strategy that consists of a reread-ing, a re-vision, a *sub-version* that is realized underneath the words (a paragram or hypogram in the terms of Saussure, or *les mots sous les mots,* for Jean Starobinski), a transposition of the graphic unities of the word that responds to the procedures of selection and combination, a combinatory of decisions of that lector-elector-selector who recuperates in each reading (lecture) the freedom of an option that revises and defines it.[17]

Reading practices, which are also writing practices, are, like the other interpretive fixes we have discussed, exercises in self-discovery that is at the same time a self-creation. The resolution of coordinates involved in each such act, a reading, is pulled together out of another form, like the word out of chaos. But chaos is not primordial, as Block de Behar also points out; the operations of chance that seem to lie at the origin of all these reading practices are themselves the result of a demonic "falling through" out of the divine and into the human form, a form defined by its separation from the divine, just as the divine is resolved through the expulsion of the human, and the demonic. This falling produces the purity of chance, and its legacy is recorded in our languages.[18]

Borges's text is, for Block de Behar, the palimpsest reservoir of this resolving act, of the precipitation of meaning out of a primordial soup of chance, which is likewise and retroactively born of that same movement. The games, the ruminations, the thoughts, the verses, the narratives, in short the interpreteritions are innumerable, and so they must be. For the interpretive fix is not merely explained with examples, it cannot be thus put to rest; we do not read *of* such a process from the fixity of the language of criticism, but rather participate *in* it, repeatedly, inescapably, as that lan-guage changes us, and changes itself through us as well.

CHAPTER ONE

First Words

Even at the risk of falling into redundancies from the start, one would have to recognize, once again, the gravitation of quotations in Borges's universe, where, unbeholden to time, though without eluding the facts of their origin, quotations allow for the repetition of several discourses at once. On more than one occasion, Borges affirmed the literary fatefulness of his destiny and, assuming that task, recognized the precedence of a writing that cannot avoid the quotation. Literary repetition reiterates and demands the affinities of a shared place, more than shared place, a common place, which—beyond distances and circumstantial differences, and on the basis of verbal coincidences—is conducive to signs of universality.

A balance of unsuspected reciprocities impels us to appreciate and recognize this repetition as a proper practice: if Borges quotes innumerable authors in his works, it should not surprise us that innumerable authors continue to quote Borges. Recourse and recurrence, from one author to the other: literary passion manages to order itself around quotations that animate an inconclusive textual game.

Borges's library multiplies, in parts, the books of others in his books and his in those of others, accumulating the potential of a partial, endless literary play. Reading Borges, one makes out the parts of disparate works, and that shared discovery—a discovery parceled between author and reader—lends itself to more than one meaning. Someone glimpses the revelation of a distant fragment, and comes to be glimpsed in turn. Fragments come and go as if transported by an endless band in which oppositions are knotted and annulled, reconciled by the same passion for quoting.

This back and forth of the quotation replicates the literary ritual, or rituals, of circulating. It is a curious tendency of quotations that they are quoted, as if each one, once invoked, reserved the imminence of a potential quoting, which is mentioned for its energy, for its efficacy, or simply because it can occur. Its simple occurrence refers it to a previous instance, like to a past time, but pointed toward a text or time to come. It returns to the beginning, only to circle back again.

Despite the secret to which Borges ambiguously refers in his story, the narrator belonging to "The Sect of the Phoenix"[1] knows that this textual reproduction seals literary continuity via the quotation; literal, in silence, the species is not extinguished. In the same way that the sense of this story is doubled, so should we understand the ambivalence of the quotation's meaning.

These are dualities that Spanish, in its good fortune, does not dissimulate: "cita" [quotation, rendezvous] designates a meeting—more than a meeting—of the text or of the heart, and, as a result of the complicity of this meeting, other passions rush forth. The words of a text mingle and cohabitate in another text and thus do they survive. If it is true that a book does not choose its lectors, it is the "e-lection" that the latter realize that affords the book an unforeseen permanence, beyond the disposition of a presumable authority. Therefore, it is not surprising that one of the century's most quoted authors should be an unknown author—one who does not exist—of a well-known book—which already existed; the quote legitimates the ambivalencies of its open statute. Borges's character, Pierre Menard,[2] consecrated reader and author, writes not another *Quijote* but the *Quijote* of another: letter for letter, word for word, its identical paragraphs authorize a meaning that modifies, according to different versions, a truth in terms. This eventual alteration of the truth is found precisely in a text that deals with truth conditioned by history; the references to the discipline make of the theme and of the discourse that articulates it one and the same hermeneutic question.

This is not an objection, on the contrary; nevertheless, one may observe that, for a long time now, Borges has been quoted too much. It is true that his lines are repeated in other pages and that passages, verses, words to which Borges restored original meaning appear in contexts that reveal, or not, the origin that the poet demands: "Every word was once a poem,"[3] and, in the same way that only the word remembers, its reiterated use attenuates the origin.

Repetition is a phenomenon that lacks novelty, as is known; in any case—and this has also been said—novelty is rooted only in the return, which suggests that the recognition of the quotation is especially appropriate—in Borges's text, with Borges—for the celebration of a centennial.[4] In its repetition it calls for suspension in a timeless time, a return to a placeless space that, as the ceremony punctually authorizes, rescinds the circumstances.

If, for Borges, quotations reveal that authors are readers who rewrite what has already been written, those turnings that found and shape his poetics approach the doctrine that Borges shared, according to which Paradise exists under the species of a library. Without departing from it, I would invoke an old maxim belonging to Talmudic interpretations that attribute to the loyalty of the quotation the recuperation of a time that courts eternity. "All who utter the words in the name of the one who uttered them"[5] not only provoke their own salvation, but also initiate a redemption without end.[6]

CHAPTER TWO

Variations on a Letter *Avant-la-Lettre*

Seul le chapitre des bifurcations reste ouvert à l'espér-
ance. N'oublions pas que tout ce qu'on aurait pu être ici-
bas, on l'est quelque part ailleurs.

(Only the chapter of bifurcations remains open to hope.
Let us not forget that all that we could have been down
here, we are somewhere else.)

Louis-Auguste Blanqui[1]

I

If the aesthetic, theoretical, and hermeneutic present is debated in the
face of the indeterminacy of works that slip between the expansive
spaces of a disputable disciplinary topography; if epistemological definitions question its limits and its doctrinal and methodological foundations;
if questions of taxonomy challenge the rigidity of inventories that fail to
encompass the inventions they seek to classify; nor oppositions justify
series because they interlace them, accelerating their differences; if other
uncertainties are not exclusive of the scientific present; perhaps it is not
necessary to remind ourselves that, since more than a half a century ago,
numerous thinkers, philosophers, and writers have been reading Borges.
They hesitated at first, interpreting as metaphors the aporias of his rhetoric of indecision, as allegories the paradoxical variations of a poetics of
preterition that grasps the imagination of possibilities and their opposites,
convinced, like some of the characters of his fiction, that historical times
interlace their differences, multiplying uncertainties, planting suspicions,
filtered through an unpredictable network that intercepts them as much as
it lets them pass through.

5

Just as *after Borges*[2] it is no longer disputed that each author creates his or her own precursors,[3] it is even less disputed that Borges creates other authors who follow him, read him, who write and therefore exist. So many poets and narrators, so many theoreticians and critics are occupied with the imagination of Borges, that the imagination of Borges has occupied the world. Understandably, a long time after Emir Rodríguez Monegal[4] wrote down the illustrious terms of that "greatest common denominator" that is his *name*, a North American critic proposed to nominate Borges as the emblem of this era.[5] There is no question about it: In such a case, I would carve in that emblematic image the inscription *ante litteram*.

It is not unusual to approach the variations of his literature's reasoned aesthetics, the diverse modulations of his intellectual poetry, which anticipated and concentrated the thought, knowledge, and imagination of the century, attending to the reticencies contained in a *transgressive writing* that has been alluded to more than once, but whose excesses would recuperate the original meaning of "to transgress": to pass to the other side, traverse margins, cross borders, *go beyond*—also in capitals, transitions that cede way to the *transcendence* that is, properly speaking, an ascension to universal terms, by which it overcomes categories, oppositions, the eventuality of differences. A contradictory transgression overcomes limits or suspends them through a bringing into relief (*relevamiento*) that, like the well-known *Aufhebung*—that Hegelian form of "to bring into relief" (*relevar*)—is overcoming and suppression, both actions at once. It is important to bring into relief that first meaning of *to transgress* because, among other reasons, that is how to understand, in a contradictory way, that his writings "read with a previous fervor and a mysterious loyalty"; those conditions of reading that define, according to Borges,[6] the classical writers. An in-fraction restitutes the fracture, reunites the fragments, animates the vigor and validity of his writings. It is precisely in that essay, "On the Classics," where he concludes by formulating an assertion that I would introduce here as an exhortation, with the purpose of controverting a permanence that neither endorses nor invalidates transgression:

> The emotions that literature evokes are perhaps eternal, but the means must constantly change, even if only in the slightest way, in order not to lose their virtue. They expend themselves as they are recognized by the reader. Thus the danger of affirming that there exist classical works and that they will be so for ever.[7]

II

Beyond the functions of reader and critic, of author and critic, or of author and reader, Borges's writing melds attributions that are presumed to be external to the textual universe, interlacing them in a threshold that extends and disappears. Neither inside nor outside, neither before nor after. A diegesis in crisis alters the spaces and times of a textuality that does not distinguish between them. Beyond oppositions between language and metalanguage, between both, it is possible to imagine variations of a semiosis that, (a)posited in the abyss, confuses references, impeding the discerning of another way out through an exit facing inward, facing backward, at the same time or timelessly. Beyond disciplinary conventions, his writing slips between literary and philosophical borders, superimposing theory and poetry, history and fiction, representation and reference, lucidity that is not only wakefulness. Without imposing, without being excessive, a spectral entity—a specter in fact—oscillates between narrator and characters, victims and heroes, hangmen and traitors, between times that do not differ, return, or coincide in the simultaneity of an instant, an *Augenblick* that, deprived of time, is not distinguished from eternity: fleeing that threshold a man is discerned on the way to a universe where space does not count, nor time, who persists in creating a passage where extension and ephemerality are confused in a reality *au-delà, à outrance*, an ultrareality,[8] an ideal reality, perfect, eternal, exaggerated, extreme.

Beyond limits, the writing of Borges e-liminates them; beyond oppositions, it requires an interpretation, succinct, in the key of *O*; different *or* the same, either the letter *or* the cipher, *or* both, it obliterates the disjunction making of alterity another identity. His imagination does not resolve the antagonism of superimpositions, suppositions, conjectures; it invents or discovers the literary space that makes place for an origin, the beginning (*principio*) of a thought that adjusts to the principles (*principios*) of a logic—if not proper, adverse, illogical—a logic that reveals the mechanisms of a reasoning secured according to rules that, albeit imposed, seem natural, or it seems natural that they be so.

What is missing are limits to this transliminal aesthetic, where definition coincides with the indefinite, the finished with the infinite, acceding to a perfection that, unexpected, does not end. In "Of Rigor in Science,"[9] the brief text (which could serve as epigraph to these reflections) endorses the cartographic practices of geographers who expose the perfection of their maps to the inclemencies of time and weather (*tiempos*), chronological or temporal, meteorological or the more intemperate storms of rain and wind that intensify beyond the times (*tiempos*) that neither grammar nor history can periodize. Another text, almost symmetrical, "The Parable of the Palace,"[10] reveals that that perverse *perfection* is not an exclusivity of rigorous sciences, and ends by risking poetry as well; the word of the poet that destroys the poem, the palace: "It was enough (they tell us) that the poet pronounce the poem for the palace to disappear, abolished and struck down by the last syllable."[11] The word (*palabra*) is the parable,[12] a "com*par*ison," a story, an *allegory* that, literally, is "another thing," but that other thing is also a word: in this story, the word (*palabra*) is *le palais*, the palace or the palate where the word (*palabra*) takes place, where it forms, and when it disappears, its disappearance drags everything with it: poet, poem, palace, parable/parabola, describing a movement, a geometric figure similar to the curve described by a projectile, or a parable/parabola similar to this plural figure. The perfection of poetry or the perfection of the cartographers' techniques insinuates the "intrusion of a fantastic world into the real world,"[13] where neither the incidences of fiction nor the networks of a parabolic or satellitic installation cause surprise. Between these networks is shaped a terminal reality, terminated, revoked by a voice that suppresses it while duplicating it, that re-vokes it (the semantics of the prefix are tricky) on the screens, in the words that are duplicated in a contradictory way, as in "the things [that] are duplicated in Tlön have a propensity to be erased and lose their details."[14]

Without outrage, without putting it in those terms, a canon such as that of Borges contests the canon. But more than joining with other contestations, its questionings are verified by arguments of a different nature from those arming the skirmishes of certain all-too-current, all-too-circumstantial academic debates. In the same essay on the classics he said:

> Thus my ignorance of Malay or Hungarian letters is complete, but I am sure that if time lent me the occasion to study them, I would find in them all the nourishment the soul requires. In addition to linguistic barriers, political or geographical barriers intervene.[15]

As well as including "*les phares*," visible, foreseeable, he illuminates authors scarcely known, discovers unknown authors, gives birth to others who, like J. Hládik in the Prague jail or like P. Menard in Nîmes, convert their success (*éxito*) into existence in a universal literature that now counts, among its glories, the statute of an author who does not exist celebrated for a work that also does not exist, signs of an apophantic poetics that, like negative theology, configures the critical and theoretical imaginary of this epoch. Borges brought together into one figure all the literary functions: just as he himself is, Menard is a reader; a critic; an author; a translator, according to some; in all cases a character. Menard exists *for* (*por*) Borges, and the Spanish preposition figures as cause, as substitution, and as multiplication, such is the fantastic polysemy of the preposition *por*: Borges for Menard, one author for another who does not exist; as if he multiplied by (*por*) zero, the number (*cifra*) that reunites all numbers, he exceeds him and exhausts him, he animates and annuls him at once.

The vanishing of the author in such functions long predates the overnight "mort de l'auteur" (death of the author)—the sentence is from Barthes who, like another death foretold, pronounces it on the basis of the accepted theories of writing.[16] A little later, on the basis of a related notion of *écriture*—although he extends it in certain ways—Michel Foucault pronounces a similar sentence by referring to "the disappearance of the author."[17] It was a great disappearance—it was not the first—but like the decree of an earlier, greater death, it precipitated the announcement of a chain of disappearances: the disappearance of poetry, a disappearance consecutive to other flagrant disgraces; the presumed and oft-proclaimed disappearance of history; or, in the best of cases, the claim of writing, which confers on it a status of fiction that neither the historians nor the writers would oppose. The disappearance of systematic difference, more rigid than rigorous, the disappearance of the *difference* in a writing that belittled even the voice,[18] which cannot even be heard amidst the bells tolling in mourning over the disappearance of absolute knowledge,[19] brought into relief by a *pensiero debole*,[20] disappearance of the referent as one more illusion. One had spoken of an *hors texte* like an *hors la loi*; it is not surprising that an aesthetics of disappearance that razes geographic and generic borders would have in the work of Borges its fabulous antecedent. In his texts, a cell in Prague borders on an entryway in Tacuarembó; a hovel in Cairo, Illinois; a slum of Buenos Aires; or a suburb of Dublin, it is all the same whether "in Oklahoma or Texas or in the region that the literati call the *pampa*."[21] If the latest edition of the *Encyclopedia Universalis* defines the current concept of globalization on the basis of a quote from P. Valéry: "Le temps du monde fini commence"[22] (The time of the completed world begins), any one of the numerous references imagined by Borges from his earliest to his most recent writings would have been more pertinent:

> But let us not speak of facts. Facts are no longer of any concern to anyone. They are mere starting points for invention and reasoning. In the schools they teach us doubt and the art of forget-

ting. Foremost the forgetting of what is personal and local. We live in time, which is successive, but we try to live *sub specie aeternitatis*. From the past we retain a few names, which language tends to forget. We pass over the useless details. There is neither chronology nor history. There are no statistics either.[23]

In that utopia of the story, although "English, French, and mere Spanish" had already disappeared from the planet, language is not the conjectural *Ursprache* of Tlön, because "the earth had returned to Latin." The anonymous character encountered by the narrator warns him that: "There are those who fear that it will once again degenerate into French, Languedocian, or Papiamento, but the risk is not imminent."[24]

For diverse reasons—critical and hermeneutic, philological or mystical—no one is surprised that the vastness of Borges's oeuvre could be identified, emblematically, with the *aleph*. More than the letter, more than the title, the story, the book, his whole oeuvre constitutes a sort of *aleph*, the first letter touching on an immense universe, the disproportionate *aleph* that is found, in places, in all places, before the beginning, before the creation, on whose account the beginning does not appear because something had already started before: a letter *avant la lettre? Ante litteram*. In Hebrew *aleph* represents, more than the letter, the inspiration prior to the production of sound, it points to the movement of the soul, a wish previous to its articulation; the Kabbalists always considered "the *aleph* the spiritual root of all letters, capable of containing in its essence the entire alphabet and, hence, all human language. 'Entendre l'Aleph, c'est proprement ne rien entendre'" [to hear/understand the Aleph is not to hear/understand anything],[25] and I turn to the French translation in order to take advantage of the verbal polysemy of a verb that, in that language, alludes to a form of grasping at once sensory and intellectual.[26]

Nevertheless, and to confirm the beginning/principle (*principio*) of that initial silence, it should not be surprising that the inquiries into the genesis of his text indicate that a space, the *mihrab*,[27] had preceded the literal, graphic, and Kabbalistic inscription of that letter. Because of that literal and figurative vision, a character of Borges, he who does not see— just as one says of Socrates, he who does not write, or of Plato, he who does not speak—sees all the earth and the whole earth sees him. The whole orb in the orbits, *urbi et orbi*. Which is the center and which the periphery in that excessive topography that suppresses the dimensions and distances that are its material? In a miniaturized domestication of the universe, the shaded enclosure, at home, in a point of the basement like the corner of the miserable hut of Funes, an enigmatic but square black hole, perhaps another *black hole*[28] where the stars of a "collapsing universe" are pulled apart, on the edge of the void, there where the world contracts, exposes itself to the horror of a blind window, of a screen like a blank page, which risks it, reveals it, hides it. A hole like an empty orbit, it becomes the bastion (*reducto*) of vision, the reduction of the visible, a résumé of the world or a receptacle where the world is concentrated into a fenced-in camp, a metaphor of the preelectronic prison, of a *prisonhouse*,[29] the prisonhouse of language where reality is held hostage by its vision. I wonder if someday someone will dare to say: "Once upon a time, there was reality . . ." as in a fairy tale, the narrator will create suspense and, condescendingly, will refer to reality like to the sleeping beauty, in a box with a crystal cover, beneath a transparent screen. Face to face, the *aleph* of Garay street, "where the entire universe was reflected"[30] threatened by demolition on the verge of disappearing; similar to the *aleph* on the forehead of the Golem, on which Judá Leon inscribed and, repentant, erased the first letter of the "simulacrum"[31] that he had made: "Made of consonants and vowels [. . .] in exact letters and syllables," the suppression of the first letter, like the suppression of a page in an encyclopedia, turns the truth (*emet*) into death (*met*), a country, a region, a continent, suppressed by a perfect version, exact (*cabal*), complete (*acabada*)—Kabbalah plays with the homophony of these letters, between them—or because it is missing a page: the *aleph*, the letter the Golem (Hebrew for an embryo, a larva, a being short of being; a mask in German[32]), the letter missing at the beginning (*bereshit*—Genesis—begins with *beth*), the title that announces that the world had begun before, before the beginning and its version. If the world was created by the letter, by the same cause, literally, it can disappear.

In 1980 Paul Virilio began to speak of an aesthetics of disappearance.[33] More than forty years earlier, the year in which Walter Benjamin committed suicide, Borges, in the story "Tlön, Uqbar, Orbis Tertius," and Bioy Casares, in *The Invention of Morel*[34]—"a perfect novel"[35] that crosses paths with that story—anticipated in a literary way that aesthetics of disappearance. A multiplied disappearance that the concentration universe would cast into the abyss, the endless precipice, that fall. "Impossible to write and think like before," says Giorgio Agamben;[36] or as Jean-François Lyotard says in the *Differend*,[37] the dilemma that has been faced by thought since the furthest reaches of time and remains detained in the *disgrace*, the dividing (*einteilen*) of a world that does not communicate (*mitteilen*), variants that do not belie the negation of Theodor Adorno,[38] to whom it perhaps did not seem necessary to negate history as well, because according to Hegel it had already come to an end in October of 1806.[39]

III

From his first books, Borges had shown his preoccupation with the relation between space and signification. But in place of the maximal minimal *aleph*, in *The Size of My Hope*[40]—that book that replicates in its title *The Size of Space*, the small volume that Leopoldo Lugones had written some years earlier on mathematical questions[41]—Borges had desired to accede, by way of the appropriation of the common tongue, to the singularity of each place (in space), of each time (in waiting, in hope), to a different idiomatic property, a language of his own, particular, which, as was already said, is the original meaning of *idiom*.[42]

At one time I had intended to analyze linguistically the impossible language (*idioma*) of Ireneo Funes; I wanted to formulate a semantics on the basis of words that, precisely because they were particular, like proper names, do not signify. Today it would be interesting to sketch out a different analysis of Borges's language, of a multilingual "Borgese" to which the transversality of his revelations is conducive. In the same way one says "the language of Cervantes" but in reverse, I would disfigure the metonymy such that in place of making reference to the language of all Spanish speakers, I could restrict it to a particular language, his, since it is that *original particularity* that we are talking about. The language of Borges both is and is not the language of Cervantes and, according to this contradictory ambivalence, Borges would be trying to approach a primordial language, at times via etymologies, at times dispensing with them:

> There are few disciplines as interesting as etymology; this is due
> to the unpredictable transformations of the primitive meaning of
> words across time. Given such transformations, which can
> border on the paradoxical, the origin of word will help little or
> not at all in the clarification of a concept.[43]

One would have to pause to consider the poetic reason of a signification that brings him close to the theories of Walter Benjamin, to the mysticism of his speculations, which lays the foundations of, among others, one of his greatest essays: "The Task of the Translator,"[44] "Die Aufgabe des Übersetzers" (utterance and demonstration of a task at once possible and impossible, since *Aufgabe* in German means both work and giving up). It is a question of one of the semantic dilemmas that preoccupied Borges and that distinguish his words with a universal poetic density. The comprehension of antebabelian language, edenic/adamic[45] because of his foreseeable blindness, the ironic association of this fate with access to a paradoxical Paradise, a species of library; the appropriation of his ancestors' iron language, which his blindness throws down into a crossroads of tongues: "the iron language"[46] similar to the "hard iron, the intimate knife at my throat"[47] ("Conjectural Poem"[48]), *un lenguaje blindado* ("blinded" and "armoured").[49] The translinguistic crossroads is prolonged in a series of names, proper or not, which reciprocally "untranslate" themselves: the red Adam, Red Scharlach, Escoto Erígena, or the Irish Irishman, and so many others.

If all thought is conjectural[50]—the thought and the declaration are Borges's—one of the conjectures I could formulate, apropos of thought and knowledge, would be as much a double conjecture as a double thought: in a certain sense, Borges knew how to reveal "the grace of thought" or "the grace of knowledge," the grace so needed by this twentieth century that fell into *disgrace*, because of the catastrophe that more than fifty years ago provoked the differend from which there is no exit. Perhaps it is pertinent to evoke, from the place of my double ignorance of Hebrew and Kabbalah, a procedure that the Kabbalists apply to the interpretations of texts. I refer to "tikkun,"[51] that restitution that demands prayer, in the middle of the night, imploring the restoration of the ruined temples, the urns broken like crystals in the night. More than a prayer, "tikkun" is the procedure that the lay lecture, *lega*,[52] cannot elude. All reading supposes an operation of fragmentation and the contrary operation, a reunion of fragments, the search for unity, the means to a restitution of *a* meaning that implies not a unique meaning but rather the union of meaning, one where the series commences and encompasses it, in unity, less secular, less fortuitous than other unities more celebrated in the last years.

From these perspectives, it was necessary that the restitution pass through German, through its idiom and, as Adorno said, when he pointed to the absurd lexical obstinacies of German that designates *philosophy* as *thought*, thus making a profit out of a deficiency.[53] To aspire, among so much disgrace, to return *grace*, to a restitution that language just like recent history still obliges and of which language is conducive. "La grace, par hypothèse, n'a pas de prix, peut-elle même s'obtenir?" (Grace, by hypothesis, has no price, can it even be obtained?).[54] Without avoiding the academic, epistemological exigencies of thought and knowing (*saber*), one would have to undertake to recuperate in thought *the grace/humor of thought* since, in their origin, it was impossible to distinguish them: *danken und denken* (to thank and to think) are terms that originate in the same voice: in old high German, *danc*. In the same way, one would have to recuperate in knowing *the grace of knowing*, since something similar occurs there, *Wissen* being not so different from *Witz*, the joke. In the end, in both cases, to claim to restore *the grace of knowledge* (*conocimiento*), or better yet, *cognizance* (or recognition), which was one of the forms of *gratia*, configuring a gesture or gratitude that passes through knowledge and duplicates it, fragmenting it along a semantic cleavage that tends not to be remembered.

They are more than coincidences, convergences of meaning in the biography of a word or the incidences of simultaneity in a single voice. *In a word*, I allude again, one more time, to the recuperation of an original meaning that accumulates, without attenuating the variations of other meanings, discovering a semantic synthesis that the fragmentation of use had disarticulated. Borges writes in Spanish, which is his language, although his *quête* or *quest*,[55] his search and questioning of universality orients his verbal imagination toward other languages and myths: he uses words in Spanish, but they can be understood in English, at times in other languages—in Hebrew, for example—a fate of translinguistic, poetic growth, because of which the same words sound, re-sound at the same time in different languages. It is one of the paths I could find in a Garden beyond or before, through which it is possible to transgress borders, and which erases them or bifurcates them: *une biffure*, as Lévinas said of thought: "La pensée est originalement *biffure*" [Thought is originally *bifurcation*],[56] the trace that crosses—erases—and symbolizes, at the same time, parts of a fractured piece that, when they coincide, incite a return to the illusion of the beginning.

CHAPTER THREE

Paradoxa Ortodoxa

Coincidences are inevitable since we are reading Derrida
and Plato on the basis of Borges.
—Emir Rodríguez Monegal,
"Borges and Derrida: Boticarios"

It is said that the pelican so loves her young that she puts
them to death with her claws.
—Honorius de Autun, *Speculum de mysteris ecclesiae*

Let us adore without understanding, said the priest.
So be it, said Bouvard.
—Gustave Flaubert, *Bouvard et Pécuchet*

In "Vindication of Bouvard and Pécuchet"[1] Borges considered
Flaubert's work to be a "deceptively simple story"; we could apply a
similar consideration to his story "The Gospel According to Mark."[2] But
the coincidences between Flaubert's work—an aberration, according to
some, "the greatest work of French literature and perhaps of all literature,"[3] according to others—and Borges's story are recognizable as something more than an appearance of shared simplicity. According to Borges,
Flaubert makes his characters read a library "so that they don't understand it,"[4] they (cornu)copy[5] it; also in "The Gospel according to Mark,"
Borges imagines the problems of a reading that is too loyal and, for this
reason, here too the risks of incomprehension should not be discarded.

The story begins by describing the primary narrative circumstances
of every introduction ("The deed occurred in the hacienda Los Álamos, in
the district of Junín, toward the south, in the last days of the month of
March of 1928"[6]), but this observation of conventional "beginnings"
constitutes a realist option in two ways: a beginning that adjusts itself to

15

the most conservative realism, which according to Roman Jakobson is the one on which he models his observations concerning the old canons;[7] and a minute and chronologically punctual geographic orientation. As far as Borges is concerned, the exaggeration of realist precision can only be a cause for suspicion. Perhaps it is more prudent to define this narration as realist *à outrance*, of an *outré* realism, better yet, an ultrarealism. (We will return to this definition.)

The character, Baltasar Espinosa, a student from Buenos Aires, is found summering at his cousin's hacienda when the storm crashes down, and the estuaries of an unforeseeable river-swell oblige him to remain in the heart of the hacienda, to share it with the foreman and his family—the Gutres—and to turn to the reading of the Gospel in order to attenuate the hostility of a forced conviviality, sidestepping by way of the (re)cited word as much the dubious proximity of dialogue as the discomforts of an inevitable circumspection.

Basically, the narrative situation ends up being quite similar to that of another story: "The Shape of the Sword."[8] In this piece as well the story transpired in a hacienda, La Colorada, it was called (although, as we may read in the previous quote from the edition of the complete works, the hacienda from "The Gospel According to Mark" is called "Los Álamos," in the first version it appears as "la Colorada"; the coincidence of the proper name cannot be ignored). But other, less striking similarities may be registered as well: the city/country opposition; inundation and isolation; involuntary closeness; the precarious Spanish of those living in the hacienda; the resistance to dialogue; the change and accumulation of narrative functions brought about by the participation of a character who takes on another narration and introduces in this way a second, distant—biblical or historical—diegesis. That introduction is crucial in that it unleashes an exchange of fundamental narrative functions: narrator for narratee; reader for characters, slippages that stratify the narration in chiasmas, weaving it into two crossed planes: in superposition and opposition, because the structure of "the circular ruins" is not only the fundamental literary articulation of the imaginative archeology of Borges but also the evidencing—by its narrative, by its poetics—of the referential fracture, the inevitability of breakdown through the phenomenon of signification. Representation as the point where the abyss opens: the sign is the origin of other signs, said Peirce, recognizing the il-limitation of semiosis as the path that, by way of the breakdown, precipitates the infinite:

One—which?—looked at the other
Like he who dreams he is dreaming.[9]

More than the common place of the Borgesian imaginary, these interlaced slippages reveal duality as a necessary condition of any literary text that, according to Derrida, prefigures its own deconstruction: presence for absence, absence for presence, truth for fiction: "any truth would be an illusion of which one forgets that it is an illusion," said Nietzsche, and there is no need to be surprised; "such truths do exist."[10]

The word installs a strategy of initiation; it is the origin, according to John, where all begins, but it would also be that revelation that begins the Apocalypse; from the beginning, the first word, "apocalypse" evokes the end: the revelation/destruction, origin and catastrophe, origin of the catastrophe, the word "apocalypse" initiating the Apocalypse recuperates the ambiguity that the mere mention convokes. "Je parle, donc je ne suis pas" (I speak, therefore I am not), Maurice Blanchot could have said.[11] If Peirce said "to know a sign is always to know something else," it would not be abusive to understand from this that to know a sign is always to know something different, something opposite. This is what Umberto Eco reiterates: "Starting from the sign, one goes through the whole semiotic process and arrives at the point where the sign becomes capable of contradicting itself (otherwise, those textual mechanisms called 'literature' would not be possible)."[12]

THE CONTRADICTIONS OF WRITING

> Littré dealt them the coup de grace affirming that there had never been a positive orthography and that there couldn't be one either. For this reason they arrived at the conclusion that syntax is a fantasy and grammar an illusion.
>
> —Flaubert, *Bouvard et Péchuchet*

In "Plato's Pharmacy," Jacques Derrida questions the contradictions that from antiquity to structuralism without interruption have denigrated the function of writing. He starts from Socrates, "he who does not write," who in *Phaedrus* traces the doubts as to the benefits of writing back to a remote Egyptian past. His contradictory ambivalence makes suspect Plato's claims about this invention of Theuth, and—even though his suspicion remains written—he does not hesitate to suspect a remedy that, created for the benefit of memory, damages it as much as it assists it; a *pharmakon*, at once remedy and poison, fixes and destroys it at the same time. "Because writing has neither an essence nor a value of its own, whether positive or negative. It acts in its simulacrum and mimes in its type, memory, knowledge, truth."[13] It is not truth because it imitates it; it is not knowledge but appearance; it is not memory but its fixation; nor the word because it silences it. Derrida deconstructs that logocentric obsession that tries to ignore the relevance of writing: its *reserve*. Nevertheless, it is that discretion and accumulation, disposition and prudence, that makes of its virtuality a virtue. Against time, writing fixes itself; it spatializes discourse, initiating controversy, giving way to an infinite textual openness: in this abyssal space time does not count. Reading departs from there, it withdraws (*se aparta*): "Reading has to begin in this unstable conmixture of literalism and suspicion"[14] and, when it is valid, it deconstructs it: "Reading [. . .] if strong is always a misreading,"[15] Harold Bloom contradicts himself, and this contradiction legitimizes the *potency* of interpretation, its power: the power to be; its possibility: the multiplication of a truth to the "nth" version. Neither literal nor notarial, concerning meaning there is no *property* but rather *appropriation* and confrontation; "the will to the contrary," which could be attributed to Nietzsche, is the condition and passion of the text. "Je suis le sinistre miroir // où la mégère se regarde"[16] (I am the sinister mirror // in which the harpy looks at herself), as if spoken by writing about itself, demanding a first person who is— "Thanks to voracious irony"[17]—subject and object of interminable contradictions. "I will speak of a letter"; thus Derrida declares the initiation of *differance* (these are the first words with which "Différance" begins), imposing in this way the introduction of the Derridean order: the letter as primordial referent, the letter that precedes speech: Derrida speaks of the letter.

From its origin—it was Theuth who invented it, either Theuth or Hermes or Mercury or Wotan or the great magician Odin, inventor of runes, god of war and god of poets; through writing the text debates; it is a debate, or it is not a text. Writing is fixed in a dual space, on the bias, between an inside and an outside, between imagination and reflection, between silence and silence, a space beyond, of transparence and tergiversation, where it (ex)poses itself in curious evidence, impugning "the fundamental epistemological metaphor: understanding as seeing,"[18] the flight of meaning, the fault through which it slips out, the failure that is neither error nor lack but rather an obstinate will to know and to be the truth.

TO HEAR ONESELF OR TEAR ONESELF AWAY: WHERE TO?

What did "the abyss that broke" and "the waterfalls from heaven" mean in Genesis? Because an abyss does not break and heaven has no waterfalls! [. . .] You must

remember, said Bouvard, that Moses exaggerated
demonically.

—Flaubert, *Bouvard et Pécuchet*

Oral discourse takes place in time, with time, like time, and these coincidences dissimulate in fluidity the abysmal breakdowns of meaning, reduce
interpretive possibilities, limit them, eliminating disconcert by a sort of
certainty: I understand because I hear, an epistemological metaphor
always more disputable albeit accepted. The suspicious Francophone
plausibility of *entendre* confounds comprehension with audition, sense
with the sensed, truth with presence, presence with the voice: "And all the
people are seeing the voices," the scriptures say,[19] and John, for his part,
transcribed the revelation of that strange vision: "Then I turned to see the
voice that spoke with me,"[20] as if the voice were sufficient: seeing in order
to hear, hearing in order to believe, are what counts as evidence. "For after
that in the wisdom of God the world by wisdom knew not God. . . . "[27]
But neither does ignorance guarantee that knowledge, as Pécuchet could
have reasoned, Pécuchet who, excited by his recent erudition, had begun
a record of the Bible's contradictions, even though he would not have proposed to deconstruct them.

The Gutres of Borges's story were illiterate, they barely knew how to
speak; Roberto Paoli speaks of their "almost zoological regression."[22] The
readings of *La Chacra*,[23] of the veterinarian manual, of *The History of the
Shorthorns in Argentina*, or of *Don Segundo Sombra*, that Baltasar
Espinosa tried to present them did not interest them. The triviality of the
stories was not distinguishable from those they lived every day: on the
contrary, when dealing with the country, they preferred their own adventures as cattlemen. In reality there was no difference. Nevertheless, when
he began to read the *Gospel According to Mark*, "perhaps to see if they
understood anything [. . .], he was surprised that they listened to it with
attention and then with hushed interest. [. . .] It reminded him the elocu-
tion classes he had received in Ramos Mejía and he stood up to preach the
parables."[24] Espinosa proceeds like Mark: he does not limit his version to
referring to deeds but rather preaches while dramatizing them: to be precise, his discourse converts the tale into action.

The naive attention of his listeners was foreseeable. They are listen-
ing for the first time to a tale; that tale refers to the story of Jesus Christ;
the initiation could not be better. Furthermore, the circumstances of this
reading reinforce credulity: they hear, they do not read. More still than the
philosophical arguments of Plato, of Rousseau, or of Saussure, objected to
by Derrida, mentioned so often by the deconstructivists, the live reading
of revealed truth concentrates in *logos* its privileged polysemy. The

eloquent conviction of Borges's character sums up the differences, in his voice is everything: reason, thought, knowledge, word, sacred word, the word of God. For these listeners—who are also unaware of the works of deconstruction—the logocentric priority is verified once again as the coincidence of voice and presence: truth in person. Logos as origin and foundation of being converts the Gutres, converts their credulity into credence. In "The Gospel According to Mark," Borges presents a sacred parody of conversion via the word: the revealed logos reveals, mediating between man and things, erasing the differences between nature/culture, country/city, barbarity/civilization. Perhaps Borges would have shared the fantasy that Walter Benjamin creates on the basis of *Angelus Novus*— a painting made by Paul Klee that belonged to him—as to the determining force of names that, in addition to representing the secret personal identity of the individual, conditions his or her biography and work.

Barthes does not exaggerate when he understands the disposition to write (a "mise en writing" we could say) to begin when Proust finds or invents proper nouns: "Once this system was found, the work wrote itself immediately."[25] It is not only for Proust that the class of proper nouns— the Name—presents "the greatest constitutive power." Cratylus[26] was already suspicious of a kind of onomastic Platonism that might as well be a patronymic, which, beyond designative singularity, more than the name of the Father that gives name to a family, configures a model that anticipates and determines nature and essence with different fates: "The proper Name is, in this way, the linguistic form of reminiscence."[27]

In poetic matter, the proper noun is not a meaningful hole but rather the very gesture of *vocation*,[28] the voice on the basis of which starts the process of gestation as a presence and a concomitant absence, since every vocation implies its opposite, and in-vocation, the appellation of an absence. Just as Barthes affirms that it is possible to say, poetically, that Proust's entire oeuvre emerged from a few names, we can risk the attribution of "that catalysis of an infinite richness"[29] to the proper name of the author who motivates[30] the work or rather—and it is not different—*motivates* by way of the work the name: "The author of Percival would be 'a Christian of Troy'?,"[31] Lautréamont would be the pseudonym of the other of Montevideo, in French, l'autre à Montevideo? Jorge Luis Borges would be the man on the border, an oxymoron between two spaces, the countryside, like in the Georgics, and the city as in the boroughs? The story's theme alludes to this confrontation.

If, in ordinary language, different from the common noun, the proper noun attains regularly to a particular designation, extracting itself in that way from the universality of the concept, in literary space the expansion of meaning comes to recuse the linguistic statute of the proper name and, with a double edge, becomes more proper[37] and more universal than ever. As literary interpretation aims to discover or invent meanings, this practice takes advantage of the semantic void in order to fill it with the greatest signification. In this way, from an a-semantic extreme, and authorized by textualization—by the operations that appropriate and are appropriated by the text—proper nouns slip easily toward a meaningful plenum. The onomastic motivation that the author attributes to his characters extends beyond the text and contaminates with meaning the proper name of the author too, who does not belong to the text itself, although he configures its constitutive frame. Everything comes to signify, as much the textual center as its borders. From the same zone, marginal and anterior to the work, Leopoldo Lugones inserts between the prologue and his poems the epigraph of *El lunario sentimental*, illustrating by way of the title the "nobility" of a procedure that, within the literary species, categorizes the proper noun above both the common and the proper:

In the old days
The Lugones were called Lunones
Because these men came
From Great Castle, and wore
The moon on their heralds.
[Tirso de Avilés, *Blasones de Asturias*][33]

When the literary condition is recognized the verbal movement is interesting, and it is double. For the poetic word, the author or interpreter claims two attributions: he or she makes proper the common noun and common the proper noun. Also inspired by "French reflections," Geoffrey Hartman formulates the hypothesis that the literary work constitutes the elaboration of a specular name, the proper.[34] Borges—Georgie to his friends—celebrates in his work a name that recalls both the agricultural labors of the *Georgics*, and the boroughs, or towns, and their echoes, reuniting the extremes. When one mentions to him such a determination, he is also delighted by the specular coincidences of his name and its literary consequences.

Different from other "read readers" (subject and object of reading, who read and are read),[35] the characters of "The Gospel According to Mark" are not properly readers because, assigning all privilege to the voice, they do not observe the silent condition of reading. Double error: neither voice of presence nor silence of reading. A case not foreseen by

Plato but that Borges encounters, records, invents. Borges and his own invent-ory, "Borges, the apothecary."[36]

This privilege of the *phoné* is not fortuitous. In *De la grammatologie*, Derrida attributes it to a *"s'entendre parler"* (hear oneself speaking, understand oneself speaking) where the immediacy of discourse, the evanescence of the oral word, the intangible properties of the phonic substance have brought about the confounding of the oppositions concerning the signifier as nonexternal, nonmaterial, nonempirical, noncontingent, capable of direct access to thought, to truth, an immediacy that neutralizes differences between outside/inside, visible/intelligible, universal/nonuniversal, transcendent/empirical.

A LITERAL DIFFERENCE

How to transmit to others the infinite Aleph that my fearful memory barely grasps?

—Jorge Luis Borges, *The Aleph*

One letter alone can contain the book, the universe.

Edmund Jabès, *Ça suit son cours*

In an earlier piece,[37] apropos of some narrative contrasts between "The Aleph" and "The Zahir," I tried to observe the extremes of an alphabetic order capable of reducing the initial totality of the orb to the wastes of a final fixity. I quoted Gershom Scholem, who defines the aleph "as the spiritual root of all letters and of that from which derive all the elements of human language,"[38] an aspiration that anticipates the articulation of sound, but implicated by the Borgesian imaginary. That "aspiration" of the aleph exceeds its literal rootedness. Without negating its nature (phonetic or physiological), aspiration extends to another form of realization, is understood as a wish, the breath of a desire, the profound aspiration, the "inspiration" that animates. The aleph is, at least, a double aspiration: a respiratory movement, a movement of the soul. Generator of energy, anterior and initial, the aleph identifies two instances of one and the same principle, instances that cipher the double key of the origin,[39] the place where the text begins: the key of aperture and a key that—as in the score—registers the interpretation, because in interpretation are found the aperture and the key. Wish and aspiration, principle and key, soul and life; I am not loathe to read in the aleph a form of totality. Edmond Jabès did not refer to the *aleph* but to the *a*, and although he does not express it, perhaps he had already speculated about these transcendent coincidences of the aleph when he defines the difference that Derrida notes, or takes note of. Without naming it, he warns: "So is it that in the word difference (différence), a letter, the seventh, was exchanged for the first letter of the alphabet, in secret, silently. Sufficient for the text to be another,"[40] or for the text to be.

In the same way as Derrida, Edmond Jabès does not formulate simply a claim for writing, but rather, recognizing its emergence, he deconstructs the illusion that impedes our distinguishing among logos-truth-presence. In French, the substitution is neither heard nor said; it is hardly even written: différence/différance, and in that operation—substitution without suppression—is verified its relevance. The a for the e. More than substitute, the preposition multiplies: $a \times e$, a substitution that multiplies the meaning of the word. It produces a dissemination of meaning that, because of it, shimmers and shatters, dispersing univocal interpretation, disarticulating definitively whatever definition. There is no origin, nor center, nor end; whatever solution, whatever exit is illusory, or pure theory.

In difference deconstruction is concretized, without distinction (a form of differing), without displacement and postponement (another form of differing), the writing is a dead letter or a letter that kills, as the Gospel says.

PROPHECY OR PROVOCATION?

> Who can tell the dancer from the dance?
> —W. B. Yeats, "Among School Children"

Some time ago, when I proposed a hypothesis concerning the silence required by a text, I noted the paradoxical condition of literary reading, a contradictory activity that repeats and is silent.[41]

In Borges's story, a reader, the reader of the Gospel—and his lectaries[42]—transgress that silent condition of reading and, by reading out loud, suspend the difference, thereby provoking logocentric fascination: the word, the logos, the divine word, are identified in presence.

Borges's theological exercises weave another atrocious version of literary passion: high fidelity puts reading at risk. Because of faith, because of identification, the fidelity manifested by his characters is at least doubled; the risk as well.

In a certain way, the Borgesian material conforms to the cycle of evangelical narration: just as Mark recounted what Peter had recounted, so does Espinosa recount what Mark recounted.

By way of the out-loud reading of the Gospel, Baltasar Espinosa, "whose theology was uncertain,"[43] Borges says, consummates a precarious con-substantiation. To his eyes, to those of his lectaries, that voice is no longer to be distinguished from that of Christ nor from his presence. Because of that same precarious union, neither are the Gutres to be distinguished from his executioners. One cannot be surprised, by the end of the work, by another crucifixion. "Espinosa understood what awaited him on the other side of the door."[44]

The characters do not speak, they do not speak to one another. "The genuine logos is always a dia-logos."[45] But the discourse of Espinosa, his presence, the conviction of his voice, revokes the hiatus of representation, constitutes an efficient *effet de réel*: none of the characters conceives of the difference. The reading of the Gospel is a mirror in which the characters fix themselves in order to *identify themselves*. Specular, or spectacular, identification is, once again, a frustrated interpretation.

Borges had already said enough. In "The Gospel According to Mark," as in "Of Rigor in Science,"[46] the more faithful the representation the more it sabotages the reference; fidelity perpetrates another "perfect crime" and, only because it is perfect, it does not know itself; if there existed a perfect reading it would mean the end of literature. The Gutres do not know the duality of the word; the presence of Espinosa, his voice, dissimulates his absence, suspends the inevitable duality that representation encloses. The reading they realize is the most innocent, the most guilty.

The word brings along its contrary: a message of civilization/barbary, of life/death, of goodness/cruelty, of truth/lie.

> What law orders this "contradiction," this internal opposition of the spoken against writing, a spoken that is spoken against itself from the moment that one writes, writes his identity in himself and extracts his identity against this depth of writing? This "contradiction," which is nothing but the relation of diction opposing itself to inscription, is not contingent,[47]

but neither is his warning new.

Given that contrariness, interpretation cannot fail to be ironic:

> Most things are not the ones one reads, one no longer understands bread for bread, but for earth: nor wine for wine, but for water, since even the elements are ciphered in elements. What could men be? Where you think there to be substance, all is circumstance, and that which seems to be the most solid is a hole,

and all holes are empty: only women seem what they are and are what they seem. How can that be, replied Andrenio, if they are all, from head to toe, nothing but one lying sycophancy? I will tell you; because most of them seem bad, and really are: such that it is necessary that one be a very good reader in order not to read everything backward.[48]

"This was and was not." Roman Jakobson tells us that this was the usual exhortation with which the Mallorcan storytellers introduce their narratives.[49] "WALK DON'T WALK." I transcribe the sign of the traffic light that, both illuminated, detain or hurry along the walking of the characters in George Segal's sculpture, the group of plaster, wood, metal, and electric light that is to be found in the Whitney Museum in New York. It makes no sense. The work, like the world, has only various senses or contradictory meanings, or else it has none.

"The allegory of reading narrates the impossibility of reading,"[50] says Paul de Man apropos of the allegorical requirements urged by Proust's narrator. From which we may derive that comprehension, as an aesthetic response, is either produced through difference, or is not produced at all. "Plus tard j'ai compris" (later I understood), Marcel repeatedly confesses; comprehension implies a postponement that the simultaneity (or instantaneity) of presence suspends.

THE ULTRAREALISM OF BORGES

Coleridge observes that all men are born Aristotelians or Platonists. The latter feel that classes, orders, and genres are realities; the former, that they are generalizations; for these, language is nothing other than an approximate play of symbols; for those, it is the map of the universe.
—Borges, *Otras inquisiciones*

Borges does not deny the initiatory property of logos. His story deconstructs it: nothing remains safe from the contradictions. Neither salvation nor order, as we already know. The Word *orders* chaos; it concludes or *institutes* it. The confusion is rooted in the nature of the word itself, which is the origin of the troubled compatibility of presence/absence, identity/difference, universal/particular. Narration exacerbates it all the more when it has narration as its theme. Confused from the beginning—there begins Apocalypse—it is already impossible to distinguish the initiation—

the beginning—from the end; the revelation does not finish with the catastrophe; in the telling it convokes it.

Displacing a dialogue that the characters could not establish, the
words of the Gospel constitute a strange quote, they penetrate the situation, they superimpose themselves on that reality but do not discard
another contradiction: without failing to be an *act* (they configure a quite
debatable "speech act"), they would also be its *model*. From which we
may conclude that, as Borges comments apropos of *Bouvard and
Pécuchet*, "the action does not occur in time but rather in eternity,"[51] a
reflection that would also correspond to his story.

Within the literary frame installed by Borges's narrative statute, the
reading of the Gospel reconciles at once model and realization: "The individual is in some way the species, and the Keats's nightingale is also Ruth's
nightingale," Borges says in *Otras Inquisiciones*,[52] and it is that coincidence that justifies the reflection that I transcribe as an epigraph.

Even without intending it, every reading approaches an appropriation
of the text. As for the author, so too for the reader—although in a less trou-
blesome form—the page is the target of the one who *writes* his own mean-
ing/a proper meaning. But, in the same way as occurs to the characters of
"The Gospel According to Mark," in the *propriety* of the reading is confounded the rigor of literalness (and I do not avoid here the associations of
cruelty and hardness) and the search for a truth as meaning, a second propriety that consists of making meaning proper/own, usurping it.

In Borges's story, literalness is a literary fiction: interpretive absti-
nence—a search for pure or primary meaning. It is the first interpretive
abuse, an impossible refinement that makes room for two aspects of one
and the same austerity; without interpretation (only a matter of a naive
conjecture), loyalty and fidelity, which try to appear as the manifestation
of faith, the observation of literal truth, give way to an authoritarian rigidity where once again "The letter kills and . . ."[53] And once again propriety is more arbitrariness than exactitude.

This contradictory ambivalence of the word and its properties constitutes the very statute of the word, the duality of a nature far from
simple. Each mention refers at least two times, since while referring to a
particular individual it never ceases referring to an archetype, a universal.
One could explain this ambivalence by considering the old neo-Platonic
contribution of the distinction later established by Peirce when he
opposed *type* and *token*. He indicated for each word the possibility of
recalling a type (the *legisign* of the luxuriant Peircean nomenclature) and
a particular object (the *sinsign*, in this case), such that each word registers
two memories, remembers two registers. But not only this. The word
token is particularly felicitous because, apart from the sixteen substantive

forms the *Oxford English Dictionary* defines for it, on the basis of its relation with *type* it weaves a semantic network that gathers up the folds of its signification. The *token* is, among other things, a *password*, a *mot de passe*, a safe conduct that trespasses through planes and, in that passage, allows the *token* to be seen in the *type* and vice versa. Different from Saussure's sign, the *token* is a *sign* that, without discarding the meaning of *evidence*, of something that is there, expresses, at the same time, the sign as footprint, the sign of something that existed and, as well, the sign insofar as it is a *presage* of a prodigy to come; the sign in all times, something that presents itself as a "memory," a present—a gift—offered especially to someone about to leave. Because of it the tenses appear superimposed.[54]

Borges's is not *the Gospel According to Mark* but "The Gospel According to Mark," and the precise mention of the article, from the title, initiates the process of actualization. The reading actualizes the text: from ideal to real, from possibility to action, from archetype to particular type, from a past to a present, on the basis of an original, the copy; but in this case, the copy is also an origin.

Referred to by the narrator-character, the biblical recitation appears "en-abîme." Model of action, it reflects itself in the story as in a mirror, faithful and inverted, and in this way the *paradoxes* begin to appear. Part of the text, the characters do not imitate a historical reality but rather another textual reality. The realist illusion of the tale does not attain to an imitation of the real but to a system of transtextual verisimilitude. Neither the mirror that hung along the way and of which Stendhal spoke, nor the life that imitates art, as Oscar Wilde preferred. If the story turns out to be verisimilar, this impression is produced because the interpretation occurs *between* texts. This *between* is the hole through which another form of reading falls. The anxiety of influence—a title from Harold Bloom—appears as the necessity of formulating at least a transtextual legitimization. Writing—sacred, in this case—guarantees a narrative event that, without the prestige of such a precedent, would lack not a little credibility.

One diegesis generates another diegesis: the metaleptic[55] slippage does not appear to occur outside the boundaries. Because of its literary nature it is natural for the character-reader to find inscribed, in the book he or she reads, his or her archetype, "like a shadow of the things to come," as Paul says apropos of the affirmations that, in the Old Testament, announce the events of the New. That is the depth of reality, a reality that is beyond, an ultrareality that—also for this reason—adds itself to the realist exaggerations of the outset.

Here as well literal reading is a risk; a fixation of writing is produced, an obsession contains a strange metamorphosis. As in Cortazar's story,[56] in "The Gospel According to Mark" the reader turns into a larva, an *axolotl* that identifies with itself, problematically, because it no longer distinguishes between who watches and is watched.

The book read in the book repeats itself as in a mirror (in a similar book) and en-abîme (in a different space). Like Don Quijote, like Emma Bovary, like Bouvard and Pécuchet, it is the fidelity of reading, literal, without difference (writing without writing: a coincidence), which determines its own mishaps, those proper to literary readers. Everything occurs between equals. It is Virgil who leads Dante in his *Inferno*. If, as Derrida says, there is no "*hors-texte*," there must necessarily without *hors-texte* be an inside-text. Like *Lancelot du Lac*, the "Galeotto"[57] that facilitated the love between Paolo and Francesca, the *Gospel* is origin and model, the archetype of a fatal relation between characters.

EITHER THE LETTER OR THE CIPHER

Among books there is no exit. If the characters try to extract themselves from the calamities of their situation by means of reading, that extraction is a plot and a trap: as if, by duplicating itself, the fiction were to negate itself. The text within the text establishes a curious transtextuality; by way of a play of mirrors it creates a flight toward profundity, but also an edge, a look out point over the abyss. The "illusion of reality" is not formed by imitating reality but by reiterating the literary condition: "One is never, then, simply in literature. The problem is posed by the structure of the edge: the edge is not certain, because it does not cease to be divided."[58]

The story begins before beginning since here as well, in the beginning is the Word, not chaos. The title, gospel, announces what has occurred and what will occur. The recourse does not appear to be exceptional. Another story from the same book, "The Intruder,"[59] indicates, from the same paratextual zone, from the aperture of those marginal texts where the story is inscribed, all the biblical, bibliographical references necessary for the quote but excessive for the epigraph: "2 Kings, 1:26,"[60] nothing more. Like in "The Gospel According to Mark," Borges specifies the references but abstains from quoting. These retrospective anticipations that simultaneously announce and suspend the reference imitate the archetypical nature of the aleph insofar as the present and past, present and absent model is both within each realization and beyond it. It was in this way that God proceeded, who—according to the *Midrash Rabbah*—in order to create the world had first to consult the Bible, previous and present, cause and effect of creation.

Interior and anterior, that transtextual ingression is its regress: the exit leads inside and back. As Derrida says, all writing is anterior; which is why with it begins history: "The worlds that propose *April March* are not regressive; what is regressive is the manner of writing their history," says Borges in "The Examination of the Work of Herbert Quain," clarifying that "the weak *calembour* of the title does not signify *The March of April* but rather, literally, *April March*."[61]

In "The Gospel According to Mark" the Gospel is interior and anterior. Because of this the crucifixion of Espinosa is *prescribed*: written, anterior, and obligatory. The transtextual mention does not distinguish whether the anteriority is only anticipation or cause. In *prescription*, the anteriority of writing is confused with causality. Its priority, because of its importance, its precedence, brings to light the opposition between the temporal and successive progression that defines the condition of the signifier, of the non-written sign according to Saussure, and writing as inversion—reversal and return—that is a form of salvation by literature. "Time recovered," reaching safety in writing, insinuates a glimpse of eternity, its resplendence as much as its conjecture.

The invention of writing by Hermes-Mercury and the reconciliation of opposites by means of the cross is a recurrent idea in the texts of the alchemists, always ready to resolve conflict by means of paradoxes. Perhaps, as Jung says in *Mysterium Conjunctionis*, the unifying agent is the spirit of Mercury and, thus, its singular spirit makes the author confess to being a member of the Ecclesia Spiritualis, for the spirit of God. This religious antecedent appears in the selection of the term "Pelican" for the circular process, since the bird is a recognized allegory of Christ.[62]

As occurs in Proust's novel, reading remits a thing to its beginning and what Paul understood as a mirror—as enigma and reversed—typology as annunciation, is not so different from what Origen understood for apocatastasis:[63] *restitutio et reintegratio* and the operations of allegorical reading; neither the one nor the other deny the "reversal and reinscription" that seems to be the foundation of deconstruction. The book is memory and divination and, speaking of interpretations, be it in Antioch or in Alexandria, repetition does not cease to be a transformation. In the same way that no book could communicate the ultimate knowledge, neither can its interpretation be definitive: "to want to limit the knowledge of the text would be as prudent as leaving a knife in the hands of a child."[64]

The interpretation of the text reiterates, revises, in each reader the (theological) problem of comprehension, of a knowledge that may be as well explicated by *tautology* as by *paradox*. For Thomas Browne, ordinary events only require the credulity of common sense,[65] mystery is the only possible proof of divinity: "I am what I am" enables the foundation of that mystery and the endeavors of a negative theology that, like *Docta Ignorantia*,[66] affirms by negating. The sacred definition affirms nondefinition, it runs through the discourse without interruption, turning around above itself. The end returns to the beginning, giving root to a paradox of knowledge capable of reconciling as much the reverse as repetition.

Analyzing the complexity of paradoxes, Rosalie L. Colie understands, on the basis of *The Sophist*, of *Theaetetus*, and of *Parmenides*, that the problems derived from the ineludibility of contradictions emerge from the proper nature of logos and the consecutive existence of two realms apparently opposed to one another, such that what is real in the one could not be so in the other: ". . . that paradox necessarily attends upon those men brave enough to travel to the limits of discourse."[67]

In the same way as paradoxes, deconstructive operations question the mechanisms of comprehension and, above all, the certainties that comprehension establishes: "Certum est quia impossibile est."[68] But neither paradoxes nor deconstruction have an end. The paradox negates itself, and in negating itself the failure of definition constitutes a kind of definition. This contradiction holds as well for deconstruction, which deliberately avoids defining itself, plays with the temptation of deconstructing itself. As Oscar Wilde says, "paradoxes are very dangerous,"[69] hardly are they invoked when it becomes impossible to elude their occurring. The paradox negates definition, it negates itself, attempting, by that auto-deconstruction, to undermine the closure of disciplinary formulas, of academic norms, of the systems that are the most rigorous means of limitation—or the means of the most rigorous limitation.

"My end is my beginning,"[70] the phrase attributed by Borges to Schiller, is inscribed in the ring of the Queen of Scotland to confirm her Christian faith and challenge in this way execution and death. The necessity of a circular route, the return to the beginning, contradiction as a specular vision, the organization on the cross as a reconciliation of opposites, impossible literalness, the impossibility of paraphrasing paradox, the inscription in the ring could also be the enigma and motto of textual comprehension.

Perhaps the greatest fidelity verifies the greatest paradox.

CHAPTER FOUR

On "Ultrarealism": Borges and Bioy Casares

(THE INTERLACING OF THE IMAGINATION AND MEMORY ON THE THRESHOLDS OF OTHER WORLDS)

For Christian Metz

Those who sleep are in separate worlds, those who are awake are in the same world.

—Heraclitus, *Fragments*

Given the circumstances, it would perhaps have been more suggestive, and certainly more appropriate, to propose a title derived from "Un drame bien parisien," the novella by Alphonse Allais presented for the first time in *Le Chat Noir*[1] in 1890, a quite disconcerting piece of the *gaité française*, which Allais had nourished with a "poetic imagination situated somewhere between Zeno of Elea and that of children."[2] As is known, André Breton includes this curious text in his *Anthologie de l'humour noir*.[3] The doubtful chromatic affiliation of the humor of this piece would be justified less by the macabre laughter than by a certain affinity with *The Black Square on White Background* of Kasimir Malevitch,[4] because of its mystic, Suprematist suppressions that unite the profusion of forms into an elemental geometrical figure and that reduce the variety of colors to black, which is not a color. Too regular, "square où tout est correct"[5] (square where everything is correct), the square paradoxically insinuates a worrying forecast of those not-so-mysterious black holes in which crumbles "the microcosm of a collapsing universe,"[6] empty plenums of collapsed stars "on the edge of nothing they give us nothing on guarantee (*nantissement*),"[7] that strange guarantee with which Breton sustains humor at the margin of these cosmic considerations.

31

In a certain way, the pre-vision of a square hole, which recalls the attempts to trace the quadrature of a circle, is close to the perplexity of the denouement of Allais's novella—without another similarity than the rules of its own discursivity. The stupor in the face of its disarticulated logic drew attention to itself once again, more recently, in a different, less spectacular, literary and disciplinary circle, off-stage, starting from a series of conferences, colloquia, and seminars where Umberto Eco has converted it into the recurrent reference of his formulations concerning "Possible Worlds." Published repeatedly in articles,[8] re-elaborated in *Lector in fabula*,[9] it constitutes a notion about which he continues to speculate in his more recent books.[10]

The expression "possible worlds" was originally formulated by Leibniz, who introduced it into philosophy as the divine act of giving existence to a real world, one which God chooses among the numerous possible worlds created by His providential mind,[11] and God felt himself free not to create the best of all possible worlds; it was only He who preferred this one to all others. As Christian Metz says, "What delimits a discourse with regard to the rest of the world, and for this very reason opposes it to the 'real' world, is that a discourse must necessarily be pronounced by someone [. . .] it is one of the characteristics of the world that it is not proffered by anyone."[12]

Actual or possible, preferred or proffered, the limits of my world are the limits of my language, and because it is known that the chiasmus is true: only if there is language will there by a world, whether of truth or of fiction. Its properties may or may not coincide with the real facts, but nevertheless it is possible to narrate them or describe them verbally— graphically, photo- or cinematographically, construct them. Defined by the discursive conditions that give form and figure to objects, they are like Lichtenberg's knife without a blade that lacks a handle;[13] they are not to be found anywhere but could come to exist some day in some place or, simply, can be described. Their discursive reality is certain; however, the real presence of an anterior posterior, or exterior reference beyond the text, with which it does not necessarily coincide, is merely possible. Each fictional character can be the onomastic origin of generations of people who carry its name without altering the archetypal docility of its aesthetic condition. A chimera is a mythological monster, a vain dream, or a gargoyle sculpted on the edge of a gothic cornice. If, because of an excess of municipal zeal, Illiers comes to call itself Illiers-Combray, the toponymic literalness of the interpretation gives neither more nor less credence to the fiction that is held in suspense. Despite the closure of the story,[14] literary entities have a tendency to exist and, even dispensing

with the fatal traps of success (*éxito*), they procure an exit both dangerous and redundant, given that to exist is already to "be outside," but outside of what?

Alluding to the enigmatic mystifications of Allais' humor, Eco does
not hesitate to assimilate it to Escher's etchings or, as he says, "to a pas-
tiche à la Borges,"[15] whom he himself has *pastiched* as few others. He also
might have alluded to the slippages of planes that, overflowing their borders, obliterating them, jump out (*asoman*), provoke awe (*asombran*), in
the paintings of Magritte, stratifying vision to the point of placing it at the
edge of the *abyss*, by means of an *optical* and logical *dis-illusion* that
trompes l'oeil and twists the mouth—"beau comme": the fixed eye
between the lips without a face of Maldoror is fixed on the spectator of
Jean-Christophe Averty, closing the breach that separates the voice and
silence, making the disjunction between the word and the gaze vanish into
smoke, both, eye and mouth, surprised at the same time. The pipe is nothing but a representation of one or two pipes; without fumes, with humor
(in Spanish they are closer, *humo/humor*), an iconic figure and a verbal
figure, both in sight, are confounded in one of those jokes specific to
fumismo[16]: "*L'Hydropathe*[17] designated A. Allais as the 'head of the
fumist school.'"[18]

More than dallying in the alternatives of a drama in which one bets
against the stereotypes of the genre and against the conjectures to which
conforms a thought controlled by the automatisms of opinion, those disciplines that occupy themselves with possible worlds are interested to
observe the unexpected moves played with by an eccentric logic that
coexists with the regularity of mechanisms fastening by reason or habit;
moves of narrative prestidigitation that divert by surprise. Unforeseeability brings to light the rules that establish the normal situation, and merely
revealing them in one stroke is enough to impugn them. Breton said of
Allais:

> Not only does he never miss an occasion to take a pot shot at the
> lamentable, patriotic, and religious ideal exasperated among his
> colleagues by the defeat of 1871, but he stands out in making
> trouble for the satisfied individual, blinded by truisms and sure
> of himself, whom he finds at his side in the street everyday. His
> friend Sapek and he reign, in effect, over a kind of activity until
> then almost unheard of: mystification. One could say that with
> them it is raised to the level of an art: it is a question of nothing
> less than experimenting with a terrorist activity of the spirit,
> which puts in evidence the average conformism of the people.[19]

A semiotics of narrative texts delves into the existence of possible and impossible worlds originated by the actions of a reader who can only *suppose* his hypothesis in silence, limited by more or less vicious hermeneutic circles. But "the observer always interferes with the phenomenon under observation,"[20] such that each of his or her possible worlds brings together the *comprehension* of his readings into a *compression* that suspends momentarily the other worlds. If in the instant of its birth, the work explodes like an event of rupture, the reader's interpretation observes this fracture and *restitutes* the statutes in which are founded thought, imagination, language, or the figures that represent them.

It is in the incertitudes of interpretation that is initiated the *quête*—which is both a search and a question, a double program, doubly problematic—of old and new worlds, of so many other worlds, without a determined time or space, the diverse universes of dreams that vigil concentrates and reduces into one sole, real world, partial and shared. In other words, Heraclites' worlds precede and cipher thus interpretation.

Ownmost, intimate, individual, the many "piccoli mondi"[21] like those presented by Eco are small worlds, the exact title of David Lodge's[22] academic satire or the "microcosms" that Leibniz had undertood "monads" to be, which is to say, those formulas that are the expression of the world and a world unto themselves, a term that was adopted by German aesthetics of the between-wars period (Benjamin, Adorno, for example) to designate the singular work of art, cloistered, without windows. It is in one of those *petits mondes* of interpretation, one of the many possible worlds of those nomadic monads in which I will try to concentrate the combinatory of conjectures of a reader of fiction and theory, a private zone wherein, like in a hole in the sky, is produced the hardly coincidental meeting of Borges and Bioy with other authors, an interpretation in the key of B (*en clave de B*), an enclave in Paris, the dramatic localization of which Borges never stopped making fun:

> We men of the various Americas remain so unconnected that we
> hardly even recognize ourselves as a reference, told by Europe.
> In such cases, Europe tends to be a synecdoche for Paris. In
> Paris one is less interested in art than in the politics of art: look
> at the gang-like tradition of its literature and painting, always
> directed by committees and their political dialectics: a parlia-
> ment that speaks of lefts and rights; another military, speaking of
> vanguards and retroguards.[23]

It is not superfluous to recognize the auspices of the genies of place—*geni loci* that turn into, in this case, our *loci comuni*. Appealing to the favors of both, I would convoke genies, arguments, and coincidences in this place, from one of those small possible worlds enabled by the theoretical drift of fiction. When dreams make out the reverse side of reality, a world lurking behind this world reveals the avatars of its hybrid statute dissimulated by the frequent control of a daily and diurnal vigil. It is Walter Benjamin who discovers in Paris or in dreams the somber thresholds of those crossed worlds, passages of transit and transition that time does not repeal. A space of time, *Zeitraum*, or dream of time, *Zeittraum*, are not to be distinguished or, as with Derrida's *différance*, only one letter differs in order to, paradoxically, mark time in space. *Passagenwerke*[24] are "works of passages" or passages under work, undecided passageways between outside and inside, or rather, *Passagenwerke*, literary passages that remit to the reader, from one author to another. They are interstices of the city in which Benjamin reveals, in part, the ambivalent, indecisive nature, without an outside, of these constructions that nineteenth-century urbanization introduced between the buildings: "such a passage is a city, a world in miniature."[25] Like paths covered by a passage, like a place of localization and permanence, galleries confront dialectically before and now. Curious itineraries of spatial or spectral intermediation oscillate between house and street, a *Zwischenwelt* that compromises, erratically, or eludes the adventures of the exterior where the multitudes grow with the private misadventures of the interior where melancholy grows.

From the liberty bestowed on him by a poetics of dreams, Benjamin is swept away by the rebellions of the surrealist insurrection. But beyond that circumstantial impression,[26] he is perturbed by a more profound illumination revealed by the utopic phantasmagorias of *L'éternité par les astres* (1872) by Louis-Auguste Blanqui,[27] "an apparition" who will be obsessively present in his thought and in his texts. In the same way as he discovers the ambiguities of a contradictory world running up and down the Paris arcades, Benjamin buries himself in the mysteries *reserved* by the worlds that Blanqui's cosmogonic speculation ceaselessly conceives. "Marx imputes to the Bourgeoisie the invention of the name Blanqui";[28] Geffroy denounces those who turned him into a monster, a specter, he says; Derrida does not mention him in *Spectres de Marx*.[29] A specter among specters, betrayed, locked up, interred in his prison-tomb, not only Blanqui disappears in the shadows of his messianic desperation. It is the men of the nineteenth century who, like Benjamin, run up and down a tunnel of phantoms in the Paris arcades.

There they meet, by way of the coincidences that reading propitiates, as if they had made a "date" (*cita*/quote); Benjamin and Blanqui meet like that, by *droit de "citer,"* a right of the city, as if the city itself had given them a date, a sentimental date among other dates, one for the two of them. "Thanks to wandering through the libraries with that collector's nose, where one comes upon those meetings that so please the surrealists, by way of the luck of objective chance."[30] Benjamin begins to admire the stellar vision or visions of Blanqui, from the moment he reads *L'enfermé* (The Enclosed), the denomination and title given by Blanqui's biographer.[31] Benjamin will no longer distance himself from the political, poetic, ethical imagination, seduced as he is by the strength of a heroic figure:

> emblematic of the permanent revolution. . . . The enigma of Blanqui: for him, the idea of revolution is mysteriously associated with an infernal vision of repetition—it is the stars who pronounce the accusation—and it is there that he enters the realm of theology.[32]

More than the rebellions of the conspirator, of the terrorist of the barricades, of the audacities of an anarchist who subverts without truce—even at the cost of his own sacrifice—French society of the nineteenth century, what impresses is the contumacy of this "New Hero." Despite the oppression and prison, Blanqui puts down neither arms nor convictions, imagining at the same time the infinite plurality of different worlds. He conjectures their astronomic collapse and the coincidences of eternal return: "The world dominated by his phantasmagorias is [. . .] modernity. The vision of Blanqui brings the entire universe into modernity."[33]

I am not aware of whether Borges read Benjamin or Benjamin Borges. Nevertheless, it would have been most possible that Borges would have had news of his writings, his thought, his interests, not only through Gershom Sholem, his friend Gerhardt, whom he visits more than once in Jerusalem and with whom he discusses at length the knowledge of Kabbalah, decisive for all three. In 1933, Luis Juan Guerrero includes in the schedule of the department of aesthetics at the University of La Plata "Der Begriff der Kunstkritik in der deutschen Romantik," and, although he does not cite Benjamin explicitly, his references to the aesthetic consequences of mechanical repetition and the "loss of aura," which are easily to be found disseminated among his texts, give us sufficient indication to presume that Borges would have known of him by that time.[34] It would not surprise me if Borges and Bioy Casares, without more references about Benjamin, would have felt the echoes of his reflection on film, for example, in that decade that ended so tragically.[35] In 1967 the press *Sur* published Héctor A. Murena's Spanish translation of Selected Writings (*Gesammelte Schriften*) of Walter Benjamin for the collection "*Estudios Alemanes*."[36]

But the conjecture does not go beyond suspicion. On the contrary, I ought to pause longer to consider the image and imagination of Blanqui, his figure as well as his philosophy, transtextualized in the works of Borges and Bioy Casares, beginning nonchronologically with the texts in collaboration attributed to Honorio Bustos Domecq: *Seis problemas para don Isidro Parodi* (1942).[37] This character ponders, much as Blanqui does, from the interior of a cell, the enigmas and conflicts, both police and political, which are brewing outside of the prison. Like the inhabitants of Tlön, Blanqui continues to be a sworn conspirator who does not cease to found, from within his imprisonment, secret societies to threaten established power. In an age of violence, he weaves plans of evasion and a *revolution* that surprises by turning and returning, a return to the beginning, an apocatastasis that when it returns, inaugurates by restituting. Published in 1940, both the story "Tlön, Uqbar, Orbis Tertius"[38] and the novel *The Invention of Morel*[39] coincide with the suicide of Walter Benjamin, precipitating a story and an aesthetic of disappearance that, paradoxically, has its origin in the multiplication of copies, in copious technical reproduction. Both narratives present various aspects in common but coincide, above all, in that they play, one and the other, with a poetics of representation. They are submitted to the paradoxical turning of talents into tatters, to the excellence of technological mechanisms of repetition so perfect as to bring about numerous parallel worlds, copied dualities that end by introducing themselves into the folds of a real world, confusing themselves with it, reducing it to one sole entity in which what represents and what is represented are no longer distinguished.

The aesthetic itinerary is similar and closely follows the progress of technology: reproduction, the reiterative pluralization of things and persons en masse, repeated more and better, risk losing their existence in exchange for perfection. The encyclopedia, the mirror, the invention of Morel captures and registers figures in movement for eternity; the characters, preserved forever, become sick and dying. Like writing in Plato's *Phaedrus* and "Plato's Pharmacy," by Derrida, the instrumental solution enhances and kills. The apparatuses that capture and register life, fix it, multiply and confound individuals, reproduce and suppress them. First the aura disappears—the loss of the separation that distinguishes, of the singularity that confers to unity the character of uniqueness. Then, that disappearance initiates another: the loss of reference, the *collapse* of the necessary duality that the referent needs to signify, a collapse that the last war showed on television, like a news item or a novelty. Metz said that "the perception of the tale as such [. . .] de-realizes the told thing."[40] Was it not Barthes who feared that the fixation of codes would "make resurge . . . a phantom, the phantom of the referent?"[41]

Not only *codifixation* risks the referent. Representation, to the same extent as it requires it, preys on it; representation and predation are reciprocal and necessary: what happens, happens through representation. According to the narrator of "Tlön, Uqbar, Orbis Tertius," the *Anglo American Cyclopedia*—"literal reprint of the *Encyclopedia Britannica* of 1902"[42]—is indispensable for the existence of Uqbar; the opposite would seem to be the case, but is not. It is significant that the *Encyclopedia Britannica* that I have at home (1973), has entries for Europe, Africa, Asia, and Oceania, but no entry for "America,"[43] nor even for "Americas," as it is so often pluralized. For the authors of this *Encyclopedia*, could America still be a utopia, a "no place," an imaginary continent, without end, like Kafka's *Amerika*, a continent still to be made? Could it be that it still makes sense to believe that one can "make America," like those who now believe in *making Europe*? In any case and in some way it worries us that the encyclopedias—be it in fiction or even outside of it—do not get any answer right.

The contradictory achievements of the instrument turn discovery into repetition and drown invention in inventory, a list that conserves and abolishes it at the same time. As Borges says: "In the poem the palace was complete. It was enough (they tell us) that the poet pronounce the poem for the palace to disappear, abolished and struck down by the last syllable."[44] In one shot, palace, poem, and poet vanish by virtue of a rivalry that the Emperor comprehends but does not tolerate. In another text, the cartographers of his Empire describe it so perfectly that the description is confused with the Empire and is exposed to its weather/time (*tiempo*) and storms (*tempestades*).[45]

The reflections of Benjamin, the imagination of Borges and Bioy anticipate forms of disappearance or desperation that the atrocious events of the decade, the forties, would confirm thousands, millions of times over, in the destruction of war and in the camps of annihilation: "a desperation doubtlessly somewhat mixed with that irony of which Blanqui found himself to be so sadly and completely deprived, or with a humor blacker than that of the surrealists."[46] Was it Benjamin who compared Blanqui's lack of irony to the strange humor of the surrealists?

Like another *Esthétique de la disparition*,[47] science and technology appear to be tied to another world. The series induces us to think of other worlds, "parallel worlds, intersticial, bifurcating, even to that *black hole* that would only be an excess of speed of this type of voyage, a pure phenomenon of velocity."[48] The theoretical speculations of Paul Virilio allude to a new order of illusion in which the unidirectionality of speed causes pilots, vehicles, troops, cities, and continents to disappear, threatened by the utopias of a technology that is dedicated to accelerating and miniaturizing its machinery to the point of unnoticeability. The elusions of acceleration constitute a different phenomenon but are fundamentally related to the same collapse.

In "The Celestial Plot,"[50] Bioy Casares's narrator (re)counts (on) the inexplicable disappearance of persons and places or their equally inexplicable reappearance; an equally strange fluctuation of possible worlds is recounted by the story of captain Ireneo Morris; a name of happy recollection, like Ireneo Funes, his Ireneo is, and with a famous last name: Morel, Moreau, *or more*. Another Morris (William?) may be seen in filigree, mentioned in the famous prologue to *The Invention of Morel*, where Borges recalls Louis-Auguste Blanqui quoting Dante Gabriel Rossetti: "I have been here before,/But when or how I cannot tell."[50] The cosmological enigmas of Blanqui haunt the shared imaginary of Borges and Bioy, who interlace prologues, dedications, characters, and other elusive quotes that appear and disappear without leaving a trace, like the worlds of Blanqui.

"The Celestial Plot" begins with an introduction in which it is told that on a twentieth of December, on board an airplane, Ireneo Morris and Carlos Alberto Servian disappear in Buenos Aires. A narrator describes the commission that he received those very same days: "the complete works of the communist Luis Augusto Blanqui,"[51] a manuscript, and objects of scarce value. Like the narrative archetype of the *Quijote*, to which the narrator alludes, the story transcribes a manuscript that, although different, nevertheless forms part of the diegesis of the story that contains it. The referential turns of the *mise en abîme* make possible worlds that duplicate them thematically and textually, pushing them to the edge of the precipice, precipitating them into the abyss at a vertiginous velocity that the irony of displacement multiplies or explodes. The narrator of "The Celestial Plot" speaks of secret societies, of ritual visits to the cinematographer, of Celtic legends and subject matters. Just like the other Ireneo, the character of this story lost consciousness. The loss was not due to the fall from a horse but from an airplane. Surviving or swooning, the accident makes him doubly suspicious: either foreigner and spy, sentenced to exile, or Argentine and traitor, to be shot without further ado. In the face of these alternatives, he prefers to confess himself Uruguayan. "I consoled myself thinking that for me an Uruguayan is not a foreigner."[52] The plot is complicated by the disappearance of a letter and some grammatical and orthographic irregularities that the narrator neither grounds nor claims: "I did not doubt Morris's good faith; but I had not sent him books; I had not written him this letter; I did not know the works of Blanqui."[53] The circular paths of the story, the repetition of situations that disconcert by their similarity (then repetition is possible) and their differences (then repetition is not possible), almost equal worlds, the slippage of one world into another, the encyclopedia that distinguishes characters, life ordered as in a library: "one epoch was occupied with philosophy, another with French literature, another with the natural sciences, another with ancient Celtic literature,"[54] and thus it goes until arriving to the works of Blanqui, which I would include in the series of occult sciences, politics, and sociology. According to his strategies of reading, it is not surprising that the narrator should transcribe literally a poem in prose—that is how he defines it—of *L'éternité par les astres*, painstakingly annotating the bibliographical references of his edition, since in this poem or essay he claims to have found the explication of the adventure of Morris. The text that Bioy transcribes is one of the quotes of Blanqui preferred by Benjamin and by his critics. I begin with Bioy's quote: "There could be infinite identical worlds, infinite worlds slightly differentiated, infinite different worlds."[55] I continue with that of Blanqui: "What I am writing at this moment in a dungeon of the fort of Taureau, I wrote and will write throughout eternity, at a table, with a pen, beneath these garments, in similar circumstances. Just so, all of them."[56] I continue with the transcription from Bioy: "In infinite worlds my situation will be the same, but perhaps there will be variations in the reason for my interment or in the eloquence or tone of my pages."[57]

Like the recurrent worlds of Blanqui, *The Invention of Morel*, "The Celestial Plot" are two among other examples from Bioy that interlace with numerous stories of Borges. In "Tlön, Uqbar, Orbis Tertius," the narrator wonders: "Who are those who invented Tlön? The plural is inevitable, because the hypothesis of a single inventor—of an infinite Leibniz working in the darkness and in modesty—has been unanimously discarded. It is conjectured that this brave new world is the work of a secret society of astronomers, of biologists, of engineers, of metaphysicians, of poets, of chemists, of algebrists, of moralists, of painters, of geometers . . . lead by an obscure man of genius."[58] In "The Garden of Forking Paths,"[59] Stephen Albert says, "time bifurcates perpetually toward innumerable futures. In one of those I am your enemy."[60] In "Death and the Compass,"[61] the story ends in dialogue: "For the next time I kill you [. . .] I promise you that labyrinth that consists in only one straight line, which is invisible, and endless."[62] And also in "The Other Death,"[63] and in "The South,"[64] and in "The Theologians."[65] Similar to the worlds of Blanqui, "which repeat without end and march in place,"[66] that turn and return to turn, making the very future a repetition of the past, the universes of Bioy and Borges interlace in a passageway where the simulacra—it is Borges who highlights the term—are confounded.[67]

If I highlight the "ultrarealism" of Borges and Bioy in the title, it is not merely a question of leaving behind the "outrism"[68] (*ultraísmo*) and extravagance of their ephemeral discourtesies by way of a more proximal reality, but rather of better observing the cleavage of realisms that proliferate on the basis of a notion of realism that does not mean the real but rather only one of the possible interpretations of this specious reality. From realism to the realisms classified by Roman Jakobson,[69] the profusion of different, parallel realities, which nevertheless co-incide with this reality, is astonishing. It is known that realism is not reality but a possible world; should it be surprising that, thanks to reading, they should all coincide within one, "chosen" world: Borges, Bioy, Benjamin, and Blanqui, reasonably imagining the lurking of worlds haunted by the impulses of technologies of representation, of reproduction, of recording. The regions, the empires, the events, the figures, multiplied to the point of an alarming or indifferent exile? A collapse into the doubtful reality of a monotonous world.[70] Indifferent, copied, reproduced to the point of exaggeration, it turned into a terminal reality, a term between quotes, period.

Several years ago I had worked on "The Ultrarealism of Borges or the Miracle of the Roses,"[71] because I felt in its recurrences the attraction of a different repetition. By way of a verbal reiterative gesture the word designated its referent, but at the same time it replicated or put it into relief. By way of this *putting into relief*, the reader of Borges came to approach, face to face, the archetype, the universal idea, an ideal reality, in capitals: Beyond, exaggerated, in extreme, an *ultrareality*.

But that was years ago. Now, even repetition has changed in the profusion of replicas reproduced by "the machines of vision,"[72] which fit the roundness of a world into a square, a square in black and white or in colors. A Beyond squared by screens dominates, domesticates the excess of a reality that is turning "sage comme un image" (wise as an image), calm as a statue, correct and loyal, installed in all media by any means necessary. Everywhere and absent, partial and whole, repeated to extremes, images cause a strange universe to conform; particular as they are, images become simply universal; they suppress the referent or they arrogate themselves as such.

Irreferent, irreverent, that universe becomes a double, insofar as it represents (does not represent), more than ever, a violated reality. Preyed on, reality disappears for the gaze, or hides itself, covered by the screen that exposes it. Trapped by the black hole and the colors of the television, the viewfinder puts reality in its sights, makes of reality its objective and shoots, twice, several times, as in the most tele-visual drama. As Blanqui says and Benjamin repeats: "At bottom, it is melancholy, this eternity of man through the stars."[73]

CHAPTER FIVE

A Complexly Woven Plot:
Borges, Bioy Casares, Blanqui

(CONJECTURES AND CONJUNCTIONS
AT THE LIMITS OF POSSIBLE WORLDS)

Anywhere out of the world.
— Charles Baudelaire, *Le spleen de Paris*

Let us admit that, by coincidence, captain Ireneo Morris
has fallen into another world; that he would fall again
into this one would be an excess of coincidence.
— Adolfo Bioy Casares, *La trama celeste y otros relatos*

It could be even redundant to try to glimpse via "The Celestial Plot," the
story by Adolfo Bioy Casares, the possibilities of connection between
the parallel worlds favored by fiction. The narrator recounts something
more than the flying "accidents" of a pilot, of one who risks a crossing
between one real space and another, similar, more or less new, more or less
other. In this sidereal, literal, austral plot, the stars—the letters and signs—
are presented as propitious for ciphered acrobatics in a kind of acronymic
chance. The narrator—Carlos Alberto Servian—only signs with his initials: C.A.S. It was precisely at the CAS. (Centre des Activités Surréalistes,
CNRS in Paris) where were initiated the first literary digressions about an
astronomic hypothesis, about coincidences that could not only be

---

This piece was presented in Paris on January 30, 1995, in the framework of the CAS/ISCAM
seminar at the CNRS, while another colloquium (organized by the same team), convoked
around the theme *Nouveau monde, Autres mondes, Surréalisme et Amériques*, had already
given me the occasion, a year before, to pose and discuss these questions.

explained by chance, though chance be what is at stake. So many coincidences (*casualidades*) would result, consequently, at the very least, in two *cases*, in French, *cas* (Latin, *cadere*) fit (Spanish, *caben*) or fall (Spanish, *caen*, Latin, *cadere*) into the same letters. Casual cases? Such coincidences might be sufficient to indicate the accord between these two cases, without even including, in the "cas" series, the beginning of Bioy Casares's second last name. The exclusion has the purpose of not giving into simplistic temptations of an onomastic fetishism more partial than elemental. Nevertheless, why not accede to interpreting these "cases" as fortuitous signs, above all those which are manifested in the literal/literary region that, "almost unexplored," legitimates the "discoveries attributed to objective chance,"[1] or simply to pure chance.

One is surprised by the appearances or disappearances within the celestial plot that this narration by Bioy Casares weaves; they come to intrigue us even more due to clues that make us suppose the existence of parallel worlds, or other worlds in which other cities, other streets, persons or their doubles, their works, entities, identities, or alterities overcome or succumb for no other reason than their simple mention or omission. Like in an atlas or encyclopedia—where a nominal omission could imply the suppression of a continent—these discontinuities put in danger a reality that only the word could save. It is difficult to overcome the stupor, better yet, the fear provoked by the compromises that close in on the word, on writing, responsibilities that do not differ from others that tend to preoccupy the Kabbalists, who know that even the mere omission of a letter could upset the order of the entire universe; by that of just one word . . .

On the occasion of the colloquium at the CAS I already evoked an aspect to which I will now only allude. I anticipated then a reality *a ultranza*—an ultrareality—repeated and accelerated by the pluralization of worlds in a culture of satellites where "the excesses of velocity" contribute to annulling or rescinding the oppositions between here and there, proximity and distance, present and past, both of these and the future, real and unreal. A mixture of histories and hallucinatory utopias of the technologies of communication favor unexpected crossings, coincidences between originals, copies, and facsimiles, that profusion of "lookalikes" that find in pluriplanetary localization a multiple exit to escape the limits of a narrow space, too temporal, too human.

More than the vicissitudes of a pilot adventuring across strange worlds, more than the errancies of Bioy Casares's narrator, who flies over a variety of narrative situations, we try to follow the profound tracks of Louis-Auguste Blanqui[2] in the literary fictions of Bioy Casares. In this strange intertextual universe, the books of Blanqui—author of the most fearsome insurrections, terrorist of the Paris Communes, the anarchist who subverts without truce, even at the cost of his own sacrifice, the French society of the nineteenth century—are required, registered, transcribed, lost, negated. Bioy's tale founds the "accidents" of the narrator's flight on the comings and goings of a group of Blanqui's books that appear and disappear from the scene in the same way as their characters or cities are introduced or vanish. It confounds the stellar mysteries with the facts of captivity, as much the oppressions of the cell as the imaginary "escapes" from that prison. The quotes excerpted from *Eternity through the Stars: An Astronomic Hypothesis*[3] count as a safe conduct that gives passage to the most unheard-of references, passageways to other worlds, as enigmatic as they are unexpected.

It is not necessary to take inventory of the texts in which this eccentric book of Blanqui, the fascination of his spectacular phantasmagorias, the rare tone of an insufficiently sarcastic irony, modulate the fantastic exercises of Bioy Casares, in accordance with the celebrated poetics of Borges from the end of the thirties. His later stories prolong this same ironic approach where the traps of mediatic irruption—which had already begun to make their disastrous effects felt—the folds and duplications of parallel worlds, occult and reveal, *re-veil* two times over, reality and its variations. More numerous are the narrations in which Borges and Bioy Casares insist on the convergence of different entities that cross paths because of "a kind of double life"—a double path—in a time that returns, claiming an eternity imitated or limited by the duration of an epoch that is repeating. "All the crossroads of heaven are crowded with our doubles!" exclaims Blanqui.[4] Those doubles abound; their limits, diffuse, are confounded; the repetitions do not differ but at the same time they are never the same. The copies gesture toward a melancholy immortality; and eternity in the light of the stars, or in the key of moon, reclaims from Blanqui's Eternity a precedent that had not been sufficiently noticed.

> Thus, thanks to his planet, each man possesses, in extension, an infinite number of doubles that live . . .[5]

Constant, "the Blanqui effect" is verified as much in the works of Bioy Casares as in those of Borges, producing, on the basis of the plurality of worlds, of the interlacing encounters precipitated by voyages, of the slippages of some into others, their suspense and their substance. *The Invention of Morel*,[6] "Plans for an Escape to Carmelo,"[7] "Venetian Masks,"[8] "Unleashed History,"[92] "The Room without Windows."[10] So many texts in which chance encounters would explain coincidence in the narratives of Bioy Casares: "Well, the idea of a collision seems extraordinary. . . . He who seeks himself finds himself."[11]

Constant as well in the imaginary of Borges: "Tlön, Uqbar, Orbis Tertius,"[12] "The South,"[13] "The Theologians,"[14] "The Other Death,"[15] "The Library of Babel,"[16] "The Garden of Forking Paths,"[17] "Death and the Compass,"[18] and so many more, the duplications and dualities could only be explained partially if not for the vision of alternative worlds enabled by and inhabited by the fabulous cosmogony of Blanqui.

In several of Borges's texts, at the beginning of "The Library of Babel" just as at the beginning of *Eternity through the Stars*, Borges and Blanqui transtextualize the same sentence from Pascal: "The universe (which others call the Library) is composed of an indefinite and, perhaps, infinite number of hexagonal galleries. . . . The Library is a sphere whose reasonable center is whichever hexagon, whose circumference is inaccessible," says Borges's narrator.[19] Blanqui, for his part, recalls: "The universe is a circle, whose center is found everywhere and circumference nowhere." [20]Also, like Borges, Blanqui returns to the celebrated affirmation, adding, in his way, further on, a few lines: "Let us say (according to Pascal), and with more precision, that 'the universe is a sphere whose center is found everywhere and surface nowhere.'"[21] Similarly to Blanqui, prisoner in the endless succession of his cells, "a librarian of genius" discovered, in Borges's story, the fundamental law of the Library. The coincidences between both authors are too numerous to be able to record them only in the reductions of an inventory. Nor should the following observation of Borges be passed over:

> This thinker observed that all the books, as diverse as they might be, are made of the same elements: space, the period, the comma, the twenty two letters of the alphabet.[22]

Meanwhile, in his *Astronomic Hypothesis*, Blanqui affirms that:

> The prodigious quantities of different combinations . . . of diverse arrangements . . . It is too much work for such scarce tools.[23]

If it were not a question of the universe instead of the Library, one would say it was Borges himself who proceeds reflecting in the terminology of Blanqui:

> It may be that I find myself disoriented by age and fear, but it is not illogical to think that the world is infinite.[24]

Or, discussing the opposite, in a dialogue held by two of Bioy Casares's characters:

—I am a writer, I answered.
—Me, I'm a cosmographer.
—What you say brings to mind my first intellectual preoccupation. It's strange. It wasn't connected with literature but with cosmography.
—What was your first preoccupation?
—Perhaps the perplexity of a boy shouldn't be called that. I wondered how it could be at the limit of the universe. It had to have some form, some aspect. Because the limit of the universe, as far as it was, exists.[25]

Blanqui had begun by warning us: "Here we enter into the full obscurity of language" and adds immediately, "One should not try to handle the infinite with language." [26]

Neither is it difficult to be surprised by this tone of transcendental familiarity, of skeptical triviality a la Jules Laforgue, of lucid fatalism, an against-the-grain tone that Blanqui adopted and that has definitively marked the writing of our Latin American and Rioplatense writers, even though Walter Benjamin had judged the writing of Blanqui to be deprived of any irony. Nevertheless, the unforeseeable alternatives and the recognition of their frequent repetitions insinuate a discursive reversal that deconstructs whatever risk of solemnity in his sentences, in the same way as he impatiently admonishes: "Either the resurrection of the stars or universal death. . . . It is the third time I repeat this."[27]

In the same way as Blanqui, the imagination of Adolfo Bioy Casares approaches the complexity of infinite space with the naturalness of one who steps out for a walk across the sky, with the same indolence of one who strolls down domestic walks—or passes over them, no less indifferent to their mysteries than to those of the streets of Paris, Buenos Aires, or Montevideo. These authors testify to the monotony of a time that only passes in order to pass again. Frequently Borges, Bioy Casares, have Blanqui appear in their reflections and in their texts. What is Blanqui doing in these lands? An apparition, an unexpected phantom, brought to life by letters.

Nevertheless, it should not be so surprising if, despite this presence, the reader of Bioy Casares or of Borges noted both the gravitation of Blanqui as well as his omission by the critics. This is not a question of insinuating a conspiracy of silence, but rather of orbits that describe paths without ever crossing in the same reader.

If words are the reverse face of the world, this reversibility rescinds it; its iterability multiplies the interlacings and the encounters become more frequent. Between rescission and multiplication, silence is installed in several of the author's voices. E-lector, he already knows it is not possible to read everything. Each reading is an option among those *small worlds* where the statutes of reality/fiction, of truth/version, and fugacity/permanence coincide: "Poetry constitutes that which is most real, that which is only completely real in *another world*."[28] It was Baudelaire who debated more than once and in more than one language:

It doesn't matter where! It doesn't matter where! As long as it is outside of this world![29]

We know that for these writers as for Nietzsche, Blanchot, Lévinas, or Derrida, literature is not only a different discourse but the discourse of the desire to be different, the desire to say as well as the desire of the self and to leave the self, to be elsewhere. Recently Harold Bloom, in the preface to *The Western Canon*—as he had already adopted it from Borges in a prior book—interpreted this desire again as an "anxiety of influence," a notion that in this astronomical context I can only comprehend as that *flux* that is the search for *influence* in the stars, but also the search for the influence of others: the poets who came before, like the first gesture, like an initial gestation.

Search for an anteriority or an authority, an*other* reality, an *exalted* reality, where alterity and ex-altation are confounded in another world, above this one. It could be the possible world, the chosen world of which Liebniz spoke, chosen, read (*elegido, leído*). Books upon books upon books that create—above that bit of reality that once existed—a superreality close to the stars (*estrellas*), close to the symbols, before bursting (*estrellarse*) and fracturing into parts. In the prison where he remained for most of his life, Blanqui contemplates a superior reality, a strange space that becomes ordinary, among the stars, the ether, eternity.

The possibility of an unfolding of simultaneous and successive worlds nourishes these writers, worried by the enigmatic nature of systems insufficiently understood, weighed down by the inheritance of a century, hobbled by boredom, by spleen, as well as by positivisms or astronomic theories and cosmogonic hypotheses. They speculated about solar systems, about infinite space, about other planets, about their origin, about their end, about an eternity in flight, which remains as *time-without-time*, in the place privileged by the symbolic imagination. Later Proust recuperates time and the aesthetic principles he formulated by way of cosmogonic speculations that are assimilated:

Only through art can we leave ourselves, know what the other knows of this universe that is not the same as ours, and whose landscapes are as unknown to us as those that might be on the moon. Thanks to art, instead of seeing only one world, ours, we see it multiplied, and insofar as there are original artists, insofar as we have worlds at our disposition, they will differ more from one another than all those that wheel about in the infinite.[30]

If it is a question of weaving together by way of well-known quotes the less foreseeable considerations of Blanqui, this is due to the attempt to diminish—through indirect intertextual references—a certain deviation and various differences that do not impede our bringing together, *sub specie aeternitatis*, the close connections that exist between Borges, Bioy Casares, and Blanqui. The evident biographical distances, the presumable ideological discrepancies would suggest, at first glance, that it is a question of contrived, forced, almost excessive approximations . . . Bring these three together? That would be "Beau comme . . ." Lautréamont would say, faced with juxtapositions forced by affinity though contiguity, an affinity unsuspected, unheard of. Bring these three together? Certainly, it would be difficult to compare them without being surprised by the combination, not so much because of the coincidences between writers from different centuries coming from distant civilizations and regions, as because of our ignorance. On the one hand, Borges and Bioy Casares, associated with the highest echelons of Argentine society, hardly militant for some tastes, genial masters of a rather lucidly parodic imagination that puts into play the speculative refinements of an intellectual approach, of an exposed erudition that, too intelligent, does not attenuate the properties of a major aesthetic. On the other hand, Blanqui, one of the greater rebels in an age that did not come up short in conspiracies or violence, nor in the mythic (dis)bordering of insurrection. Feared and forgotten, dangerously popular, a revolutionary in a time of revolutionaries, a history of barricades, more ardent than incendiary, sacrificed by a means in which neither combative dissidence nor sacrifice were scarce.

There exists, without a doubt, somewhere, among the errant globes, brains sufficiently more vigorous as to be able to comprehend the enigma that is impenetrable for ours. It is necessary that our zeal continue in its mourning.[31]

In different texts, several times Borges makes reference to *the communist Blanqui*. For his part, Bioy includes long quotes from *Eternity through the Stars* in his. On the other hand, Walter Benjamin, in Paris, learns of the existence of Blanqui, of his phantasmagorias, of the reach of his revolutionary commitment, of his accusations and invectives against the different forms of oppression that dominated the society of the time. Blanqui becomes a decisive reference in the thought of the Jewish German philosopher who, like Bouvard and Pécuchet, the Borgesian characters of Flaubert, or like whichever of the doubles of Blanqui, does not cease copying and copying entire pages from that strange book that is *Eternity through the Stars*. So much so that one can no longer avoid the impression that the lookalikes that pullulate among those pages, that the multiplied doubles that haunt them, seduce and confuse the reader to such a point that he cannot extract himself from the duplications and turns himself into a lookalike, in order to copy, to imitate, to become, in his turn, one of those "new individualities," "of other ourselves." Those were the id-entities conceived by the imagination of Blanqui, by means of which he tried to flee from the enclosures of his prison or from the temporal miseries of all, but which did not succeed in bridling the vehemence of his revolutionary passion.

In *The Cipher*, Borges includes "A Dream," a short poem in prose that, beyond proper names or their absences, contains the essence of the figure in flight of Blanqui:

> In a deserted part of Iran there is a not-so tall tower of stone, without doors or windows. In the one room (whose floor is of earth and which has the shape of a circle) there is a table of wood and a bench. In that circular cell, a man who looks like me writes in characters that I do not understand a long poem about a man in another circular cell who writes a poem about a man who in another circular cell . . . The process has no end and no one will be able to read what the prisoners write.[32]

In only a few lines, Borges sketches the outline of a poetics in images that he shares with Blanqui, rounding out an anonymous vignette that biographically ciphers the image and fantasies of the prisoner, of the "enclosed one" as he was called, in several dungeons. Nevertheless, and beyond the reiterated allusions to text and figure, to development and structure, in other passages Borges quotes and ponders explicitly the integral name of Blanqui—here as well it has been repeated and will be repeated:

> In that chapter of his *Logic* that deals with the law of causality, John Stuart Mill reasons that the state of the universe at any

moment is a consequence of its state at the previous instant and that for an infinite intelligence the knowledge of *one instant alone* would be enough to know the history of the universe, past and future. (He also reasons—Oh Louis-Auguste Blanqui, oh Nietzsche, oh Pythagoras!—that the repetition of any one state would bring about the repetition of all the others and would make of universal history a cyclical series.) In this moderated version of a certain fantasy of Laplace—he had imagined that the present state of the universe is, in theory, reducible to a formula, from which Someone could deduce all of the future and all of the past. Mill does not exclude the possibility of a future exterior intervention that will break the series.[33]

Borges makes numerous allusions to Blanqui and, precisely, on more than one occasion, in relation to one of the themes that matters the most to them. For example, when he enumerates three doctrines apropos of the Eternal Return: the first, astrological, is from Le Bon; the second makes reference to Nietzsche; the third, which is grounded in the enumeration of simple bodies, is the one formulated "by the communist Blanqui."

Of the three doctrines that I have enumerated, the best reasoned and most complex is that of Blanqui. He, like Democritus (Cicero, *Cuestiones académicas*, second book, 40), crowds with facsimilar worlds and with dissimilar worlds not only time but also interminable space. His book is beautifully titled *Eternity through the Stars*.[34]

The references are frequent and the coincidences—grounded in a similar aesthetic conception, doubly cosmic—as surprising as they may be, are not fortuitous. Even when one tries to explain them via the logic of the library—in the same way as it has been attempted to explain chance by way of the displacement of airplanes and the dislocation of airports—the argument does not seem sufficient. Without a doubt, Bioy, Borges, and Blanqui are writers who have read a lot, perhaps many of the same books. A cellmate of Blanqui's declared: "My co-detainee Blanqui. . . . He is the greatest *devourer of books* that I have encountered in my life."[35] Their quotes (*citas*) are really *rendezvous* (*citas*), literary and sentimental encounters in those passages—textual, ritual, passwords—where lives and voices cross paths, verbal passes from one author to another. The quotes are fragmented and confounded with one another, they multiply, they slip between various cases and things (*cosas*) that are also causes. Blanqui mentions Tacitus, Horace, and Virgil, but among these classics does not mention Cicero, whereas Borges and Bioy, each one for his part, refer to the same passage that both quote from Blanqui:

> To plea to Blanqui, in order to praise the theory of the plurality of worlds, was perhaps a merit of Servian; I, more limited, would have proposed the authority of a classic; for example: "According to Democritus, there is an infinity of worlds among which some are not only similar but perfectly equal" [Cicero, *Primeras académicas*, II, 18].³⁶

As well,

> Or if not: "Here we are in Bauli, near Pozzuoli. Do you think that now, in an infinite number of exactly equal places there are meetings of people with our same names, bestowed of the same honors, who have passed through the same circumstances, and in ingenuity, in age, in aspect, identical to us, are discussing this same theme." [Id., II, 40]³⁷

Bioy Casares refers to various sources, but, especially in the story that interests us, he ceaselessly invokes Blanqui. "The Celestial Plot" begins with a paragraph that inscribes the key from the start:

> I received in these days a parcel post; it contained three volumes *in quarto* (the complete works of the communist Luis Augusto Blanqui).³⁸

Further on Blanqui appears again in a more extensive passage:

> I bid farewell to Morris. I promised him I would return the following week. The matter interested me and left me perplexed. I did not doubt Morris's good faith; but I had not written him that letter; I had never sent him books; I did not know the works of Blanqui . . .
> My ignorance of the works of Blanqui is due, perhaps, to the reading plan. Ever since I was young I have understood that, in order not to be dragged along by the inconsiderate production of books and in order to attain, even if only in appearance, an encyclopedic education, I had to read according to an immutable plan. . . .

The "mystery" of the letter incited me to read the works of Blanqui. I quickly realized that he was included in the encyclopedia and that he had written on political themes. That assuaged me; in my plan, immediately after the occult sciences come politics and sociology.

One early morning, on Corrientes Street, in a bookstore run by a blurry old man, I found a dusty bundle of books bound in brown leather, with golden titles and fillets: the complete works of Blanqui. I bought them for fifteen pesos.

On page 281 of my edition there is no poetry. Although I have not read the work entirely, I believe that the writing alludes to *L'éternité par les astres*, a poem in prose. In my edition it begins on page 307 of the second volume. In that poem or essay I found the explication of Morris's adventure.[39]

The editorial and bibliographical data is false, they belong solely to Bioy's fiction. Nevertheless, and with a literal minuteness that the narrative does not frequent, the narrator, a lookalike of Bouvard, of Pécuchet, of Pierre Menard, pauses and launches into a quote from *Eternity through the Stars*. Lookalike of Blanqui and of Bioy Casares, he himself, the reader, although he is writing, cannot do less than transcribe both:

There could be infinite identical worlds, infinite worlds slightly differentiated, infinite different worlds. What I am writing at this moment in this fortress of Toro, I wrote and will write throughout eternity, at a table, on a piece of paper, in a dungeon, entirely similar. In infinite worlds my situation will be the same, but perhaps there will be variations in the reason for my interment or in the eloquence or tone of my pages.[40]

Individuals, doubles, multiples wholes and fragmentary copies. Hypothesis of Blanqui or inventions of Morel, of Morris, or of Bioy: the universe put into pages or screens, exhibiting the world, hiding it; ambushing and lying in wait. It is there and is not, like the worlds, peoples, and cities, trapped in the celestial plot (*trama*) or trap (*trampa*). At the end, Blanqui comes forward:

At this hour, the entire life of our planet, from birth to death, is detailed, day by day, in the myriad of sibling stars, with all their crimes and disgraces. What we call progress is enclosed in each earth within four walls, and vanishes with it. Always and everywhere, on the terrestrial place, the same drama, the same decor, on the same narrow stage, a noisy humanity, infatuated with its grandeur, believing in the universe and living in its prison as if in an immensity, in order soon to sink with the globe that it had carried, with the most profound disdain, the burden of its pride. The same monotony, the same immobility in strange stars. The universe repeats without end and marches in place. Eternity interprets, imperturbably, in the infinite, the same representations.[41]

CHAPTER SIX

Theoretical Invention in Fiction: Marvels, Miracles, and the Gazes of Miranda

> The cause is posterior to the effect, the reason for the voyage is one of the consequences of the voyage.
> —Borges, "The Flower of Coleridge"

For some time now theory is spoken of as if of a voyage, a veering, or rather, if one takes into account, within the same semantic field or sea, the twists of an interpretation adrift or oriented by a jetty, a *quebramar* in Portuguese, the *jetée* with which Jacques Derrida designates it in French, that maritime or speculative construction that channels the sea, directing the sense of the course in the water, or of the discourse. This essay deals with the "*quebramares*," with the voyages of discovery or invention—which in the origin are not distinguished—with the current that does not distinguish either, that comes and goes "like the air in the sky and the sea in the sea,"[1] like the texts that throw themselves, without greater warning, into other texts like theory into fiction, forms of knowing, of *seeing*, of an American imagination where "writing about writing is the future of writing,"[2] the double, multiple forecast with which Haroldo de Campos sees and writes, says and foresees.

Perhaps is would have been appropriate to place the title under an interrogative, to pose the question more than once of which could be the attributes of a Latin American critical discourse. To wonder if the century's end, in which so many ends coincide, would be the appropriate cultural instance to claim, again, the particularity of a writing that, like other contemporary phenomena, is evermore unaware of specific arcs, continental, regional, national, rational boundaries, and to discuss the creative ambiguities of the critical nature. Nevertheless, it is perhaps opportune to examine yet again a question that has become an urgency, as much due to the pressures connected with its production as to the relief that makes them stand out.

Different from the sermons of so many terminal discourses, about poetry, philosophy, absolute knowledge, history, reality, reference, the drum roles of critical discourse seem to resonate everywhere "before our eyes."

Finally, almost at the end of the studies of literary communication, criticism emerges as a privileged object of study. From an attention focused on the author, then on the text, or from the attention dedicated to the reader by a new historicism, the relevant interest in the critique was foreseeable. From the author to the work, from the work to the reader, from the reader to the critic, critical appreciation, like communication itself, describes a path that ends by not ending, because by including in the last phase all the anterior ones its own dynamic returns it to the beginning. It is not necessary to say that the category of author is present in the critical text, doubly present, because the critic pauses to consider it or because he himself is an author, because that duality is extended to the work that is the object of examination and, at the same time, is confounded in one and the same writing with the work of the critic. Because the critic is, above all, a reader who is in turn read; for the sake of being read he is in turn an author and thus the recursivity of the circuit is neither truncated nor closed.

It would not be a matter of claiming, then, the property of a geographical jurisdiction, that for being continental would not for that reason be any less provincial, nor of marking territorial boundaries where policing or disciplinary customs would authorize or not the universal circulation of these works. More than insisting against doctrinal dependence—which exists—or thematic dependence—which also exists—against the absence of a strong American thought, when that absence is a planetary lack, against the imitation of a philosophy resisted from afar, it is proposed, moving beyond those studies that date back to a nineteenth century criticism certain of its positivistic researches, which continued for a large part of the past century, that we *observe* the interactive integration between similar writing, the aesthetic and theoretical coincidences of knowledge and creation that, in the last years, are assimilating different genres into a single textual entity.

A PARTICULAR HISTORY

It is known that since the first periods of colonization, decrees from the Inquisition had prohibited the importation or printing of fictional novels.

Nevertheless, there arrived to the Americas in the bodegas of the galleys of the Spanish merchant fleet: books of science, physics, and math, of Greek and Latin, and of religious and philosophical themes. Legally, the "books of romances and false stories"[3] were intercepted by the frequent Royal Decrees. On April 4, 1531, the House of Contracts directed a Royal Decree to impede the arrival to the Indies of "books of romances, of vain stories, and of profanities such as that of Amadís and others . . . because it is a bad practice for the Indians to learn reading putting aside the books of sounds and good doctrine and, reading those of deceitful history, to learn in those bad habits and vices."[4] The severity of the exclusions, as is known, came to be justified by certain commentators, who recognized that, on the one hand, "the Spaniards were opening wide the doors of European culture to the Indians," such that if these ordinances prohibited "books of Romance of profane subjects and fables," they did so "with the purpose of protecting the Indians, who, because they were ignorant of Spanish customs, when faced with novels in the form of printed books, could have lost faith in the printed word and, as a result, in the Scriptures."[5] In 1536, the Queen complained that "in the execution of this [policy, W.E.] there was not the care that there should have been."[6] At times the severities of the Spanish Crown's censorship were even brushed aside by pointing out that "the mania of persecuting books was universal at that time,"[7] such that it was not exclusive either of the Spanish Indies nor of that epoch. For example,

> Father Labat, having returned from a brief stay on the island of Saint Thomas, already advanced for the 18th century, bought there a shipment of books brought over by the Dutch. 'I took those books—he writes—not so much in order to read them as to impede that they read them, and that the book make an impression on spirits weak and already sufficiently lost. I went leafing through them during the trip and threw them into the sea as I read them.[8]

On the one hand, given these precedents, it would have perhaps been impossible to foresee that over the years it would be precisely fiction that would attain its greatest expression in these territories. On the other hand, over time there was manifested a progressive nonchalance for generic and regional categorizations, making the provenance and location indifferent in favor of a common "literary world."

As a parable of this situation, we will only recall, among many examples, the appearance in the 1920s in Rio de la Plata of Borges's *Inquisitions* (1925), the essays that were intended to relieve the term of "*sambenitos* and the smoke of bonfires." Nevertheless, as far as Borges is concerned, the risks of literariness do not cease to be ironic, to the point that his own inquisitions were handed over to the censorship of those who wanted, by way of his book, to liberate the term.

It was he himself who tried to impede the circulation of the book, first, later excluding it from his *Complete Works*. Without being ignorant of the incontinencies of mechanical reproducibility, he did everything possible to avoid the conservation of the book, from the destruction of the copies to which he had access, to making the contradictory gesture of acquiring them in antiquarian bookstores, ordering them, confiscating them, in order to do the same. Or he accomplished the same task but reversed, writing other books in order to counterbalance them by way of an alterity that he administered in his own way. Later would appear *Other Inquisitions*, which differ in an ambivalent way from the actions imposed by the ecclesiastic tribunal. This second book displaces the first inquisitions by means of new investigations, eluding the doctrines that his writings had tried to disarticulate or had succeeded without trying, contributing to the extinction of "the terrible flame of absolute knowledge."[9]

The reasoned imagination of his writing gave place to a literary form that recuperates interpretation without discarding spectacle in speculation, or the reflection of thought in that of a mirror, or imagination in theory. He would not speak of the invention of a sole genre because, engaged between the image and the idea, he is not interested in distinguishing between genres or canons or codes, those conventions that Christian Metz denominates the formal machines of historical and social content: "To name, to classify: here begins our problem, that of cultural taxonomies."[10]

In the paradoxical "Warnings" that Borges includes at the end of *Inquisitions*, its author proposes to have recourse to "a rhetoric that would start not from the adjustment of the current literary happenings to the already fixed forms of classical doctrine, but rather from their direct contemplation."[11]

BETWEEN TWO MEANS

After the copious data compiled by Emir Rodríguez Monegal in *Borges par lui-même*, it would be redundant to note that Maurice Blanchot, Michel Foucault, Jacques Derrida, Jean Gennette, as well as Jean Baudrillard, Hans Robert Jauss, Emmanuel Lévinas, John Barth, Paul de Man, Harold Bloom, Gianni Vattimo, Jean-François Lyotard, Umberto Eco,

Paul Virilio, Jean Bessière, Douglas R. Hofstadter, and so many other thinkers, writers, and doers of the second half of the twentieth century start from the considerations and fictions of Borges. Everything *passes* through Borges, he is the obligatory passage, the transit and initial cause. So many poets, so many theorists and critics occupy themselves with the imagination of Borges that the imagination of Borges has occupied the world. It is not in vain that a North American critic[12] proposed "to nominate Borges" as the emblem of this age. I have proposed to add to this emblem the inscription *ante litteram*, but that is another story, which has already been alluded to.

For this reason, more than in the theoretic discussion, in the validity or caducity of systems, in "the explicit breakdown of the subject, putting in parentheses the ennunciative mechanism,"[13] in the advances of an "epistemological anarchy," we would have to delve into the alternatives of a certain cultural history that favors this critical primacy. We would have to wonder at the same time about a second grade attempt at "invention" on the part of critical discourse in Latin America, which is not limited to the existence of a recognized textual category—more than a genre because it overflows it, is more and less than two, because it overlaps them—and confirm the "grace/humor" (*gracia*) of Borges's imagination, in which are contracted (the term is less felicitous than the action it denotes), thought and knowledge as forms of a poetic writing.

Without risking, at the start, that "metonymic practice of history"[14] guaranteed by one singular work and one sole proper name, the intellectual imagination of Borges anticipates and condenses the fiction and knowledge of at least a half a century. In as much as the narrative, poetic, essayistic masterpiece eludes the facility of historicizations and categorizations of genres that his genius supercedes, criticism does not elude its time. Nor is it a question of denigrating theory, as Stefan Collini does, attributing to it, in his introduction to Eco's *Interpretation and Overinterpretation*, the individual success in American (North American) academic life where cultural diversity and the principles of the market "Have contributed to making of this second order mass of reflection designated by the word 'theory' the central intellectual arena where reputations surge and where battles for status and power are played out."[15]

Nevertheless, one of the principle attributes that distinguishes Borges's writing is neither the theoretical questioning not the entry of different philosophical doctrines, nor a critique of the thought or judgment that resolves—or not—the narrative intrigues or the truth of his poetry.

Perhaps the poetic invention of Borges is his Latin American and universal aspiration, the search for a *transgressive writing*, a transgression that means—it is its first meaning—"to pass to the other side," through frames, margins, boundaries. A form of "passing beyond," a transcendence that, at the same time as it *reveals* the limits—which are the requisite of definitions—makes them disappear:

—beyond traditional *literary genres*, that writing supercedes or suspends definitions, interlacing categories.

—beyond the attributions of reader and critic or of author and critic, or of *author and reader*, his writing superimposes functions presumptuously considered exterior to the textual universe, introducing them, crossing them with the properly textual functions of *narrators and characters*, confounding them.

—beyond the possibilities of distinguishing thought from imagination in areas, his writing slips between disciplinary boundaries: *literary, philosophical,* or between *theory and poetry,* or between *history and fiction,* interlacing them, or between *reality and its representation* (two forms of interpretation), or between *vigil and sleep,* or between times that do not *differ,* return, or coincide, disappearing into an instant that, in its lack of time, does not differ from eternity. Borges's writing annuls the differences between names and numbers, making *the other from the same,* making of alterity an identity, both doubtful.

In this aesthetic "without limits" of Borges, even *words or things* are confounded, rescinding an opposition that should be ironic. A lack of limits is produced that attains perfection and on the basis of this is demonstrated the coincidence of *the indefinite with definition,* confounding, contradictorily, *the finished with the infinite.*

The excesses of a canon like that of Borges revise and resist the impositions of the canon. Without excluding the masters, Borges throws light on authors barely known or unknown, brings to the light (gives birth to) others who, like J. Hládik, a playwright in jail in Prague, like Pierre Menard, critic and novelist in Nîmes, make of their literary existence a parody of universal literature that counts among its glories the statute of an author who does not exist celebrated for a work that also does not exist, or that is not his. They are signs of a *negative poetics* that, like negative theology, configure the theoretical and critical imaginary of this epoch.

Borges has brought together in one sole figure all the literary functions. Like he himself, Menard is a reader, a critic, author, translator according to some, a character in all cases. He exists for/because of/by (*por*) Borges, and the preposition functions as cause, as substitution and as multiplication: Borges *por* Menard, one author *por* another who does not exist; as if muliplied by zero, the number that reunites all numbers, it exhausts him, suppresses him.

This vanishing of an author in functions that are similar is quite prior to the already noted "death of the author" (1968). The sentence is that of Roland Barthes, who pronounces it on the basis of well known theories of writing.[16] A little later (1969), on the basis of the same notion of *écriture*—although in a certain way he impugns it—Michel Foucault pronounces a similar condemnation when he refers to "the disappearance of the author."[17] These were neither the first deaths to be announced nor the most lapidary.[18]

The disappearance of the oppositions that defined the systematic differences of doctrines more rigid than rigorous, the disappearance or postponement of *difference* in a writing that claimed to denigrate the voice, bells of mourning for the disappearance of definitive knowledge, sublated knowledge, that is to say, for a *pensiero debole* defined—interpreted— by Gianni Vattimo. Disappeared the referent, or the referential illusion vanished, neither does thought venture to impose. It is not surprising that an aesthetic of disappearance that razes boundaries has its fabulous antecedent in Borges's work. In his texts, a cell in Prague borders on a foyer in Tacuarembó; a city in Africa on a district in North America, or a slum in Buenos Aires blends into another in Dublin. Historiography is the same as cartography, reading or writing associates and condenses, obliterates, literally, distances. If the *Encyclopedia Universalis* defines the passing concept of *globalization*, so recent and often cited, on the basis of a quote: "*Le temps du monde fini commence*" (The time of the completed world begins),[19] the oxymoron is from Paul Valéry, and he justifies it. It would have been more pertinent to illustrate this by way of any one of the numerous a-geographical references that Borges imagines from his earliest to his most recent writings: "You might say that a passport does not change the character of a man."[20]

THEORETICAL DISENCHANTMENTS: SECULARIZATION AND GLOBALIZATION

The complicities that have defined the critical statute are complicated in the present day by other dualities that confirm as much the hybrid nature of the critic as the excesses of his or her irregularly reticent condition.

Today a preeminence of criticism would be explained by the disappearance of "*les phares*" (the enlightened ones), to allude in the terms of Baudelaire's visual rhetoric to the absence of new writers and thinkers of greatness; too simple, a mechanics of compensations would explain away a reason as debatable as it is transitory.

The preeminence of criticism before the theoretical legitimation of intertextuality does not rival, in general terms, with those excellences of the writer, such that even when his irradiation orients the cultural movements of a period, the antagonism between creation and criticism, original and derivative writing, work of the imagination and intellectual work, is not maintained.

Comparing Barthes's anxiety at the idea of writing a novel, or the substitutive search in the pleasure of the text, with the efforts of Eco, who yearns to write more than one novel in which he introduces, "as certain as science," the recourses of a theoretical foundation that he himself or his colleagues elaborated. The revelations of writing of Jacques Derrida, which impugn disciplinary categories and stereotypes, speculating on the texts of writers such as Mallarmé, Artaud, Genet, Ponge, and Celan reconciles philosophy and literature in a double reflection that does not deny either of the two. Just as for Kant,[21] "all the capacities of the soul can be reduced to three: the 'faculty of knowledge,' 'the sensation or feeling of pain or pleasure, and the faculty of desire," "the crisis of criticism" is a change that comprehends those capacities comprehended in different forms.

Other factors would be the buttressing of doctrines, the rigor of systems, neopositivist optimism—the ingenuous and erudite confidence in methodological solutions and in ideological models that exalted the critical function until the 1970s—have declined. Nevertheless, this decline, suggestively, entailed a reduction in the preeminence of criticism.

We could not discard, as a consequence, other historical circumstances in addition to these epistemological conjunctions and locate in less disciplinary reasons the relevance of a phenomenon that has been attributed to the flourishing of human sciences in one of their greatest apogees.

Despite the fact that in this field definitions have become elusive, that the resistance to theory[22] is an inherent condition of the nature of theory itself, it would be necessary to recognize that critical discourse starts from literary discourse and, consequent to the ambivalencies of that indefinable, or at least "endless," "nature," participates in the logical fallacy of a de-*fin*-ition without *fin*ality—because it does not end—without end, because it is not of use. Part of the "ineffability" of beauty is its "undecidability," the rejection of a concept conceived in the short term, the urgencies of a thought that makes use of concepts for which the objects "criticism" and "literature" are not always circumscribable.

If art has been defined as those productions that a community understands as art, if the definition of literature does not promise much more, the criticism practiced by the art of judgment could be adjusted to that vagueness, that errancy of meaning that depends historically, socially, on other definitions that do not manage to be formulated, and as such maintain themselves in this radiant precariousness.

The critical necessity that literary institutionalization requires does not undermine its diffuse statute, on whose oscillations the canon depends, at the same time as it is the canon that depends on the critical activity. This reciprocity of circular dependence does not discard the ups and downs of the market since, if indeed the validity of a mediatic literature is irregularly recognized, what is not in debate is the fact that the mediatic space is recognized as the most "natural" for criticism. Its functions of mediation, between work and reader, between author and reader, find in today's globalization of techno-scientific communication a stability and authority that the tradition did not assign it. The media consecrate these attributions of mediation with jurisdictions of universality that are their own. Criticism finds itself in its element in the media, between two media/means, and it is that between-two wherein are consolidated its mediacritical or mediacratic settlements, which extend over all that is mediatic and over what is not, in order to assimilate it.

THE LIMITS OF CRITICISM

In this way the theme that has existed for more than twenty years has acquired, in this tele-techno-scientific culture,[23] dimensions of an exaggeration that was not foreseeable. Properly speaking, the competence of today's critic is not so different from that of the original critics. Reconsidered the problems of the constitution of the canon, reconsidering "the quest of the author" as "a critical question": Who is critical in a literary arena that has extended its critical arrogance to the point of not knowing its limits? Who is not?

It is no longer a question of the practicing critic of whom T. S. Eliot spoke but rather of a literary practice that since Borges—without overlooking passages of the *Quijote*, of Baudelaire, of Mallarmé, of Proust—does not lend itself to exclusions of authority or genre. From its beginnings the critical task implied historically the consideration of themes that until the present have not ceased to be "the themes" of a labor determined by the orientations of literary theory and its problems: the question of the author, truth and fiction, identity and alterity in writing, the plurality of voices in the text, its reception, the rigidity or flexibility of the canon, among others.

The relations into which the writing of creation enters with critical writing have become close to the same degree that critical writing has been assimilated to theoretical writing. Inscribed in the limits, its liminal function is constituted as an epistemological question: "The word *criticism* signifies more an investigation of the limits of knowledge, that is to say, of that which cannot be formulated or is ungraspable."[24] Its position as *tiers arbitre*, or third in discord, who has to resolve a plaint between two orders, would fit if it were a third, an arbiter, except that it does not involve a plaint between two others, but rather it is the critic who participates in the condition in which both parties find themselves. His thirdness is, without doubt, his natural statute and the recognition of his semiotic condition, the third term, the figuration of an *orbis tertius* that criticism carries to planetary dimensions.

Without claiming to carry out an inventory—since such a proposal alludes to invention—nor to recur to the dangers of taxonomic procedures, but rather to deconstruct on the basis of the critical function whatever taxonomy that tries to register and describe taxatively the critical function, it behooves us to recall the arbitrariness that results from the dualities among which we debate:

—The critic installs himself between the author and the reader but, without eluding the network of implications of his work, participates in the attributions and requisites of both and, in a certain way, neutralizes the opposition by way of a third position that involves them both.

—The critical texts is found between the text of creation, without ceasing to be itself a creation, and the theoretical text, without ceasing to be theoretical. A convergence organized by forms of knowledge that pass through the imagination or through reason producing a third form of reasoned imagination that defines the predominant characteristic of contemporary literature.

One could attribute to the vigor of the imagination *the weakness of a thought* that recognizes hermeneutics as the manifestation of contemporary knowing: "The contemporaneity of hermeneutics, which is thought of for good reason as the philosophy of modernity,"[25] a knowing that distances itself from philosophy in order to come closer to history, to the accidental variability of circumstances, in order to disembowel the textual truth. Vattimo attributes to the discoveries of interpretation the mission of a transcendent nature: "The history of salvation and the history of interpretation are far more tightly bound than the Catholic orthodoxy would like to admit."[26]

—In effect, he attributes to hermeneutic intermediation an eternal safe passage: "salvation occurs through interpretation,"[27] navigates between different times. The critical gaze make the past resurface in the present of reading, an ephemeral time that is prolonged or not according to how the critical examination manages to consolidate it. In this sense all criticism is responsible for continuity, is posterior to the literary texts it deals with, a *posterity* that is consecutive time and suspension of time: heaven. It is, in this sense, that the present of critical interpretation keeps vigil over the text, suspending the difference between times that have passed or, equally, times that will pass.

—Although it is known to be ephemeral, critical writing scrutinizes a knowledge and, at the moment of finding it, it finds it but without going beyond conjecture, beyond an imminent revelation that remains under suspicion, or a supposition that, in the terms of Charles Sanders Peirce, would be an *abduction*. Neither deduction nor induction, the hypothesis is a sequestering of reason, a supposition that is valid for only a short time, a certainty that is not prolonged for much more than the clarity produced by a lighting bolt. Like the horizon always in flight, one hypothesis is displaced by another hypothesis that is left behind only to be in turn superceded by a new hypothesis, and so on successively: each epoch, each critic, each reader *supposes*.

Critical supposition may be an abduction, or it may prolong the work thanks to an infinite interpretation, like unlimited semiosis, the successive comprehension of which Peirce spoke. For this reason, despite the apparent tautological construction, it would not be merely redundant to propose *the hypothesis that interpretation is a hypothesis*, a conjecture, a supposition that turns back on itself, a logical figure but also a game of the imagination, "a play of musement."[28] I have already said that in this age, when *positions* becomes less and less drastic, when *oppositions* are defended with indifference, it would be possible to find in *supposition* the personal procedure valid for approaching that scarce reality of reality that is ours, the truth that is ever less convincing, conditioned ever more by a plurality that puts in evidence the dangerous limits of a unique truth.

A hypothesis, a supposition, in both expressions is revealed—from the (in)formation of the word—an operation that lies beneath the text. *To suppose* means to interpret; *to interpret*, a way of understanding (*entender*). I do not believe that "understand" in English is associated with this hypothetical position (localization) but, without a doubt, comprehension is bound to a perspective that is opened from within this plane, which is not of inferiority (*under*) but rather of profundity. From the pro-found depths, the foundation to which one accedes only with difficulty.

We spoke of the anagrammatic strategy that consists of a rereading, a re-vision, a *sub-version* that is realized underneath the words (a paragram or hypogram in the terms of Saussure, or *les mots sous les mots*, for Jean Starobinski). A transposition of the graphic unities of the word responds to the procedures of selection and combination, a combinatory of decisions of that *lector-elector-selector* who recuperates in each reading (*lectura*) the freedom of an option that revises and defines it.

Between the cloister and the century, between the university and the media, there remains no cultural space in which the management of criticism does not mediate or inflate itself. If their differences are recognized, they are becoming ever less noticed in this century that has consecrated, paradoxically, secularization as its basic condition, razing the regimes of cloisters in a progressive secularization that leaves no ground for the sacred, for separation, for the discernment that is the key of the critical exercise. Discernment is the separation, the distinction, the pondering that our age has put aside. That is why I cited Eco as a paradigmatic example of this secular explosion. His literary ambition that extends in voluminous novels the information of his readings, the deeds of not-so-ordinary bibliophilia: the collector of old books chooses little known facts, the least known of an extravagant library rescued from dereliction or deluge. Among the novelties of technical prowess whose novelties no longer astonish, one is also not too astonished by the results of relics found by an encyclopedic archeology that brings together equally mirrors with mirages in a deep swell, that *mare magnum* where the "reader-navigator" confronts the tempest, various tempests.

America is configured from the remains of the shipwreck, with the pieces of an embarcation and a library: those cherished books that, close to the New World, Prospero rescues from a storm that can be seen as a sign from Providence—which is how Columbus interpreted them in his *Diario*, the logbooks of another voyage he claims as his own. From within his own perplexity, Emir Rodríguez Monegal, the greatest Urugayan critic and greatest critic of Borges, confessed a few years ago:

> It has taken on so many twists and turns since my birth in the border town of Melo that at times I think of myself as a bizarre combination of spectator and actor looking at a play in which I am simultaneously a performer and a critic.[29]

A rare combination in which the terms are inverted. It is true: Manuel Puig, Severo Sarduy, and others say—write—that they have been invented by Emir. I transcribe here the fragment of a letter from Manuel Puig who, playing with the ruins and voices of Babel, joins with Sarduy in the explicit recognition of that common authority who overflows the critical function:

> Well, the Puig Bulletin ends with the announcement of his next novel, of a crime novel stripe, currently shooting on location in

perverted Buenos Aires, it's a sort of thriller.[30] Do you remember MGM's slogan for the premiere of "I'll Cry Tomorrow" with Susan Hayward? It went like this: "A Film shot on location: inside a woman's soul." Well, the same could said of my crime novel. Ok, Emir, this time answer me please. In Paris Severo and I were in agreement that we are both your inventions. It wouldn't occur to you to disinvent me for some mysterious reason?[31]

Although they do not say so in the same words, both are aware that "it is the other who makes you a writer," and in this case "the other" has a name. It is not so frequent that recognition be that explicit.

Playing a plurality of roles, the considerations and realizations of Emir were an advance on the cinematographic excellencies of Peter Greenaway, a film director who makes of the image his world or of the world an image, on the basis of the books that he saves from the *Tempest* and the shipwreck; he saves them and shows them. Prospero—John Gielgud—gives his voice to the other characters, evoking the search for a unity that the idiomatization of language revokes. Like the critic in the literary space that was his own, Prospero interprets all the functions, speaks for all the characters. In the film, the voice of Prospero is that of all, the books of mirrors (*The Book of Mirrors*),[32] the gaze (*mirada*) is that of Miranda.

This is also so of the poetics of blindness that Derrida outlines: the blind man becomes "the great blind man." In the exploits of Latin American thought it is the woman who sees or the woman who looks, or both: "*volonté de savoir comme volonté de voir*" (the will to know like the will to see), as Derrida said.[33] Before shining forth in the film, Prospero was the image from which derived the great symbols of Latin American ideology,[34] which since the end of the last century the continent has adopted as its own: the saga of Ariel, of Prospero, Caliban, and, last but not least,[35] it is now time to start Miranda's clock. The admired and admirable gaze (*mirada*) of Miranda, which brings together, in a single aesthetic dazzling display, imagination and knowledge, the stupor prior to study, the miracle of the gaze (*mirada*), amazed by the magic of Prospero, by the conversion of the scattered parts of the shipwreck into the images of a world to be made.[36] Between Europe and America, between Ariel and Caliban, between fiction and theory, between his memories of a past world and the foundation of a new time, Miranda[37] dreams, idea and figure, all of humanity:

O wonder!
How many goodly creatures are there here!

How beauteous mankind is! O brave new world,
That has such people in't.[38]

Bessière, apropos of "the formal play of Alejandra, by Ernesto
Sabato," spoke of "the fable of blindness,"[39] referring to those characters
with whom he is concerned in "the paradox of the tale." Dealing with that
between-two that is the ambivalent space of Miranda, one could speak of
"la fable du regard" (the fable of the gaze) as *fábula* and *habla* (fable and
speech), a *parable* (*parábola*) of his lucid vision (in Spanish the three terms
recall the same origin, which associates fiction with the word—*palabra*).
It is those tensions and oppositions that orient the critical activity, the
presence of the critic, a mediation that makes of its condition an eternity
hard to define, a concept hard to determine, which feeds the air of this
age—"those airy nothings"[40]—the debilitation of a theory that brings
with it a theory of debilitation, the decline of strong structures, the resistance to doctrines, to the radicalisms that vanish into reconciliations more
apparent than real, and which even the fainting of anterior adherencies
fails to scandalize.

If it was indeed Heidegger —and no wonder—who insisted on the
etymology of the word *Occident*—the land of sunset, of the fall—and
despite the fact that it occurred to Oswald Spengler to sketch out a biological theory of history, of its progressive decline in *Der Untergang des
Abendlandes*, nevertheless the philological coincidence does not go
beyond a felicitously infelicitously etymological analogy that the current
stage of the century's intellectual history confirms. Though coincidental,
it pertinence does not cease to be real.

It is language proper, it is proper to language to favor these circular
effects, these voices in echo. Apropos of the hermeneutic circle, Hans
Georg Gadamer said:

> The hermeneutic rule according to which the whole must be
> understood on the basis of the particular, and the particular on
> the basis of the whole, comes from ancient rhetoric. It is the
> hermeneutics of modern times that has transposed the art of
> rhetoric onto the art of understanding. In both cases it is a ques-
> tion of a circular relation.[41]

The critic must be attentive to the recourses of the hermeneutic task, the
discovery of a past that, unknown, surprises with its strangeness the evi-
dences of a present, the search for meaning, the conjectures and conjunctions of comprehension. The invention of critical discourse takes into

account that hermeneutic requisite, a *hybrid* condition in which participates nature as crossed, a chiasmus that opposes extremes and reconciles them in a different species only because it has the property of assimilating the others, in the same way as it assimilates into its hybridity *hybris*. Cross and excess, a double condition that philology does not confirm but that propitiates the secularization of an interpretation that cannot be understood merely as "a logic of individual discourse,"[42] but in the double sense with which it has played since the beginning, rescuing classical dualities that contemporary thought recuperates.

All of which is to say that the scholar, researcher, professor, critic interprets, but so too does the actor, pianist, author who—through the mediation of transtextualities, carnivalizations, parodies, quotes—does not cease to be an intermediator of the tradition that he or she confirms or refutes, which is the same action with a different opposite:

> The eyes speak,
> words look,
> looks think

says Octavio Paz in "To say: To do,"[43] recalling, in another part, that the best that we Hispano Americans have done we have not done in the domain of politics and economics but rather in that of literature and the arts.[44]

In that crossroads of the senses (of various synaesthesias or homonyms) is rehabilitated, as Abdelwahab Meddeb[45] recalls, the priority of the imagination as a form of knowledge, postponed by the privileges of intellectual procedures and the seduction of their reasons, always partial. The duality of interpretation is found in the foundations of knowledge, that double vision, reasoned, and aesthetic, that is part of the imagination, of culture, where reflection can be a meditation but also the image reflected in the crystal, a mirage or a duplication in water, speculation as abstraction of reason, a strategy in finance or a figure between mirrors. As *theoria* was in the beginning: a contemplation close to spectacle, to theater, before ever being contracted into a disciplined discourse of knowledge. These are forms of "*escrever*," of writing and seeing, that approach each other and coincide, that separate and adjust themselves, an expectation, in more than one language.

CHAPTER SEVEN

The Ironies of a Blind Seer

What will the indecipherable future dream? It will dream
that Alonso Quijano can be Don Quijote without leaving his town and his books. It will dream that a vespers
of Ulysses can be more prodigal than the poem that narrates his travails. It will dream human generations who
will not recognize the name of Ulysses. It will dream
dreams more precise than today's vigil. It will dream that
we will be able to do miracles and that we will not do
them, because it will be more real to imagine them. It will
dream worlds so intense that the voice of just one of its
birds could kill you. It will dream that forgetting and
memory can be voluntary acts, not aggressions or gifts of
chance. It will dream that we can see with our whole
body, as Milton wished from the shade of those tender
orbs, his eyes. It will dream a world without machines
and without that painful machine, the body. Life is not a
dream, but it can become a dream, Novalis writes.
                              —Borges, "Alguien soñará,"

OF MERE TITLES

When dealing with more than one vision, with a divided vision, or
with a diffuse blindness, it would not be difficult to allude, despite
the passage of several decades since its publication, to a binary that, in its
English title enables as much the *acuities* of insight as the limitations of
blindness. Verified by the facts and the reflections that analyze them, the
foresights of Borges, those surprising anticipations of his intellectual
imagination, his provocations or prophecies that as much the theories as
the histories of his century continue to confirm, ever closer to his poetics,

we would not have to think of Paul de Man nor of the foundations of
Blindness and Insight, and yet they surge, by way of reductive, almost
mechanical associations, from a rereading that neither directs them nor
puts them aside.

It follows from this that, reviewing the variations of a literary perspicacity that impede dialectically aesthetic forms articulated by unforeseeable contradictions, paradoxes that resolve into coincidences, I would
not avoid getting even with a theoretical position whose controversial
critical elaborations continue to mark the well-trodden mystery of conjunctions that do not attenuate opposition but, on the contrary enter into
it in order to treat as finished a game that, in reality—or in its allegories—
does not end.

Nevertheless, in the first place we would have to resolve a question
of terms or, rather, "of mere titles," as Borges says in "The Blind Man."[1]
In the same way as one of the first books that Borges wrote was titled
Inquisitions,[2] a mention that he inscribed as a kind of threshold in order
to make way for a new literary space not conditioned by the deviances of
history, where he declared from the beginning his intention of unburden-
ing the concept of the violence of conversions, of exiles, and of bonfires,
it would be more simple to unburden *blindness and insight*, as much as its
adverse combination, of semantic "occupation" (*Besetzung* the Germans
would say, as if referring to the occupation of a city by an enemy army or
by themselves) that reduces them to the simplifications of one sole
authority or one sole author.

In the second place, it would be necessary to make way for a hypothesis. Despite the fact that that he does not usually say or indicate it, it is
certain that Paul de Man was well acquainted with Borges's work. It may
even be supposed that he came to know him personally when Borges was
invited to Harvard as the Charles Eliot Norton Professor in 1967, a university where de Man was himself professor between 1950 and 1960 and
from which he does seem to have distanced himself too much afterward.
Furthermore, at Yale University, more than a colleague, de Man had been
one of Emir Rodríguez Monegal's friends (1969–1985). Rodríguez Monegal has been the most fanatic Borgologist, Borgian, Borgist, even in the
early days when Borges was only appreciated by a limited group of con-
noisseurs. So much so that not only was Emir the scholar most knowl-
edgeable concerning the life and work of Borges, as Umberto Eco
recognized while Borges was still alive,[3] but also some one who, for many
reasons, biographical and literary, slipped that third person—the proper
noun constant in his dialogue—toward the first, a slippage legitimated by
recurrent quotes in a discourse that identified the two men beyond mere
grammar. At times his interlocutor could become perturbed by the

impression of a personal, almost pronomial alternation, the gradual metamorphosis of one person into another. In those conversations, Emir was slowly transformed into the prized dummy of a distant ventriloquist: quotes of Borges, anecdotes, but above all the humorous tone that conformed to an unexpected physiognomy, the gestures adequate to another facial features, of a voice that is duplicated, like another face, before one's eyes.

There is no doubt that for years de Man had known of the existence of Borges's work. In 1964, in the *New York Review of Books,* de Man had published a brief review on the appearance of *Labyrinths* and *Dreamtigers,* titled, "A Modern Master: Jorge Luis Borges"[4] which begins with a quote from William Butler Yeats:

Empty eyeballs knew
That Knowledge increases unreality . . .

If indeed it figures as an epigraph to his article, it is only when closing that de Man make a lateral allusion to Borges's blindness, a mention that does not justify the strength of that epigraph, attenuated by the reference to a suffering from which the critic wrests importance. He mentions the blindness as a natural lack owing to the years of the Argentine writer who, nevertheless, were not so many and, indeed, he would live for many more.

Rereading the article, one finds strange the thematic unbalance in favor of the epigraph and, returning to peruse de Man's other essays, included in the mentioned book, it is also strange not to find there even one sole reference to Borges or to his blindness. More suggestive still is that in the posthumous publication, *The Resistance to Theory,*[5] Borges figures only two times in the index of authors, both corresponding merely to mentions, not strictly textual, of their author. One is from Wlad Godzich, who announces from the prologue that de Man had planned to write a book of essays about classic authors like Montaigne or as modern as Borges.[6] The second mention appears in an interview[7] (RAI, Italy, 1983) with Stefano Rosso, translated from the Italian and included at the end of the book. When de Man tells him that "I feel perfectly at ease writing on eighteenth- or seventeenth-century authors and don't feel at all compelled to write on contemporaries," Rosso reminds him that nevertheless, many years before he had written an article on Borges, to which de Man replies: "Well, it was suggested to me . . . Certainly I would be at any time ready to write on Borges, certainly on the fiction of Blanchot, but if you ask me on what contemporary French authors . . . I could possibly think of myself writing on Calvino."

It is the only mention, in his entire oeuvre, of an author demanded by his interlocutor and included in an eventual list, as if his interest for Borges had been only accidental, isolated, and distant. He takes his distance: "It has been suggested to me," and, bothered, lets go of the name as of a red hot coal, passing quickly to other authors to whom he had attributed similar possibilities, engaging a barely contingent future.

Anecdote, the omission or postponement should not pass unnoticed. Above all if one keeps in mind that, in the 1964 review, de Man, when trying to define the stories of Borges, considers that it is not possible to compare them to other stories or moralizing fables because, he says, "their world is the representation, not of an actual experience, but of an intellectual proposition."[8] He formulates a quite similar consideration apropos of the nature of representation, starting point for the ambivalencies of the aesthetic process.[9]

In that review of 1964, de Man, among a few stories, commented on "The Garden of Forking Paths,"[10] a story in which Borges has the narrator say:

> I know that of all the problems, none of them worried and worked him like the abysmal problem of time. Indeed, that is the only problem that does not figure in the pages of the *Garden*. He does not even use the word that means *time*. How do you explain that voluntary omission?
>
> I proposed several solutions; all insufficient. We discussed them; in the end, Stephen Albert said to me:
>
> —In a riddle whose theme is chess, what is the only word that is prohibited? I reflected for a moment, and responded:
>
> —The word *chess*.
>
> —Precisely, said Albert. *The Garden of Forking Paths* is an enormous riddle, or parable, whose theme is time; that recondite cause prohibits it from mentioning its name. To *always* omit a word, to recur to inept metaphors and obvious paraphrases, is perhaps the most emphatic way of indicating it. It is the torturous way preferred, in each of the meanderings of his indefatigable novel, by the oblique T'sui Pen. I have confronted hundreds of manuscripts, corrected the errors introduced by the negligence of copyists, I have thought to reestablish the primordial order, I have translated the entire work: it is apparent to me that he does not once use the word *time*.[11]

And the narrator of the story continues hypothesizing on the meaningful omissions of words, of deeds, of times, in the narration of a story that, retrospectively, seems to coincide with other events that were reproduced in those same years, variants of the adverse perception of the *purloined letters*,[12] letters, of the alphabet or missives, as evident to the eyes as they are unnoticed.

Nevertheless, it is not only the omissions of the critic that are so suspicious, but also his repetitions:

> In Lukacs's story the villian—time—appears as the hero . . . The reader is given the elements to decipher the real plot hidden behind the pseudo-plot, but the author himself remains deluded.[13]

As much in *Blindness and Insight* as in his review of Borges, the same de Man said that the artist has to put on the mask of the *villain* in order to create a style: time or mask, the villain is present in his texts even though the author dissimulates (himself). However, it does not seem to me necessary to make a minute comparison between overly faithful coincidences that, in this case, do not require the attention of an investigation or inventory. More than the coincidence of a single critical slight of hand, the prolonged and careful attention he dedicates to the story "Theme of the Traitor and the Hero,"[14]—one of the least well-known and least commented on of Borges's stories in those years—shows that de Man could not avoid interpreting that the omissions, which are not only decisive for Borges's aesthetic, were also frequent and revelatory for his characters as much as they would be for de Man or for the reader who was capable of deciphering the real plot hidden behind a false plot.

In the first place, Borges's story, which is from 1944, also begins, like the review of 1964, with an epigraph from Yeats.[15] In the story, because of one of those narrative strategies of universality, Borges's narrator prefers not to define the circumstances:

> Details, rectifications, adjustments are missing; there are zones of history that had still not been revealed to me; today, January 3, 1944, I make it out like that. [. . .] Let us say (for the sake of narrative comfort) Ireland; let us say 1824. The narrator is called Ryan, he is the great grandson of the young, the heroic, the beautiful, the murdered Fergus Kilpatrick.[16]

One tolerates in the intrigues of the story that a narrator is not differentiated from a historian. In "Theme of the Traitor and the Hero," that character, also ambiguous, who is his descendent proposes to investigate the tragic attack that ended the life of an exemplary revolutionary. Nevertheless, he discovers that his ancestor was not the admirable conspirator that the fatherland venerated but rather a traitor discovered in compromising circumstances, who also was not murdered, victim of a terrorist attack, but rather was judged in secret, accused, found guilty, and executed with the same discretion. After long hesitations, the narrator decides to cover up the embarrassment of a past of betrayals and instead of declaring the truth:

> He publishes a book dedicated to the glory of the hero; even that, perhaps, was foreseen.[17]

Between veracity and its versions, he discovers the theatricalized execution of his ancestors, glimpsing among the different circumstances the dramatic model of *Julius Caesar*, the tragedy perpetuated by the "English enemy," William Shakespeare, but he prefers to remain silent about the discovery. In contrast, faced with a similar situation, Ortwin de Graef, a student of literature of the University of Lovaina, Belgian like his countryman Paul de Man, did not succumb to the temptation of the complicity of the model and, opposing it, preferred not to remain silent about the revelations of his investigation.

One cannot fail to notice that among Irish writers paradoxes abound, and it is insinuated that Life imitates Art much more than Art imitates life. Borges's narrator does not hesitate to imitate one of the most illustrious of the Irish.[18] Carnivalizing that affirmation, the narrator says: "That history would have copied history was already sufficiently astonishing; that history copies literature is inconceivable."[19] Nevertheless, it would not be surprising if theory copied literature; moreover, it is predictable that fiction be ahead of it. It is only a question of verifying, then, that the coincidences between the fiction of Borges and the theoretical contributions of de Man are numerous and notorious.

It seems disconcerting, on the other hand, that one should omit mentioning Borges as blatantly as one comes to cover up the guilt of a past in collaboration with the enemy. Perhaps this as well Borges foresaw: he anticipated the history of his reticent chronicler, some of the directions of his thought and the ethical fluctuations of an intrigue. Like the historian of the story that he was familiar with, who preferred to omit the betrayal and the scruples, de Man kept secret the violence of his past collaboration with the enemy, his debts to Belgium and Borges. Faced with this silence, his colleagues, his friends (who loved him, who believed him worthy of greater feelings), conjectured, without confirmation, that de Man's secrecies could be due to the discretion observed by one who might have suffered the tribulations of resistance. The ambiguous relations between history and literature, the turbid options that are proposed in "Theme of the Traitor and the Hero," are multiplied in the biography and reflections of the infamous Belgian critic. When he speaks in general of the blindness of the critic, who "in his blindness, turns the weapon of his language upon himself,"[20] perhaps he intended to say that also silence—which is language—can produce that reversal, a low blow that language gives the one who uses it without noticing the uncontrollable derivation of the duplicities it implies.

It is well known that in an epoch in which various transtextualities, carnivalizations, and polyphonies legitimated palimpsest writings, the displacement of themes and texts are all still of importance, and the interest in fragments of writing is a common metaphor. It is not a question then of demanding rights of textual exclusivity or of anachronistic registers, less so now, when the electronic perfection of the media of communication are obliterating the referent, accumulating copies and reducing the complexities of representation to images that, on the screen, present one reality for another, as immediate, as unmediated.

In *The Anxiety of Influence*,[21] Harold Bloom begins his book by recalling quite summarily that Borges had said that poets create their precursors.[22] I do not know if Bloom knew that this is one of the most often quoted sentences of Borges, and if he only mentions Borges in passing in order to make this frequency appear obvious. It is possible that de Man does not mention him for reasons of the same appearance of obviousness, or because he experiences as much the fear as the desire of that anxiety. It is rather significant that de Man and Bloom suppress their reference to Borges. In those same years, Michel Foucault began *Les mots et les choses*[23] affirming that "this book was born from a text of Borges's," and continues elaborating his thought on the basis of "The analytical idiom of John Wilkins."[24] Several years ago, Jean Bessière made of "Borges and the Fable of the Sphinx: From the Enigma to the Enigmatic," the title and beginning of the preface to his book on *The Enigmaticity of Literature*.[25] Douglas R. Hofstadter and Daniel Dennet, in 1981, not so far from here, Bloomington, begin *The Mind's I*[26] by transcribing the entirely of "Borges and I." That pronoun that, in English, juxtaposes at the same time Borges with an author, with himself, and with an eye—*The Blind's Eye*—adding to the pronominal ambiguity one more semantic twist, necessary to return to blindness and the ambiguity of its visions.

BLINDNESS: A POINT OF VIEW

Despite dealing with Borges, with the foreseeably uncontrollable derivations of whichever of his themes, I tried to concentrate this reflection in depth on one precise point and nothing else. One of the properties presented by his work, however, one condition that determines the validity of its emerging currency, is precisely that, in its depths, the elements that seem independent cross one another, subjacent, comprehending the universe. One begins to study his blindness and ends with the entire world, or does not end, like the world, another globalization that he did not mention but that, in part, his perspicacity or perspective, a point of view—or two—of his blindness, already foresaw.

Nevertheless, in the same way as one knows that his imagination does not tend to elude the attraction of contraries, the contrariness of his blindness contracts according to its own specious, lucid mechanics. It begins by being a sequestering of logic, a species of abduction—from the Arisotelian to the Peircean—and ends by being intelligibly revelatory. The confrontation would not surprise so much but for the intermediation of a third term, which is not mentioned but implies both—the contraries both are and are not opposed.

This three-point contrariness is the one that substantially determines a thought and a poetic that, in his work, are terms that are also not opposed. If indeed they are aspects of an intimate conviction, its causes are, more than interior, anterior. They proceed from before and, above all, would seem to proceed from outside. In the first place, the contradiction that his name, his *proper name*, formulates, would have been the beginning of his writing:

> Who can tell me if in the secret archive
> of God are found the letters of my name.[27]

In the same way that his blindness is not only a genetic and biological condition, personal, particular, his own, proper, name (a property both proper/own and distant), orders his universe according to an onomastically significant key. His name constitutes the formula of the oxymoron that ciphers the entirety of an oeuvre that adopts and articulates it speciously. In the form of an analogy to the contradictory property of the name, his *blindness* was an adoption or an inheritance (another property both proper and alien) that Borges rehabilitated as a proper condition of his vision: "Blindness is a cloistering, but it is also a liberation, a solitude propitious for inventions, a key and an algebra."[28]

In the contradictory articulation of his proper name, *Jorge*, there is a reference to the countryside. The insistence in being called by his nickname, *Georgie*, not only claims the familiarity of his English origins, but also, in English, is affiliated to Latin. The paradox of the allusion is double: it alludes by way of English—and not Spanish—and by way of a familiar, informal invocation—and not erudite or classical—to Virgil's oeuvre. In the other nominal extreme, in Borges it is the city that is alluded to (Borges, Burgos, Bürger). In *History of Night*[29] one of the poems is titled "G. A. Bürger," "(both of his dates are in the encyclopedia)," says one of Borges's verses in parenthesis; and it is easy to verify: (1747–1794). Curiously, a *lapsus calamae* of Willis Barnstone[30] inscribes as his title, in the place of G.A., abbreviation for Gottfried August, the initials G. \L., and the same occurs in the French edition,[31] as if both authors and languages were confused. The Italian edition,[32] in contrast, appears as it does in Spanish, "G.A." The city and country cross one another, ciphered onomastically in his proper name; an inheritance that demands, a *required/loved* (*[re]querido*) atavism, with its greatest affects, filial and etymological. They initiate the play of opposites that are conjugated throughout his oeuvre, uniting two extremes in a third entity, the unity that extends them to the point of comprehending everything, country and city, the common place, the plot that gives it its place.

The oppositions starts out from a personal combination but then distances itself from it, in the same way as, in his blindness, Borges does not recognize a particular biographic circumstance but the presence of his elders, times of other times that make themselves present. He actualizes the past and realizes a vision. The urban space and the rural concentrated in the oxymoron of his name, and all of time, the entire universe, in the eyes and their orbits. *Urbi et orbi.*

They are personal circumstances with which he conceives or pulls together a universality that overflows the particularity of his space and time. The *blindness* is grafted onto a genetic memory and both at the same time, blindness and memory, make of the past the present. I quote two poems—*en pendant* though the years: "A Reader,"[33] where he says: "forgetting / is one of the forms of memory, its vague basement, / the other secret side of the coin," and the other poem, "The Blind Man,"[34] says: "Memory, that form of forgetting." It is the same for the reader or the blind man, forgetting and memory, blindness and vision, letters written or read. His writing contracts common oppositions in a *double bind, a double blind, a vision and an insight,*[35] *two visions,* however, at the same time a vision and a privation, an interior vision, private, more profound, more perfect. A vision that, deprived of the sensitivity of vision, both is and is not an interior vision: insight; vision and lucidity; lack of vision or blindness.

They are opposite and correlative terms, that is to say, they exist in function of a greater or lesser reciprocal dependence, contradictions that are resolved by *an ironic mediation,* the indispensable third term between two opposites, because the imagination of Borges realizes what Thomas A. Sebeok analyzes on the basis of one of the best-known premises of Charles Sanders Peirce:

> Peirce adapted the designation "semiosis" (in a variant transcription) from Philodemus's fragmentary Herculanean papyrus *On signs*, where the Greek equivalent occurs at least thirty times . . . , to represent a type of reasoning or inference from signs. He endowed the term with a definition of his own as an action or influence, "which is, or involves, a cooperation of *three* subjects, such as sign, its object, and its interpretant, this tri-relative influence not being in anyway resolvable into actions between pairs."[36]

From his vanguardist writings, in the times of the Spanish and Latin American *ultraism*, Borges passed from perplexity to fascination when observing that words not only could have several meanings but also that this plurality could comprise contrary meanings. A fascination that, those years past, disclaiming violently his first books, did not diminish. On the contrary, it is one of the few obsessions other than semantic ones that continued to be among his most lasting. In "Brodie's Report," the eponymous story of one of his last books of stories,[37] Brodie assimilates the peculiarity of the language of the tribes to that of our language; the text is in Spanish, but nevertheless the report says: "Let us not marvel excessively; in our language the verb *to cleave*[38] means both to rend and to adhere."[39] More than fifty years earlier, his stupefaction when faced with the same phenomenon was no different:

> The fact that they exist is enough to test the provisional and tentative character of our language faced with reality [. . .] In algebra, the sign more and the sign less exclude each other; in literature, contraries become siblings and impose on consciousness a mixed sensation; but not less true than the others.[40]

The hallucinations of his blindness that extend those of dreaming to the wakefulness of his vainly open eyes; the will or valor of anticipating it, first, and the resignation facing the fatality afterward; the certainty of the lucidity in darkness; the memory of the shadow of forgetting; its elegy; the reading not distinguished from writing; are topics run through by an ironic network that multiplies constant references and preferences in poems, books, essays. Like the ambivalencies of his memory, the ambivalencies of his blindness are so frequent as to discourage, as useless, the catalog.

When Borges formulates the *In Praise of Shadow* or records the *History of Night*, it is not merely a question of affirming that resignation but of exalting the proud *belonging* to an courageous kin: his literal ancestors (Saxons or Gauchos, both warriors), or his literary ancestors converge in *the myth of the blind poet*.

It is with difficulty that the coincidence of fatalities must be attributed only to chance, a license of reasoning in which Borges does not believe. He attributes his blindness to God—in whom he also does not believe—to diminish the arrogance or enjoy a chosen liberty. For this reason he oscillates between a God (indefinite but with a capital G) or the god (definite but with a lower case G) who, like in Plato's dialogue, chooses the poet to whom to bequeath the blindness that Borges recognizes as the perfect instrument of another poet. In "The Other," a poem from *The Other, the Same*,[41] "the other" itself is the title of the poem or of the title that he bequeaths as much to Milton as to another blind poet, model of poetry and blindness, who was the first, Homer, or the other who is he himself:

The pitiless god who is not named gives:
To Milton the walls of shadow,
To Cervantes exile and forgetting.[42]

In his lecture "Blindness," Borges does not say that Oscar Wilde said it—because he did not say it—but rather that "it was said": "The Greeks maintained that Homer was blind in order to mean that poetry should not be visual, that its duty is to be auditory."[44] It is Borges who has Wilde say that it is not important if Homer existed or not, but rather that the Greeks preferred to imagine that he was blind in order to insist on the fact that poetry is above all musical, and that the visual in a poet can exist or not.

The series of enthusiasms, stubborn or blinded (he includes, in passing, Tiresias, who, prophesizing, provoked the blindness of Oedipus), is extended to other Argentine writers:

My blindness had been coming on gradually since childhood. It was a slow, summer twilight. There was nothing pathetic or dramatic about it. Beginning in 1927, I had undergone eight eye operations, but since the late 1950's, when I wrote my "Poem of the Gifts," for reading and writing purposes I have been blind. Blindness ran in my family; a description of the operation performed on the eyes of my great-grandfather Edward Young Haslam appeared in the pages of the London medical journal the *Lancet*. Blindness also seems to run among the directors of the

National Library. Two of my eminent forerunners, José Mármol and Paul Groussac, suffered the same fate.[44]

Blindness, a limitation inherited from his elders, made him slide, from the standpoint of that noble and double genealogy: arms into letters, the country into the city, prose into verse, free verse into classic meter; and by way of that adverse itinerary he intended to return to the language of his elders. He says so in an autobiographical essay in which he connects blindness with the mnemonic virtues of verse—other "*mémoires d'aveugle*," Derrida would say[45]—and the tendency to return through poetry to the story, where a narrative thread, an argument, could lead it like a sonorous thread, a *leitmotiv* between spaces and walls that do not see, quotidian environments that he passes through without recognizing, converting known objects into enigmas, no less threatening for being familiar, only more frequent. A blindness that textualizes its surroundings as "the exercise of commentary illuminates the text by adding it to the text and, in a certain way, hiding it."[46]

In poems, in talks, in dialogues and interviews, Borges attributes to blindness the necessity of having replaced the visible world with the auditory world of the Anglo-Saxon language, of having given himself over to the study of the tongue of his elders, poetry, classic verse, narration, but above all "the Germanic studies of England and Iceland."[47]

Already in *In Praise of Shadow* he had attributed—and with gratitude—to his blindness the dedication to study "the language of iron," Anglo-Saxon, Icelandic, the epic of his ancestors. But speaking of that language it is also necessary to recognize that it constitutes an *iron language*,[48] the language of iron similar to "the hard iron that slices my chest, / the intimate knife at my throat,"[49] according to the translation of the "Poema conjetural" ["Conjectural Poem"]. The translation is quite close but, for the eye-ear of a English-speaking reader, *iron* (*hierro*) cannot fail to be allude to the *ironies* from which Borges does not distance himself. Neither could *blinded*,[50] in those circumstances, fail to be associated with *blindado* (armoured).

Even if it is a legitimate play, it is not merely a question of playing with words or letters: In "A Vindication of the Kabbalah," a text published at the beginning of the thirties, Borges wrote: "it occurs in the verses, whose ordinary law is the subjection of meaning to euphonic necessities (or superstitions). The coincidental in them is not the sound, it is what they signify."[51]

When he names Adam, Borges—who confesses with sorrow to not knowing Hebrew—does not lose the idiomatic opportunity to qualify him as "Red Adam,"[52] or to recognize that "the stroke / was the blood of

Adam, a first day,"[53] or to remember the earth, the dust of which he is made. In Hebrew, earth is *Adama*, red is *Adom*, and blood is *Dam*, one more semantic dimension for the name, for the man, for the relation of his substantive condition with the earth.

It is interesting to observe that, Borges being one of the authors who most often and best elaborated the figures of contradiction (syllepsis, oxymoron, chiasmus, antithesis, attenuation, paradoxes), also engaged himself in dissimilar forms of a tricky, transversal repetition, through more than one language. Pierre Menard could be the paradigm of the procedure, but without attaining those archetypical levels; for example, in "From Someone to No One,"[54] Borges says: Johannes Eriugena or Scotus, that is to say John the Irish, whose name in history is Escoto Erígena, or rather Irish Irish."[55]

The same model of "different repetition,"[56] could be distinguished in the name of Red Scharlach, one of his most famous characters, the protagonist of "Death and the Compass."[57] After *Red (rojo)*, *Scharlach*[58] means "scarlet" in German. *Rojo Rojo* is a good forename and last name for the presumed assassin of a political story blazoned across four letters, the tetragrammaton, which is formed on the basis of Kabbalistic clues apt for discovering the ritual deaths of rabbis, Hassidic wise men, specialists in the *Sefer Yesirah,* and other books of Jewish mysticism. Although Adam, the man, also tolerates that strange synonym and promotes others: "In Latin, *humanus* was related to *homo*, although not directly derived, and the form in which both proceed from an ancestor of *humus*, 'earth,' is one of the obscure questions of Indoeuropean linguistics."[59]

Borges, Bioy, like other Rioplatense writers who preceded them, Jules Laforgue, Lautréamont, Supervielle, recur with suggestive frequency to a figure that, despite having been adopted by advertising and continuing to be stalked by the weariness of its insistence, maintains its ironic strangeness. As if it were natural for the word to dissimulate its history and reserve for poetry the revelation of its truth, its past, its origin: "He who discovers with pleasure an etymology," goes a verse of "The Just Ones,"[60] and it is not the first time that Borges alludes to the happiness of that class of discovery where the word turns historical or vice versa.

On one occasion I preferred to catalog that rhetorical procedure as an "intraduction,"[61] the figure that hinders languages and differences, a figure that, if one had to assign it an origin, would be originally rooted in Rio de la Plata. It does not cease to be coherently contradictory for it to be just a "figure," the strategy of literariness of which meaning makes use in order to rescue a common truth from among different words. Interidiomatic, it denominates the impossibility of translating a sign that, without abandoning its language, remains in between, a term comprehended between two languages, two languages that cross each other like two swords of iron, words like swords, *two-edged words*. The *irony* of an interior translation, or anterior, that remits to an edenic or adamic language, where "My viper letter,"[62] forked and seductive, will tempt the poet who procures, beyond idiomatic limits, to recuperate the comprehension of a prebabelic language.

Joyce is another blind writer who searches through invented words an identity that supercedes the jurisdictions of a conventional linguistics:

> He learned something of all languages and wrote in a language he invented, a language that is difficult to understand but that is distinguished by a strange music. Joyce brought a new music to English. And he said valorously (and mendaciously) that 'of all the things that have occurred to me, I think that the least important is that I became blind.'"[63]

BLIND GAZES

It is likely that Borges managed to say it in Indiana, when he was here in 1976, a visit from which there remain recorded dialogues. He said in one of those conversations, "I have never looked for a subject. I allow subjects to look for me, and then, walking down the streets, going from one room to another of my house, the small house of a blind man, I feel that something is about to happen, and that something may be a line or it may be some kind of shape."[64]

In the same way that he neither searches for nor rejects the themes that present themselves, he posed no resistance to his blindness coming to meet him and, from that point on, Borges elaborated a poetics of blindness, *a different vision*, as if his whole life, since his birth, he had been awaiting it, like one who awaits a reimbursement: blindness and irony in a single gift. Despite the fact that his blindness progresses from the moment of his birth, from before, he prefers to give it a date; he dates it to 1955 and from then on he celebrates both. In that "Poem of the Gifts" he said:

> Let no one diminish by tear or reproach
> This declaration of the mastery
> Of God, who with magnificent irony
> Gave me, at the same time, books and the night.[65]

Irony is of God, but God, like the maker in lowercase of the title, who is confused with the author, fuses his irony with the irony inherent to irony, as if it were a metal in an alloy of similar elements. According to Borges, the relation with divinity is no different from the relation that Ion, the gifted interpreter of Homer, describes in the *Ion*. In that dialogue, Plato describes *enthusiasm*, the overflowing of a god in the expansions of a muse who inspires the poet, who inspires the interpreter and inspires the listener. With the same magnetic force of the Heraclean stone, interpretation propagates itself, like a breath. The chain of the enthused of which Ion spoke is like Borges's chain, a chain of iron, a chain of ironic works that neither Socrates nor Plato would have de-authorized.

"A Reader" (*In Praise of Shadow*)[66] is not the only work he dedicates to one who is, like Don Quijote—another reader—his literary hero par excellence, remembered in his autobiographical essay, in his talk on blindness, in so many poems. He understands that to inherit blindness permits him to recuperate another inheritance: the forgotten language of his ancestors.

> I gave myself over to the study of the language of iron
> used by my elders, to sing
> swords and solitudes.[67]

Because forgetting is, for Borges

> one of the forms of memory, its vague basement,
> the other secret face of the coin.[68]

Iron is displaced from memory, which is ambivalent, to the language, which is as well, of "the music of the Saxon iron" (as he says in the prologue to *The Iron Coin*, 1976).[69] The coin, a metal with two faces, is a metaphor of memory and forgetting; blindness, which is double, is a metaphor of foresight and its visions. In the language that is his and is other, the words, like swords—written in English they are barely distinguished—like the "double axis of iron," mark the entrance or exit of the labyrinth (Gr. *labrys*), the dualities of language that irony mediates, as if this duality had its emblematic figure in blindness.

"A great poet of the eye" or a great poet of the gaze is what Derrida could have said of Borges, insofar as a philosopher, such as Derrida himself, would be a great thinker of the eye: "*Idein, eidos, idea*: the whole history, the whole semantics of the European *idea* in its Greek genealogy, we know it, we see it, assigns seeing to knowing."[70]

Words combine (*hacen juego*), twice over. Borges had envisioned, like the Kabbalists, an absolute writing in which every word counts. Blindness enables that interior vision, more than a mystical ascension it gives him access to a *pardes*. In Hebrew, it is the acronym formed by the initials that name the four readings necessary for enabling the comprehension of the sacred text; *pardés* is the same word that designates Paradise, a garden in the form of a library, the Eden that assures perfect comprehension; by way of the writing that does not see, one approaches the truth that is also not possible to see, although he makes it out as archetypes, and it is with them that Borges began the first stanza of his poem "The Golem."[71]

In that poem, that stanza, which is the only one of his entire work that he would like to have remain, he names Scholem twice. With Gerhardt—as he preferred calling Gershom Scholem—he had conversed twice in Jerusalem, and had read attentively his book *Major Trends in Jewish Mysticism*.[72] Attentive to the knowledge of the Kabbalah and to the imagination of the Golem, however, Borges says he names Scholem because he had not found another name that rhymes with Golem. This cannot be understood as a trivial commentary and, as transcendent, it would be inevitable to associate it with a rhyme that stands out in the *Divina Commedia*. Hatzfeld[73] recalls that Dante only names Christ three times and, although rhymes with Christ are frequent and easy in Italian, in the *Commedia* Christ only rhymes with Christ. It is not absurd to think that the relation between Golem and Scholem is also the discovery of an identification in rhyme that has for Borges, an erudite poet, scholar of the *Divina Commedia*,[74] all possible mystical resonances. *Golem*, the word in Hebrew, appears in Psalm 139, 5:16 of the *Book of Psalms* of the Old Testament, and has been the object of different or disputable translations: "substance," "inchoate mass," "imperfect," "embryo," among others.

"*Tes yeux voyaient mon Golem*"

goes the French translation,[75]

> Thine eyes did see my substance,
> yet being unperfect;
> and in thy book
> all my members were *written*.[76]

In the ancient version of Casiodoro de Reina, it says:

Your eyes saw my embryo,
And in your book were *written* all those things
That were later formed,
Without lacking any of them.[77]

"Golem" in modern Hebrew means "larva,"[78] which would not be difficult to associate with "mask" in German.

Several times Borges said that the poem was related to "The Circular
Ruins,"[79] the story that reveals the hallucinations of dreaming, of thought,
of imagination, and of memory, as the key to an aesthetic in which *mise en
abîme* questions reality and fiction in the same turn, in the same vertigo;
the sign as origin of an unlimited semiosis that affects with unreality all
instances in which man participates.

In one of the passages from Borges's Golem:

The rabbi looked at it with tenderness
And with some horror . . .

. . .

. . .

*How did I fall upon adding to the infinite
Series yet another symbol? . . .*[80]

In "The Abduction at Uqbar,"[81] Eco considers that, although he
assumes that Borges has not read Peirce, it seems to him a good Borgesian
procedure to assume that books speak to one another. Personally, I suspect that this propalation came to Borges in a more direct manner than
Eco supposes. It is true that, as he affirms, "many of Borges's stories seem
to be exemplifications of that art of inference that Peirce called abduction
or hypothesis, and that is nothing other than conjecture."[82]

But what seems to me even more suggestive is the assimilation
between the foundations of illimited semiosis and the aesthetics of the circular ruins. Both may be explained, in Peirce's words, by the fact that a
sign is something "which determines something else (its *interpretant*) to
refer to an object to which itself refers (its *object*) in the same way, the sign
becoming in turn a sign, and so on *ad infinitum*."[83]

In the short text "A Dream," the vertiginous unlimitedness of that
infinite circularity is condensed by Borges in a few lines: "In a deserted
part of Iran there is a not-so-tall tower of stone, without doors or windows. In the one room (whose floor is of earth and which has the shape
of a circle) there is a table of wood and a bench. In that circular cell, a man
who looks like me writes in characters that I do not understand a long

poem about a man in another circular cell that writes a poem about a man in another circular cell. . . . The process has no end and no one will be able to read what the prisoners write."[84]

Lector and interlocutor of Scholem, always studying the Kabbalah, Borges could not fail to know that every word counts, that names and things exist by virtue of a literal combinatory both wise and mystical. But, most of all, he is fascinated like his character by the aleph, the letter with which all begins, even before the beginning, the sign that represents in Hebrew the first movement of the larynx (like the "sweet spirit" of Greek) that precedes a vowel at the beginning of the word but that, because it is the spiritual root of all letters, contains in its essence the whole alphabet, that is to say, all the elements of human language. In this way the whole world depends on a letter. And Borges imagines this verbal dependence visually, in a story, "The Aleph," that designates as much a world as a book, as much a title as a story. *The Aleph*, in which the poet—author, narrator, and character—is at the root of an orb: "I saw in the Aleph the earth, and in the earth once again the Aleph, and in the Aleph the earth,"[85] "one of the points in space that contains all points," a point of view that the letter fixes.[86] That is why aleph is the letter that the rabbi inscribes in the forehead of the Golem, initiating a combination *emet* that means "truth." When he wants to destroy it, he erases the first letter, and in this way what remains is the word that means "death," and the Golem crumbles, like man, made of dust, into dust.

Through absolute writing, a perfect machine, the Golem was created (the first, in Writing). Its death, one not true, puts in evidence the simulacrum of writing that, for Borges, is a simulacrum of memory.[87] With the death of the Golem life is interrupted, semiosis comes to a halt. In *A Sign Is Just a Sign*, Sebeok asks:

> If objects are signs, indefinite regression to a suppositous *logos*, and if interpretants are signs marching in progression toward the ultimate disintegration of mind, what is there left that is not a sign? (. . .) In a celebrated article he published in 1868, Peirce anticipated and answered this question, contending "that the word or sign which man uses *is* the man himself," which is to claim that "the man and the external sign are identical, in the same sense in which the words *homo* and *man* are identical. Thus my language is the sum total of myself, for the man is the thought." [88]

Despite his magical wisdom, the rabbi did not concede the word to the Golem, nor did he concede language or thought:

> Despite such high witchery
> Man's apprentice did not learn to speak.[89]

For this reason, deprived of the sign, in the Scriptures, the Golem is an in-form-ed entity, a *larva*, another of the words that accumulate several different and opposed meanings. The Romance languages inherited from Latin the meaning "phantasm, specter, spirit of the dead who haunt the living, embryonic form, particularly of insects, mask." The Golem is anterior or posterior, man remains in the middle; between both extremes, his life. The Golem will exist on the basis of the word, and will cease to exist on the basis of it. It will be or it will cease to be, a chrysalis or the spirit of the dead.

It is that double gift—poison in German, like Phaedro's *pharmakon*—a poison and a remedy, a simulacrum that resolves simultaneously, ironically, memory and forgetting; a simultaneity in an instant, the *Augenblick* that is the *coup d'oeil,* a blink of the eye, the furtive gaze that permits him to apprehend and install eternity in an instant; to know in an instant his world, a knowledge that is the origin of the paradoxical relations between now and eternity. For Isaac Luria and other Kabbalists the paths of the firmament were clear, and he traveled them (seeing his way) with his mental eyes, more an interior vision than a mystical ascension . . . It is a primacy that is verified, in Greek ontology, in such terms as *idea, eidos, theorein*. To refer to the same notion, Plato and Aristotle speak of the "eye of the soul." The figure is quite similar to the one used by the Kabbalists.

It is not necessary for the observation to be of a theoretical order, but it explains in part the intellectual imagination, the reasoned fiction that defines the universe of Borges. Or as he himself defines his fortune and misfortune:

> My lot is what is normally called intellectual poetry. The word is almost an oxymoron; the intellect (vigil) thinks by means of abstraction, poetry (dreaming), by means of images, of myths, or of fables. Intellectual poetry must knit together those two processes. [. . .] Thus does Plato in his dialogues . . . The master of the genre is, in my opinion, Emerson.[90]

Blindness has attenuated the world of appearances, approximating it to another interior world, private, doubly deprived by circumstances and peripateticisms, by timelessness and future, as he says in his talk: "I said to myself: as I have lost the dear world of appearances, I have to create something else: I have to create the future, what happens to the visible world that, in fact, I have lost."[91] Beyond time, beyond its happenings and successions, a species of revelation of truth arises in the Idea:

> At the end of the years I am surrounded
> by an obstinate, luminous mist
> that reduces things to one thing
> without form or color. Almost an idea.[92]

Permanent like the idea, free of fugacity and contingency, writing shares with the coin and with arms both iron and ambivalencies. We mentioned his veneration for myths, Germanic languages and literatures, where Odin, god of war, inventor of runes, crosses—like Borges, like Cervantes, like Lope—arms with letters.

So many are the personal, biographic, conjectural, and poetic references that I will only recall that in "Pierre Menard, Author of the Quijote," the famous author is only the author of chapter XXXVIII of the *Quijote*, precisely in the one in which Cervantes "deals with the curious discourse that Don Quijote gave on arms and letters," and a fragment of two others (IX and XXII).[93] His Pierre Menard is, without doubt, one of the most quoted authors of the century, perhaps the most important of contemporary literary history. An author who did not exist and who not only wrote some fragments of a work that already existed, but who also did not write it.

It is true that, for Borges as for the tradition that precedes him, in the same way that God created man, man is capable of creating other beings in his image and semblance, subjected, in the same way as

> Gradually was seen (how we)
> imprisoned in this sonorous net
> of Before, After, Yesterday, Meanwhile, Now.[94]

In "Signs,"[95] one of his least cited poems, Borges brings together signs, ciphers, syllables, metals, secret names. "Signs" ends with a verse:

> I can be all. Leave me in the shade.[96]

"The Golem," as he says, the poem that meant the most to him, begins with a reference to Cratylus and to the literal image of a rose, quite different from the roses of Ronsard, of Laforgue, and from all the roses that poetry multiplies like another "miracle of the roses" that, like the Golem, reproduce themselves, grow, and succumb. Borges's rose is, like

"The Profound Rose" of Milton, "The Unending Rose,"[97] an inter-minable rose, archetypal, "that the Lord will show to my dead eyes,"[98] like the one that flowers in the quote of Angelus Silesius.

In the same way that the blindness of his lifeless eyes anticipates the fore-sight of his timeless life, it returns to him paradoxically the language of his ancestors, a language of iron melted across languages and their par-ticular differences by the irony that multiplies meanings to the point of filling to the rim a single sign, wherein begins the infinite of signification.

In the prologue to *The Other, the Same*, Borges recalls his encounter at Lubbock, on the edge of the desert, with a tall girl who asked him if, when writing "The Golem," "had he not intended a version of 'The Cir-ular Ruins'; I responded to her that I had to cross the entire continent to receive that revelation, which was true."[99] Both compositions recall the vertiginous character of the dream in the abyss of a dreamer who is dreamed to the same extent that a reader is read, or in the gaze of the rabbi who contemplates his Golem, suspecting that, in the same way that he looks, he is also looked at by God. The reader, miraculously, making the gaze his or her own, returns it or puts it away again.

CHAPTER EIGHT

Symbols and the Search for Unity

. . . for all the things [that is, the Sefirot], and all the
attributes, which seem as if they are separate, are not separate [at all] since all [of them] are one, as the[ir] beginning is, which unites everything "in one word."
—Commentaries of the *Sefer Yezirah*

To fix our ideas suppose players playing with dice . . .
—Charles Sanders Peirce, "Design and Chance"

Don Alejandro once aspired to be a deputy, but the
political bosses closed the doors of the Uruguayan Congress to him. The man got irritated and resolved to found
another Congress of much more vast reach. [. . .] Don
Alejandro conceived the idea of organizing a Congress
of the world that would represent all people of all
nations.
—Borges, "El Congreso"

For some years now it has seemed of interest to me to invoke the genies
of place. Close to Hollywood, Los Angeles,[1] it would have been
opportune to speak of the angels to whom today's reflection[2] and imagination[3] have dedicated so much recurrent attention. I do not know if it
was satellite networks or the ubiquitous messages of an explosive mediatic
communication or the readings of Walter Benjamin or the angelic prolif-
eration of Paul Klee, or if it was, above all, cinema that gave birth to this
new advent of angels, but I would dare to conjecture that any one of these
reasons, tightly related to one another, is not alien to it.

It is hard not to notice the bibliographical, cinematographic frequency, the notable works in which angels abound and, if perhaps few

today would wonder if "ten thousand of them could dance on a needle's point" or "why are they not more interesting than the bewildering varieties of insects which naturalists study,"[4] what is of interest is their status of intermediation between two worlds, the transmission of messages in silence that is attributed to them, their movement between the visible and the invisible, the announcement that bears witness to other realms, their constant fugacity that is also permanence. The ambivalencies of the angelicological condition turn out to be generally valid for attending to certain aspects of cinematographic language and the properties of the word in the electronic image. Said or written, mute or in movement, the word is seen. Silence and voice, word and thought, coincide in *a single vision*, a disquieting move that erases the frontiers between seeing and dreaming, saying and thinking, saying and desiring, showing and telling; all at once.

The word put into an image synthesizes differences, crosses limits: the eye that sees, hears; the image in movement contracts voices and figures; in film, showing and saying do not require each other like opposite or rival actions. The animation of film that is emotion and movement, *motivates* the word (*le mot*, in French, says it all). Everything is in view. The image shows and says, shows what it says, concurs to realize the miracle of the gaze (*mirada*), an elegy of the gaze, *ad miration*. One sees, one hears, one reads, one looks, everything is seen and there is nothing behind or outside of this vision. What would bishop Berkeley have argued faced with that impression of the senses? For him these too would be "truths so clear that to see them it is enough to open our eyes."[5] In an *Augenblick* the *correspondences* that angels establish also allow us to glimpse an instant of eternity. Film breathes this neo-angelic air that brings to light another *vaste clarté*, as if the stars of a seventh heaven vaguely illuminated the seventh art that, in the meantime, turns the image into time.

Beyond the figures animated by light and movement, film diffused new hybrids of verbal and visual images, promoted different aesthetic tensions enabling vision, registering, as of not so long ago, the metamorphoses of the written words that transformed into things that represent, magisterial images demonstrating the magic of a movement, a prestidigitation that the nature of language did not know. Suddenly the image is no longer the illustration of diction but rather goes on to be the impossible vision of its idea. It is in film that where the apparition of the "invisible man" was not unusual, nor ghosts unheard of.

Similar to the evangelic annunciation of gestation, a new gesture of deixis announces another *language of angels*. A communication by way of messengers who also engage themselves in a rite of passage, require passwords to slip around borders, between outside and inside, on the limit of fiction, on the edge of the beyond, between heaven and earth. Suspended, they suspend the schematic dualisms that reduce to opposition biological, grammatical, literary genre; they discur in an interior language that film makes visible.

In film, angels also pass in silence, meditating, midway between god and human, mediating between spaces and species, they cross them. Some legends had it that angels were so numerous that they distanced themselves from God, were separated from the divinity, and fell, converted into demons. These falls from a divine space to a human space multiplied legends, theories, and doctrines that agree in recognizing one and the same fracture: either it was the separation that provoked the fall or it was the fall that provoked the separation. In both cases the catastrophe is consecutive: separation gives origin to the diabolical (Gr. *diabolos*[6]: "that which disunites, separates") and the re-union re-establishes the symbolic. From this comes the union between different universes that the symbol recalls. For Peirce that is precisely the objective of the semiotic universe, the Third Universe that "comprises everything whose being consists in active power to establish connections between different objects, especially between objects in different Universes."[7] His Third Universe could be the Orbis Tertius inscribed in the ancient cartography or in Borges's story, where the "aerial nothings" are crossed with Brute Actuality.

In this epoch of synthesis—or *sans*thesis—perhaps the convocation of the Fifth Congress is of interest as a topic, which is a theme and a common place, adequate for observing the diversities of a present that, without being ignorant of them, tends to throw them together. Although it sounds tautological, we meet in a reunion[8] that is at the same time a re-union, the agglomeration wherein is observed as much the diversity of elements as the movement of turning back, the return to a unity. A species of secular, institutionalized apocatastasis remits us to an initial and anterior instance, since "all the things [that is, the Sefirot], and all the attributes, which seem as if they are separate, are not separate [at all] since all [of them] are one, as the[ir] beginning is, which unites everything 'in one word.'"[9]

Word and thing all at once, the *common place* attenuates differences, assimilates them into one and the same *affinitas*: neighbor, similar because next. Shared, the same limits reduce differences between word and image, between the object referred to and the object that refers, between performative and constative discourses, between language and metalanguage, between theory and fiction. It is not to be verified only in one language: a process of synthesis vanishes the limits between different languages by way of a semantic cross-fertilization dissimulated between words that are syntactically close. It is not a recent process but it anticipates—poetically—the excessive suppressions at the end of a millennium, at the end of a century, that did not skimp on them. Among so many reiteratedly foreseen ends—of oppositions, of referents, of poetry, of theory, of history, of wars[10]—a reality disappears, overwhelmed by the specters of its representation. Daily the technological image confounds reality with nothing. Since this confounding is not noticed, the disappearance is double and rekindles. In other terms, two ancient quarrels (the images, the universals) in one sole question. Does the globalization of images universalize the failure of representation? Everything appears or disappears in that square *black hole*[11] of screens that allow one to see that they do not allow one to see, where "the microcosm of a collapsing universe"[12] crumbles, "vacuums full of collapsed stars," "on the edge of the nothing that offers nothing as a guarantee,"[13] the strange guarantee with which Breton sustains black humor on the margin of the abyss.

It is fair for semioticians to broach this work of reunion and synthesis of diversities in a *congress*,[14] because no one will forget that since its origin, *congressus* designated in Latin, as it does today, the "action of meeting," even when it has been adopted later, in our languages, with more scabrous meanings that will not be invoked here. Only when it loses that erotic meaning of an initial union gone bad, *congress* goes on to designate, more austerely, a reunion of specialists who, in this case, were convoked to study the synthesis that comprehends diversity, a logical or anthropological operation of long history and remote myths that confirm the antagonistic character of the world as revelation of the symbolic vocation. Here "congress" alludes to a fact, a story, a name, and a thing; like the *I think* of Peirce, denotes "the unity of thought," underlining that "the unity of thought is nothing but the unity of symbolization-consistency, in a word (the implication of *being*) and belongs to every word whatever." [15]

As much as Sebeok may have said that "'symbol' is the most abused term" and "in consequence, it has either tended to be grotesquely overburdened . . . or, to the contrary, reduced . . . even to absurd nullity,"[16] it is known that the oscillation between "replenishment and exhaustion,"[17] in addition to being the prevalent aesthetic diffusion, is our disquieting quotidian practice. It is not necessary to remark that we are discarding any intention to add to *symbol* new meanings. Still more, toward the end of suspending the excesses of its semantic profusion, we try to rescue here one of the meanings that *symbolon* had in its origins, and that the numerous and varied contexts, interpretations, and theories, gradually mitigated.

Neither similarity nor contiguity, for Peirce the symbol is a sign which refers to the object and denotes by virtue of a law. There is another important corollary which may be drawn from the law of symbols: "This infinite Symbol being necessary denotes not the contingent facts of the universe but the absolute law in all its detail and unity to which the universe is subjected."[18] It is in this legal, conventional aspect that Peirce points to that the symbol would be opposed to the notion that "chance is indeterminacy, is freedom. But the action of freedom issues in the strictest rule of law."[19]

"Chance changes everything & chance will change that" says Peirce in the same essay. From this comes the thesis that chance[20] is really operative in the Universe. That phenomenon that Peirce denominates tychism is a form of falling, a fall that other languages still conserve (Fr. *choir*. Ital. *cadere*, Span. *caer*). It is a luck, a hazard, a fall, a part of its evolutive cosmology, but that fall is also the fatality of the symbol. In several senses it is its lot: a "chance" and a fall, another syllepsis that reunites in one word contradictory meanings that, in this context, cannot be avoided, nor do they surprise. Just as Borges's "Ingenuous One" confessed to be amazed that:

> There is not in the orb one
> Thing that is not another, or contrary, or nothing.[21]

David Brodie repressed his amazement before the possibility that there could coincide in a name meanings both different and at the same time opposed. One need not be surprised, however, that "the verb *to cleave* means both to rend and to adhere."[22] One and the same verb means "to separate" and "to unite," an example of several edges because, like *congress*, it designates and illustrates at once segmentation and union. Borges underscores that single word in a series of examples in which he speaks of a congress and of carnal union, without saying that in Latin a single designation did not distinguish them.[23]

The consequences of these *falls* still affect us, and although the versions of the loss of innocence are among the most dramatic and repeated, one need only recall that for the Greeks this *chance-fall* referred initially to the game *of kubos*, the throw of dice, later it was a *pass-word*,[24] a sign of recognition or of hospitality in a shared community, before giving birth to symbols. *Knucklebone*, in English, *osselets*, in French, and *taba*, in Spanish. They are the names of a game of little bones that, also found in prehistoric caverns, remit to an ancient and universal rite, and it is this ancestral game that we are wagering in this essay alludes to symbols, to falls, fragments, fractures, breaking of the vessels, or crumblings of towers, a provocation of linguistic differences, of dispersions and carnal or spiritual reunions, of congresses, a ludic and theoretical series that, according to Peirce, runs through stages of *tychism* (fall), *synechism* (continuity), terminating in *agapism*, "the thesis that love, or sympathy, has real influence in the world and, in fact, is 'the great evolutionary agency of the universe.'"[25]

The myths coincide in imagining similar falls: angels who plummet to earth, expelled inhabitants of *pardes*, the punished androgynous hybrids of Plato, the vessels are broken and the towers crumble down and, in all cases, a cause explains the event by reasons of the pride and rivalry of human knowledge with a superior one.

Like in archaic times, universal communication, without limits, of the present, would be verified in the heavens; today, without going Beyond—in capitals—in the satellites. An anterior common language, without fissures, first; the division in languages or sexes, as a punishment, after. In the "Symposium," Aristophanes, less an author than a character of Plato, speaks of the pride of the *androgynes* who, being our ancestors, sharing our human nature and condition, were not like us. In that past, no sex was distinguished, or three were recognized rather than two. As if, foreseeing the rigidity of oppositional paradigms, philosophy would have already appealed to a third order of discourse apt for overcoming the binary logic of contraries, of the yes and no.

Its form was different:

> The form of each human being as a whole was round, with back and sides forming a circle, but it had four arms and an equal number of legs, and two faces exactly alike on cylindrical neck; there was a single head for both faces, which faced in opposite directions, and four ears and two sets of pudenda, and one can imagine all the rest from this. It also traveled upright just as now, in whatever direction it wished; and whenever they took off in a swift run, they brought their legs around straight and somersaulted as tumblers do, and then, with eight limbs to support them, they rolled in a swift circle.[26]

It was in such a way that Zeus decided to "cut each of them in two" so that they would be "weaker and at the same time more useful to us [. . .] by having increased in number, and they'll walk upright on two legs."[27] Sacrifice of unity or thirdness, the loss consists of a division into two. It is for this reason that "Each of us then is but the token of a human being, sliced like a flat fish, two from one; each then ever seeks his matching token."[28] Perhaps for that reason as well, Peirce, "An American Plato,"[29] without further clarification affirmed that "the general answer to the question What is man? is that he is a symbol."[30]

As I have already said on a number of occasions, the Greek word for *tessera*, for *token*, is *sumbolon*: the reunion of the parts corresponding to a knucklebone, an earthen pot, or whatever other object broken in two; each one of these parts fits with another, such that it becomes proof of the anterior sentimental affinity, amical or amorous, of those who possess it.

"Words are symbols that postulate a shared memory," says Borges in "The Congress," one of the stories from *The Book of Sand*: "The mystics invoke a rose, a kiss, a bird that is all birds, a sun that is all the stars and the sun, a pitcher of wine, a garden, or the sexual act."[31] The words of the narrator announce the end of "The Congress," a story that takes place in Montevideo, in Uruguay, a small country, and, secretly, comprises the universe. The fidelity of the quote reveals the dualities that the word in Spanish combines. *Cita* (quote/*rendezvous*) is the sentimental and intellectual meeting, transsexual or transtextual, biblical sin or Greek banquet, text or sex, the secret of "The Sect of the Pheonix,"[32] or of "the pleasure of the text."[33] Who would wonder if angels speak? Sex and word reconciled from the beginning as diversity and unity in one and the same *knowledge*[34] immediately after the fall, when *yâda* in Hebrew means both "to know" and "to lie down" with the beloved one.

"Type or token," type or part, the universe broken into pieces by knowledge, the separation of fields and disciplines. The ambition of the androgynes, like the divine emanations that make boats or vessels explode (*breaking of the vessels*),[35] like the tempest that shipwrecked utopia, the ship, and the books of Prospero, blowing up "a brave vessel, / Who have no doubt some noble creatures in her, /Dash'd all to pieces, . . ."[36] There are no gods who will withstand the challenge of (pre)potency, and symbols shatter in order, perhaps, to one day be reunited. Faithful to his Muse, Aristophanes, between jokes and interludes, before ceding the word to Socrates and Agathon, repeats that the lover wishes

> to join and be fused with his beloved, to become one from two. The cause is that this was our ancient nature, and we were wholes. Eros then is a name for the desire and pursuit of wholeness. And as I say, before we were one, but now we have been dispersed by the god due to our injustice as the Arcadians were dispersed by the Spartans. So there is fear that if we should not be well ordered toward the gods, we shall be split in two again and go around like the people molded in profile on tombstones, sawed in half through the nose, born like split dice.[37]

Dice and *sumbola* at the same time. The French translation is curious: it translates *anthropon sumbolon* as it figures in the text with *tessère d'homme*. The footnote of this French translation clarifies:

The translation is not literal. The Greek word is *symbol* but its proper meaning is lost in French, whereas for us the Latin *tessera* evokes a more concrete image. Essentially it is question of a tablet, a cube, a knucklebone, of which two patrons each kept the half, transmitted thereafter to their descendents; when one of these two complementary fractions of the whole one would approach the other (this is the etymology), there would be established the existence of anterior bonds of hospitality.[38]

If the relation between the symbol and the trinity appears recurrently, it is not solely sue to "compulsive drive" to return "to the excitation of excessive triplicities" of which Umberto Eco and Thomas Sebeok speak in their preface to *The Sign of Three*,[39] nor is it due to having suffered a "triadomania," that infirmity against which Peirce warns when he confesses that "I have no marked predilection for trichotomies in general," although he admits that "there is a not uncommon craze for trichotomies."[40]
Nevertheless,

nobody will suppose that I wish to claim any originality in reckoning the triad important in philosophy. Since Hegel, almost every fanciful thinker has done the same. Originality is the last of recommendations for fundamental conceptions. On the contrary, the fact that the minds of men have ever been inclined to threefold divisions is one of the considerations in favour of them.[41]

If I pause yet again over this trinitary economy of Peirce's thought, it is not only on account of their having renounced or overcome the paradigmatic binarisms of the Saussurian structural articulations, but rather because it is a question of returning to unity from thirdness by way of hybrids and divisions, of recognizing "intermediary tertias," of the intermediation that the present day propitiates with an unusual extension and frequency. "A centaur is a mixture of a man and a horse. Philadelphia lies between New York and Washington. Such thirds may be called Intermediate thirds or Thirds of comparison" says Peirce in the same text, and it is that mention of hybrids as a *tiers arbitre* or third in discord, one distant to the dilemma, the foreigner—a status sheltered by "the figures of alterity" or of geographic illusion, the place that gives a place to fiction, which is of interest to highlight here.

It could have been foreseen that, having overcome the rigorous limitations and systematic abstractions imposed by emphatic theoretical formulations, the research in course, of and about the present day, would articulate disciplines, would contextualize knowledge, reconciling a current cultural search that is not verified in an isolated medium but among *different media*. For this reason, in addition to distinguishing each *medium* in particular, what is of interest is a *new medium, another medium*: the one that is *intermediate*. A hole is opened, that is formed and is a figure between two: between natural and cultural, between outside and inside, between secular and sacred, between showing and telling, between visual and verbal, between oral and written, between journalistic and literary, between scientific and poetic, between doctrines and fictions, an intermediate space, mediated and mediatic, where historical, theoretic, and aesthetic imagination comes together endeavoring to combine those fragments, restore fractures, resolve fractions and cracks. The massification of the media is understood in another sense: media are in everything and everything is in media. Two cracks: *two media between two media*, two divided by two between two divided by two; simplifying, one divided by one equals one, that is to say, three times one. In all cases it is a question of dividing, of *middle* points, of *mi-lieu*, a place between two, in "the brief vertigo of the in between," as Octavio Paz said.[42]

Despite the necessity of knowing, of analyzing, that is separating, of applying doctrines and disciplines, contemporary realizations tend to look for that unity—more than unique, initial—that claims to recuperate, on the basis of the diversity of knowledges and languages, some coincidences that the epistemological and aesthetic conditions of the contemporary condition legitimate. Current reflection is debating among diverse media, is throwing itself in the middle, in the crossroads, the place of crossing and intersection where differences are confounded out of proximity, where it is no surprise that coincidence, which is one form of co-incidence, would be routine.

With all reason, Eco, with the famous image of a Babel crumbling on the cover of his book *In Search of the Perfect Language*, on beginning the introduction warns:

> The utopia of a perfect language has not only obsessed European culture. The theme of the confusion of languages, and the attempt to remedy it thanks to the refinding or invention of a language common to the whole human race, runs through the history of all cultures.[43]

They are the first words of the book, perhaps without intending to, they extend into a necessary volume, the search that Borges summarizes in some lines of "The Congress":

I stayed in a modest pension behind the British Museum,
to whose library I would run morning and afternoon, in
search of a language that would be worthy of the Congress
of the World. I did not overlook universal languages; I
looked into Esperanto—which the *Lunario sentimental*
qualifies as "equitable, simple, and economic"—and
Volapük, which wants to explore all linguistic possibilities,
declining verbs and conjugating nouns. I considered the
arguments in favor of and against resuscitating Latin,
whose nostalgia has not ceased to perdure at the end of the
centuries. I lingered as well in the examination of the ana-
lytic idiom of John Wilkins, where the definition of each
word lies in the letters that form it. It was under the high
cupola of the hall that I met Beatrice.[44]

Ten years ago, quite close to the Research Center for Language and
Semiotic Studies that Thomas A. Sebeok created, it occurred to Douglas
Hofstadter to dedicate a voluminous book to Bloomington and to propose formulas of a "Magic Cubology"—there continue to be implied
more cubes, flagstones, and rubrics—recuperating[45] in his metamagical
way the polysemic possibilities of a firm or fragile tessera or symbol.

He gives an account[46] of an alphabet in which the letters that have a
distinctive graphic function would cease to differentiate, would represent
as much one phenomenon as another, "A Total Unification of All Typefaces,"[47] "the trick is to achieve *completeness*: to fill the space."[48] Hofstadter and Kim spent years drawing what a friend called "ambigrams,"
one more aggravative that Saussure did not foresee in his denegrations of
writing. For that reason, that unification is not totally distant from the
"differances" of Derrida, although their authors are not aware of them.
Nor is it distant from the "spirit," maker of all writings, from that literal
aspiration required by the articulation of the aleph and that gives birth to
all letters, or from the aleph of Borges, synthesis in diversity to the letter.
"The 'A' spirit"[49] that Hofstadter describes demands a singular "Platonic
essence" that recognizes that "the platonic essence reveals something new
about the spirit without ever exhausting it." Hofstadter further recognizes
that "the shape of a letterform is a surface manifestation of deep mental
abstractions."[503] With the arrival of computers, "to have an 'A' making
machine with infinite variety of potential output is not in itself difficult,"[51] and it is no longer impossible to think of approaching "the vision
of a unification of all typefaces."[52]

In May of 1994 a congress of academies in the *Real Academia
Española* imposed on us, against our will, the elimination of letters

belonging to our alphabet.[53] It was argued that there existed an urgency to accede to a universal Latin alphabet but, different from a *lingua perfetta* toward which humanity continues to direct its worries, universality in this case is of interest in order to facilitate the connections between computers and databases. Eco wonders: "But would it be possible for a supernational entity (like the UN or the European parliament) to impose an International Auxiliary Language as lingua franca [. . .]. There are no historical precedents."[54] One has the impression that "Every few centuries we have to burn the Library of Alexandria," as one of the characters of "The Congress" says.[55] Sometimes the fire begins with the letter.

In the *Phaedrus*, Thamus, the Egyptian king, was right to doubt the invention of Thot or Hermes. Writing, the first technology dedicated to registering and conserving fugacity, was intended to represent, to make present what is absent. Effective, secret, suspect. As a remedy, it brings together the dangerous ambiguity of the *pharmakon*; as an instrument, the dangerous ambivalencies of the servant. The Golem is animated by the letter and with the obliteration of the letter it crumbles; made of earth, of dust, it falls to earth, like the dirt that forms it.

As the century passes, we believe ever more that we believe ever less. Nevertheless, this increasing discredit that disparages representation, from rhetorical discourses to the images that dissimulate them, reinforces perhaps a belief in circumstances: immediate circumstances, indisputably immediate, which, present, without need of representation, are there, without claiming to be able to foresee the uncertainties of a Beyond more or less sure, without claiming to accede to the prolonged wishes for utopias more or less isolated or fantastic. It is these circumstances that, adverse to the mere speculations of political fantasies, contemplate the radication in a place, celebrating the arguments of common places, in the present—like a present—the place in which we are.

> The Congress of the World began with the first instant of the world and will continue when we are dust. There is no place in which it is not.[56]

It is not a question of bringing to life the *furore etimologico* nor of consecrating a perfect language in which names, as Cratylus wanted, would be in a natural or necessary correspondence with things, nor of giving oneself over to "an unbridled hunting of etymologies,"[57] as Eco warns against, in order to demonstrate remote relations or philological coincidences of roots with which the nineteenth century more than sufficiently nourished its historical, philological, and biological investigations. It is interesting to trace, nevertheless, some common lines in contempo-

rary thought, to propose a synthesis of diversities that would attain a
unity beyond theological consecrations, overcoming the facileness of
binary oppositions or the limitation of a numeration that, triadic, only
adds a term to the series. We do not speak of *unity* in order to reduce three
to two or two to one, but rather in order to recuperate "one," more as a
beginning, as the commencement of an open series, than as quantitative
limit to a monotheistic unity: "I will not extend this speculation much
more since it could be offensive to the prejudices of some who find themselves here," I might say, paraphrasing Peirce.[58]

One, a commencement, an origin of creation, a ludic beginning, of re-
creation, after the ending where words match, combine, and wager those
combinations, as if one played anew in order to engage symbols with
poetry, with knucklebones, or with dice. "A toss of the dice will never
abolish chance,"[59] summarizes in a verse a world, or two, their destruction, their sudden fragmentation, and their restitution by transidiomatic
means, re-veiling by means of some cubes thrown at hazard the profound
coincidence beyond the differential surface of languages.

The symbol is found aplenty in the intersection of two spheres of
existence, combining exterior, interior, the physical and spiritual world,
the visible and the invisible. Perhaps it alludes to the androgynes, to the
fall and luck of symbols, to the suspicious law of chance, to the toss of
dice, of two dice or of one and the same die duplicated by different languages in one and the same verse, and the possibility of *restitution* (a key
word) by poetic *intraduction*. That is the figure with which I designate on
the one hand the impossibility of translating and on the other a most profound translation beyond the meanings that the names segment or simplify. In this task, it is the difference of languages that is in play.

Far from the deplored positivist yearning for finding an *Ursprache*
that would explain genealogically a common origin, intraduction stands in
Borges, in great poetry, as an example of synthesis in diversity. It is a
search—poetic, theoretical—for the remaining traces of a unique, initial,
anterior, interior, indivisible language. The presumption of a prebabelic
nominal unity that appears recurrently in his essays constitutes a starting
point for his fiction.

Borges discovers the magnificent *irony* of God on the basis of a language of *iron*, of his armored (*blindado*) language which is that of a *blind*
man, speaks of *red Adam*,[60] of many other reds juxtaposed in his own
names: Red Scharlach. Those crossed words stake claim to an edenic or
adamic language, where *My viper letter*,[61] forked and seductress, a split
tongue of "departure" and "arrival," a safe conduct that fools customs by
way of a symbolic key, will tempt the poet who procures, beyond linguistic limits, to recuperate the com-prehension of a language if not

unique, at least united or universal. By way of an extravagant onomastic-semasiological dispositive, the poet or the philosopher challenges borders, impugns the rigor of a history, parodies basic linguistic properties (arbitrariness, linearity). He does not transgress, but neither does he observe, the syntactic norms in favor of an almost perverse semantics, extending consecutiveness not as an effect and not in time but rather in a place (place, not space, Ger. *Ort*, not *Raum*).

There it is possible to return to these circumstances, to highlight the *place* that enables the relation between material elements; the continent[62] that makes the meeting possible, orienting ourselves first to the West, the point from which points are defined, secondly, to the West of America, near Los Angeles. For this reason I have said for some time now I have not rejected the temptation to venerate the *genii loci* and I invoke them, quoting Walt Whitman, thanks to an epigraph from Sebeok:[63]

> Solitary, singing in the West,
> I strike up for a New World.

From this nearby far-West, two times west, two times occidental, west on west, *double the double u*, a U-turn returns us to the beginning when we spoke of the dualities of that chance-fall. It is inevitable to recall that the Latin *occidens* is the present participle of *occidere*, a verb composed of *ob-* and *cadere*, the "fall" to which we have been referring since the beginning, a fall that, without ignoring the others, refers to the setting of the stars, of the sun especially, whose setting place is the occident. This time, however, it is not a question of a *decadence of the occident*, although that fall is double too.

CHAPTER NINE

The Paradoxes of Paradoxes

Now we do not define each deed that incites our song;
we cipher it in one sole word that is the Word.
　　　　　　　　　　　　—Borges, "UNDR"

In this case it would be valid to modify the formula of the Hebrew superlative, since it is not only a question of distinguishing a level of superiority that exalts a king of kings for being the greatest, or a song of songs that was the best and is his. Despite these grammaticized excellences, it is necessary to point out that the superlative used here is not applied in order to exalt in the same way. Similarly, Borges announces in his book *Prologues*[1] the presentation of a "prologue of prologues." I would be interested in anticipating by way of this double plural the apex of paradoxes that Borges's oeuvre and its author multiply, those of a Borges, who writes, and the other, who also does.

I would not want to attribute solely to the Balkan hospitality of Hans Ulrich Gumbrecht, to his convocation to reflect, in Dubrovnic, in 1989, on "Collapses, paradoxes, cognitive dissonances," the necessity to recur thematically to Borges's paradoxical imagination with such *naturalness.* Above all because, attending to themes of this nature, naturalness could be alarming. It is true that if unforeseeability constitutes one of the conditions of the paradox, then dealing with paradoxes one need not speak of Borges nor, dealing with Borges, would it be necessary to speak of paradoxes: "in the Koran there are no camels; this absence of camels would be enough to prove that it is not Arabic."[2]

For this reason, these reflections are initiated in the *key of preterition,* a figure that seems to me more paradoxical than paradoxes themselves, although, as it is limited to accessory metadiscursive rhetorical recourses, one does not always remember that in saying that one does not say what one says, the rhetorical figure reveals one of the complicated dualities that are a condition of the word. Between paradoxes and preteritions would be the sententious occurrence of the first and the perverse redundancy of the second, two of the scarce differences between figures that have in common an ambivalent autoreferential *renvoi*: without interrupting the consecutiveness of discourse, they are terms that remit it to itself, formulating a verbal autoreferentiality at the same time as they suspend it. The suspended reference remains and does not, goes and comes, as much what one says as what one does not say is said, is negated, and is maintained.[3]

Paradoxical literature has always existed, but there are works and moments in which this frequency explodes, and it is already difficult to pass them by, their lights and blinding flashes. Borges is a paradoxical event of such a kind that his analysis would overflow the specifics of whatever description, or the limits of inventory. Because of the logical vastness and variety of this recourse, one of the first problems would be to pose again the question, Where to begin? But the beginning, in the same way as the end, once mentioned, moves away. There is always a discourse or witness that refers the phrase, the judgment, the solution, the catastrophe, like the messengers who recount the calamities of Job to Job and believe, or say, that they exist only to recount to him his misfortunes. Through the word, even the greatest disasters, verbalized, are normalized. From the moment that someone recounts it, once it is named, the ending becomes a deferred end, postponed; through the phrase, mentioned, the beginning also becomes posterior. Because of something "at the beginning," at the beginning of Genesis, as "*Bereshit*" was translated, does not begin with aleph but with the next letter. In the indicative ambiguities that deixis claims to avoid, the uttered beginning refers to itself from the beginning, two times: "In the beginning was the Word." In the same way, in the oft-discussed "*Ceci n'est pas une pipe*," the initial autoreferentiality formulated as deixis (*ceci*: this) is part of an indication of circularity that problematizes the formulation. Perhaps more than the Beginning, it was in the End that there was the Word: "*début*" is a beginning that in French would seem to negate the end from the beginning. Hegel had always observed this complex circularity: "The result is the same thing as the beginning because the beginning is the end (*parce que le commencement est le but / weil der Anfang Zweck ist*)."[4] Similar to the designation "the perfect crime,"[5] one does not take into account that once it is said, it ceases to be perfect, although it does not cease to be a crime. Its perfection, perfection itself, would not tolerate the commentary; because of the mention, not only would it be known, but the perfection is destroyed and it is only a matter of a crime; without the mention it would not be known and would not even be a crime.

It is in the recognition of this naturalness or paradoxical nature that is rooted one of the obstacles that impede the comprehension of Borges's vision because, precisely, his paradoxical imagination is as *natural* as his *blindness*, because, as well, his *vision is paradoxical*. That precariousness of his biographical, genetic, hereditary condition has been so often alluded to that it would seem obvious at this point to speak of Borges's blindness, above all when he himself accepts that contradictory gift "from God, who with magnificent irony / Gave me at the same time books and the night."[6] He says he accepts it without thinking, without sorrow, like the days and the darkness. It is not a question of resignation; hesitating among shadows, Borges praises them, like Oedipus, he makes out in this way another light. Borges, who never boasted about the pages he had written but rather about those he had read,[7] has no compunction about demanding the virtues of his defect. "Escrever é uma forma de / ver" for Haroldo de Campos,[8] although neither for him, creator of concrete poetry, does seeing manage to evidence the truth. For some time now the theoretical and methodological statements that insist on the question of the observer have been numerous. It is possible, as a consequence, to consider Borges as a paradigmatic observer: perspicuous, clever, lucid, and blind, the paradoxical observer par excellence.

When Borges presumes that Oscar Wilde "realized that his poetry was too visual and intended to cure himself of that defect," he was not referring only to Wilde. Mostly he is also speaking of himself when he recalls that Wilde had said to himself:

> The Greeks maintained that Homer was blind in order to mean that poetry should not be visual, that its duty is to be auditory. [. . .] We may think that Homer did not exist but that the Greeks liked to imagine him blind in order to insist on the fact that poetry is before all music, that poetry is above all the lyre, and that the visual can exist or not exist in a poet. I know of great visual poets and I know of great poets who are not visual: intellectual poets, mental, there is no reason to mention names.[9]

The irony of his verses, like the discretion of confidence, does not diminish a stubbornness that is no more paradoxical than it is literal, because poetry brings together those contradictions of the written word. In the first of his last poems, Octavio Paz said:

Poetry
is said and is heard:
is real.
And hardly do I say
is real,
it dissipates.
Is it more real that way?[10]

From the beginning Borges was determined by contradictions. Like
few others, his is an adventure properly verbal, nominal: "His adventure
is having been *named.*" In this case it is Geoffrey Hartman who, inspired
by "French reflections,"[11] quotes J. P. Sartre and validates his hypothesis
on the notion that the literary work constitutes the elaboration of a specular name, the proper name proper. Nor did Roland Barthes exaggerate
when he understood that in Marcel Proust the decision or disposition to
write his novel begins in the moment in which he finds or invents proper
names: "Once he found the system, the work was written immediately."[12] For this reason we can say that the "constitutive power" of the
name, of the proper name, may well have consolidated the great literary
adventure of Jorge Luis Borges—Georgie, to his closest friends. An
adventure in which he risks more than the opposing forecasts of a proper
oxymoron that celebrates in his texts the bestowing of necessary names
in order to recall in a contradictory way the labors of farmers, the barbarous victories of *gauchos* on the plains, and the travels through villages
and suburbs.

Onomastically ciphering country and city, the extremes that his texts
reconcile interminably, Borges used to rejoice recalling the literary consequences of this specular expansion of his proper name, of his own name,
as a natural phenomenon, as part of the denominative pact that "slips
between the yes and the no,"[13] the allusions of poetry and the verbal ver-
tigos of the quotidian abyss.

If *"le sententie fuori del comun parere"* (sentences outside of
common seeming) can be considered paradoxical, the legitimacy of rescuing the contradictory constants of his texts or of his person remains per-
manently in question. It is already known that the observation of this
constancy is a *common place* of criticism that is not worried about falling
back into the same topics, registering, immutably, *mirrors and doubles,*
deciphering enigmatic *writings,* reciding in a cosmos that is assimilated
into paradise ordered under the species of the *library.* The same *tigers*
abbreviate a limited bestiary, stalking through *infinite labyrinths,* control-
ling acts of violence framed in the sly adventures of *chess,* partly open cells
in the prisons engraved by G. B. Piranesi or dissimulated with spatial

humor by M. C. Escher in fixed corridors and useless staircases. It is difficult to blaze a path so well marked, discover the discovered, invent outside of the inventory. As if what were required were the *genii loci* that Borges appeared to avoid, the poor protector genies of my land, the scarce intellectual ascendant of Indians who were confused from the beginning, men or Indians, Indians or beasts, Indians with soul or without, Indians without *h* or with *h*, as Francis Drake registers them;[14] so many ab-original confusions appear determined by the paradoxes of an occidental discovery by accident, of a *dis-orientation* to the letter. America continues to be utopia, an id-entity always in flight.

As for Borges, the greatest paradox is precisely that the paradoxes and the *topoi koinoi* are not distinguished. In the past, in more recent times, criticism has not ceased to indicate the paradoxical frequencies of a dubious eccentricity. A little while ago, the *Magazine Littéraire*,[15] which dedicated once again a special issue to Borges, brought together an abundant series of articles in which I believe that nobody failed to observe the variants of his paradoxical imagination.

It is not strange that the author of a character-author who is the author-reader of a character-reader should be the great author of this age, author of the author of a *Don Quijote* identical to that of Cervantes, although superior. It is strange, on the other hand, that Pierre Menard, one of the authors most analyzed in recent times, is no more than a fictional character; even more strange is the fact that his partial and unknown oeuvre—no one read or even managed to see the draft that he himself destroyed—should provoke so many commentaries and so much praise. It would not surprise us if it turned out to be a matter of emblematizing as well the perplexities of a critical exercise that does not hesitate to pronounce on texts that it does not know—or that do not exist—in the same way that it simulates not knowing texts that it does in fact know.

It is not an exaggeration to affirm that Borges's entire imagination is articulated paradoxically, and it would even be paradoxical to do away with this articulation. How to avoid then the common sense that paradox avoids? How to observe, in that "alliance of words, the artifice of language through which ideas and words, which ordinarily oppose and contradict each other, come to approach each other and combine with one another in such a way that they surprise the intellect,"[16] if novelty, surprise, is rooted in the fact that here are confounded common place and genies of place, doxa and paradox? Once again the paradox is paradoxical, and tends to accredit itself ambivalently; yes and no, one diction against the other, they oppose and support each other in a reciprocal way. Indeed, paradoxes are most dangerous,[17] hardly are they invoked and it becomes impossible to interrupt their occurrence, whenever it occurs. Once again, what is said is said against itself, like Plato, "*accusing*[18] writing in writing," a less well known version of the liar's paradox, which does not cease to be belied because it is not merely coincidental that *mention* and *mendacious* are hardly to be distinguished: Who is *L'homme qui ment*?[19] Literature accuses itself of tempting him, and the accusation is as much burden as justification, since not only in Latin does *accusing* recall the *cause*, and all of Borges is a cause for contradictions.

I do not know if Borges, in the same way as the metaphysicians of Tlön—who "do not search for truth or even for verisimilitude: they search for amazement"[20]—only searched for amazement because amazement is all too natural for Borges, so much so that it surprises him that amazement can still surprise. When referring to the admirable perfection of a poem, the narrator hits on the idea of commenting on "the true, the incredible."[21] The consecutive incompatibility of the oxymoron is neither suspicious nor noteworthy in an author who is so well *read* (in both Spanish and English, one who reads much is not to be idiomatically distinguished from one who is much read). Among so many inexhaustibly bookish references in his literature, among libraries, books, poems, stories, letters, where everything is quoted, it is not unusual that the contrarities of a topsy-turvy world should abound. Nevertheless, the inadvertence of the oxymoron goes beyond the recurrences of a narrator well planted in the literary universe. "Incredible" is also the most frequent commentary even for the normal events registered by the certitudes of everyday information. As much about the news that appears in the press as among the informalities of spontaneous communication, it is said of everything that everything "is incredible." Not only in fiction is "truth stranger than fiction," it is in media less literary—journalistic or historical—that truth seems even stranger.

Other oppositions form part of known and established structures: *History of Eternity*[22] or *The Other, the Same*,[23] are titles that are adjusted to the well-known rhetorical reconciliations of titles to which, like so many other authors, Borges tends to accede. As if from the title itself an author would cipher, as *mot-de-passe*, the "No pasarán" [They will not pass],[24] a contradiction that defines ambivalently the condition of literature, of art in general, that converts into equivalents the terms of the tragic alternative and, without discarding them, maintains it. Before Socrates and after Hamlet, in the strongest moments as much of philosophy as of poetry, to know and not to know, to be and not to be, although they oppose one another, do not exclude one another.

Attentive to the inevitable contradictions of an antonymic semantics, Borges deconstructs, from his first writings, the conflictive accumulations of an *undecidable* language: "Let us not marvel excessively; in our language the verb *to cleave* means both to rend and to adhere," he translates thus, between two languages, the observation of an Anglophone character, a fracture similar to the indiscernible irreducibility of the properties confronted by the oxymoron: "the public and secret representation."[25] It is an "inversion" in narrative structures, where a narrator uses the correction of grammatical rules to occult under a third person the folds of his own betrayal, using the double edge of the word-sword, the word as thought in English: (s)word(s)word(s)word(s).

Starting out from the title of the story "The Form of the Sword,"[26] the segmentation becomes less abusive. It is a question of a story that has as a protagonist an Irishman whose name is hidden until the end but whom they call in the hacienda "the Englishman." In the same way as the sword cuts on two sides, the word identifies problematically nationalities, identifies victim and executioner, a confusion that the narration enables and grammar guarantees. Barely a minimal prestidigitation, a pronominal transition (third person for Latin, *persona*)[27] and the cases appear to be interchanged: a name for another, a man for another; the displacement manages to make the fundaments of reason oscillate. How to know if they identify with one another because they are distinguished from one another or if they identify with one another because they are no longer distinguished from one another? In either the narrations or in history, little can be extracted from the *confabulations* that nourish writing. Derrida says that

> writing does not have its own essence or value, be it positive or negative. It is played in the simulacrum. It mimes in its type memory, knowledge, truth. For this reason the men of writing gather under the eye of god, not already as wisemen (*sophoi*), but in truth as pretend or self-proclaimed wisemen (*doxosophoi*).[28]

In "Theme of the Traitor and the Hero,"[29] the play of challenges is joined contradictorily between the possibility of searching for truth in theatrical representation (*Julius Caesar*, an imperial tragedy set in Ireland) and the juggleries that historical research does not avoid when, on discovering the crime, it hides it. Once again history and poetry confront one another: if a crime is registered, it is the version of the historian that says the last word or does not say it, even when the crime occurs in the middle of a fiction, as in this case. The two discourses remain vacillating between diegesis and mimesis, between history and poetry, between verity and version. It is too well known that history as well has its origin in writing. That is the first *inversion* of writing, its *investissement*. The figures take shape in *chiasmus*, an *x*, the letter that obliterates identity or represents it ambiguously in the anonym that cannot sign its name; the incognate identity of the crossed figure.

In another story, "Three Versions of Judas,"[30] access to the mystery of knowledge, to the knowledge of the mystery, is even more capricious. Truth passes through three versions according to which what was even greater than Christ's sacrifice on the cross was the sacrifice of Judas, who betrayed him. Because of a betrayal, similar to *"le Christ en gloire,"* his damnation is eternal: the three versions are those of Borges's narrator, against the four of the Gospel. Beyond the uncertain probability of the hypothesis it is the faith in the word, it is the word that counts, not the number or the name. In truth, and for God in eternity, those differences are minor. All differences, even the religious ones. In "The Theologians,"[31] the absentminded mind of God

> is not interested in religious differences either, as far as taking one theologian for another. [. . .] for the unfathomable divinity, he [Aureliano de Aquilea] and Juan de Panonia (the orthodox and the heretic, the abhorrer and the abhorred, the accuser and the victim) were one and the same person.[32]

Acccording to Harold Bloom, if the misreading fits the reading ("Reading, if strong . . . is always a misreading),[33] its deconstructive operations of *reversal and reinscription* could also be applied to writing. It is a recurrent recognition that the twentieth century has multiplied on the basis of diverse notions and doctrines. Nevertheless, several decades before, the erudite offensives of Lautréamont and "the viper Letter" in which Jules Laforgue wrote, spatialized a poetry that inscribed itself ambiguously *between* different texts.

When Charles Sanders Peirce said that "A sign is something which we know by knowing something more,"[34] he understood by it, doubtlessly, that by knowing something more one would know something different, such that the knowledge of that difference necessarily implies the variations of an inevitable opposition. In part, this is what Umberto Eco reiterates when he considers that, "Starting from the sign, one goes through the whole semiotic process and arrives at the point where the sign becomes capable of contradicting itself (otherwise, those textual mechanisms called 'literature' would not be possible)."[35]

Like the imaginary regions of Tlön, where a book that did not include its counterbook would be considered incomplete, in the universe ordered by Borges, or in his ordered universe, everything occurs or is explained by mechanisms of contradiction. Beyond the interiority of the text, a story is limited by another story to which it is counterposed ("The Aleph"/"The Zahir"). A letter (*aleph*) is unfolded into two signs (*yod*) that confront each other; a book against another book: *Other Inquisitions* (1952) against *Inquisitions* (1926). There remains in specter the disquiet of a prohibited book, submitted to the censorship of its own inquisition: the book that is object of the most severe interdiction, that of its author, despite his intention of writing it only to relieve the concept of "*samben-itos* and the smoke of bonfires," separating it, "purely by coincidence," from those other, more famous, more atrocious *inquisitions*. Although historical, they do not cease thereby to be the same. Is it a question of words, of rhetorical figures, of books, of religious abuses, of absurd criminal abuses?

> Paradoxes exist to reject such divisions as those between "thought" and "language," between "thought" and "feeling," between "logic" and "rhetoric," between "logic," "rhetoric," and "poetics," and between all of these and "experience." In paradox, form and content, subject and object are collapsed into one, in an ultimate insistence upon the unity of being.[36]

In this way Borges discovers in the semasiological reserve of one and the same word conceptual divisions, internal oppositions, and although lexical propriety registers and authorizes them, adverse coincidence recalls incompatibilities of meaning that the pragmatic reductions of context tend to attenuate or discard. Usage avoids those semantic collisions that the dictionary guarantees but that the speaker prefers to forget. Beyond those objections, Borges's language has its foundation in simultaneous usage, at the same time, of different, contrary meanings. That simultaneity discovers in the instant an instance of eternity. It is "The Secret Miracle,"[37] a story in which Borges makes of the "temporality" of time a secondary condition of permanence. It is the moment in which the fugacity of *maintenant*, of "now" is detained, *se maintenant*, maintaining itself. The diegesis of the story initiates it at dawn, when "the armored vanguards of the Third Reich entered Prague."[38] The story was written in 1943.

Elsewhere but by similar mechanisms, his textual strategies manage to dissimulate in one and the same unity philosophical, religious, political, historical, personal, circumstantial antagonisms. Of him as well it could be said that he considered human beliefs to be like children's toys,[39] since for him as for Coleridge all men are born either Aristotelians or Platonists. The latter believe classes, orders, and genres to be realities; the former, that they are generalizations; for these language is no more than an approximate game of symbols; for those it is the map of the universe.[40]

One of the most suggestive uses of that paradoxical reserve is constituted by the production of opposed and simultaneous meanings, which is one form of the principle property of the term but which manages to disarticulate it in a literary use that reaches the apex of meaning (*Literature of Replenishment*) at the same time as its refutation and questioning (*Literature of Exhaustion*).[41] One meaning *against* another: Do they impugn or support one another? One meaning *for* another: Do they multiply or exclude one another? "This text, then, begins from/by/because of (*por*) the word from/by/because of (*por*)" recalls Derrida.[42] The fable, "Fable," by Francis Ponge, two times fable, is a poem of (the) truth. Nevertheless, not only in the complexities of a poem is it possible to verify the singular cross of irony and allegory with which Derrida celebrates Paul de Man. Whatever word, the mere voice, evokes and revokes at the same time. "The action takes place in an oppressed and tenacious country: Poland, Ireland, the Republic of Venice, some South American or (o)Balkan state"[43] which the ambiguity of the conjunction convokes. A *mysterium conjunctionis* is to be verified in this conjunction (*conjunctionis oppositorum* par excellence), a word almost not articulated, a vocal cry that the letter imitates in the original and primary emblematic circularity of its elliptical trace: multiplication of meanings that attract and reject each other in opposite directions, the oval nucleus from which proceed all contradictions.

Perhaps in the word *cipher*[44] is rooted one of the keys of the word, its gematric or geometric virtuality, the representative aptitude of a word that names the number, the secret writing of a figure that is number and secret, quantity and silence, each one of the numbers and its set, that one with which the enumeration begins, part and whole, the void in Arabic (*sifr*), nothing and the circle that encircles all of the plenum, the apex, the zero: O the letter, 0 the cipher/numeral.

His preoccupation for these different tensions into which opposite meanings enter, that ironic bidirectionality that is the power of meaning, or potential meanings, is hindered by the paradoxes of identity and difference that, although they are among the oldest formulations, are not for that reason the least disquieting: "They do not know how the discordant accords with itself, agreement of inverse tensions, like in the arc and the lyre."[45] It is precisely in the mouth of a foreigner that Plato affirms being to be both one and several, both hate and friendship make its cohesion. In

"Funes the Memorious,"[46] the protagonist of one of Borges's master showpieces of epistemology-fiction suffers, like "A Reader,"[47] "the passion of language."[48] The suffering is as strong as the attraction. Funes is a gaucho from my country who "since that afternoon when the blue-black horse threw him [. . .] he lost consciousness [. . .] Now his perception and his memory are infallible."[49] And for that reason, precisely, he is incapable of thinking what it is to remember and forget. He lies prostrate in an obscure corner of the rancho because he cannot tolerate, he cannot conceive that "the dog of three fourteen (seen in profile) would have the same name as the dog of quarter after three (seen from head on)."[50] For Funes, "the generic symbol *dog* is an archetypal exaggeration."[51] The question is as old as the word. Although Parmenides does not, in the alternatives of his dialogue, manifest it in such a perturbing way, I am not sure that Plato any more than Parmenides had not foreseen the occurrence of this native rustic passion.

The problem is posed poetically when Borges recognizes that the individual is in some way the species, a duality that is dissimulated under the same name: "Keats's nightingale is also Ruth's nightingale."[52] By virtue of one sole word all times coincide, eternity and an instant; all space, the universe in a point; in one word, a word that is also a letter: the aleph. There begins the conflict.

It is worth recognizing in the homonymic lability of the word one of the decisive reasons for the paradoxical constancy. It is in the tendentious and inevitable confrontation that is produced in the interior of the word, of the word with itself, that is rooted the origin of so much contradiction:

> Language says the opposite of what we try to say. We attempt the singular, and its says the universal. But it does not maintain only an opinion against ours; because it says the universal, what it says is true; it refutes our opinion. Hegel, in the decisive conclusion of his analysis of sensible certainty, says precisely that language has "divine nature because it is absolvent, because it absolves us of unilateralness and makes us say the universal, the true."[53]

In the same way that "The true theme of poetry, although always secret and never explicit, is poetry itself,"[54] Borges's writings elaborate the conflict of that dual and contradictory condition, of the paradoxical ambivalence of the word that distinguishes and confounds, that rescues and annihilates at the same time. "How to Undo Things with Words" would be a necessary title to complete some that are already circulating.

For example, in the "Parable of the Palace,"[55] the narrator discloses the variants of an obliteration literal insofar as literary: the word suspends the thing or, if the thing is in turn a name, the name of a name, it names it two times, through two voices, a species of *re-vocation* that makes it disappear like the palace that, described by the poet, remains suspended, that is to say, does not remain.

Without making any reference to the dream of Caedmon,[56] or to Coleridge's poem, Borges recounts the story of a Yellow Emperor (he does not name him) who accuses a poet (he does not name him) of having robbed his palace (which he also does not name). "In the poem the palace was entire [. . .] It was enough for the poet to pronounce the poem for the palace to disappear, as if abolished and annihilated by the last syllable."[57] Because of this double *lack* (of the palace, of the poet), the Emperor did not hesitate to have him killed. In the same way as with the poet of the story, for whom the poem brought about immortality and death, by means of the word one palace is destroyed and another rises, like the successive temples of which Nietzsche spoke, which were capable of being placed and displacing themselves at the same time. By virtue of the same word, things begin to exist and cease to exist. The word re-presents them, and by means of that contradictory prefix, the things are not present (which is why they are represented) and are there again; they are presented two times. But as the parable recounts, all representation is suspicious, in reality there are no two things alike in the world.

The "Parable of the Palace," beyond Borges's page, alludes to more than one *pala*bra (word), parable of the *pala*ce or, a *para*bola of the *pal*abra itself. More precisely, a *para*dox of the *pala*bra, a repetition of the word that contradicts it while repeating it and that designates as much the vault of the palace that the emperor constructs and the poet makes disappear, as the "palate" (Fr. *palais*) where the word "takes place." When the repeated particulars are crossed they are sublated, like another form of *Aufhebung*, which exalts while degrading, disclosing even while suppressing, describes and destroys at the same time. If it is known that all paradox tends toward self-contradiction and toward selfdestruction, the word can do no more and no less.

Between a *counterfeiting* that is to imitate and *contradict*, Borges does not hesitate and insists on both procedures, such that from the moment they are said, facts become counterfeits.

> But let us not speak of facts. No one is interested in facts anymore. They are mere starting points for invention and reasoning. In the schools they teach us questions and the art of forgetting.

[. . .] The images and the printed letter were more real than things. Only the published was true. [. . .] After walking for fifteen minutes, we turned to the left. In the distance I made out a sort of tower, crowned with a cupola. —It is the crematorium — said someone. —Inside is the death chamber. They say that it was invented by a philanthropist whose name was, I believe, Adolph Hitler.[58]

For that reason, from his first writings to the most recent, Borges laments that "there is not one sole beautiful word, with the dubious exception of 'witness,' which is not an abstraction."[59] Perhaps Borges doubted, anticipating in those terms, what Lyotard asserted several decades after: "the unstable state and the instant of language in which something that should be able to be put into words has not yet been."[60] And if the witness professed the vocation of *martyr* (from Gr. *martur*: "witness"), doubting the word, believing in the sacrifice? If, as has occurred so many times, victim and witness coincided? What testimony can a victim present? What words could he or she find for so many losses, for so much destruction? *"Il ne trouve pas ses mots"* (he does not find his words), it is not only that he cannot find them. And if he found them? *"Il ne trouve pas ses morts"* (he does not find his dead), when there is nothing but damage, any pronouncement will be useless. Nor would silence be less useless. Like the dilemma of the crocodile[61] ready to devour a baby, it has no solution.

Lyotard defines the *differend*[62] as a case in which the plaintiff has been deprived of the means necessary for his argumentation, and for this reason is turned into a victim. He wonders if the victim has the means to establish that he is a victim. What tribunal can judge him when no tribunal and no right foresaw the nature of a crime that shatters any legitimate state whatever? "There is no other witness than the victim, no other victim than the one who has died."[63] Witness and victim disappear at the same time and there is no possible or attenuating plea for the crime. If it is still necessary to convince, argue, deliberate, verify, only rhetoric would remain safe from the disaster, because it is one of its origins. Neither theory, nor history, nor poetry. After Auschwitz, nothing.

Proofs wear out the truth[64] and make it barely *probable*, that is to say, as true as it is uncertain. If it were necessary to prove such a crime, the means would invalidate themselves. Once again, Hamlet is right to put on a *dumb-show*;[65] for one who debates with himself in the confines of a tragedy, a comedy could well be *The real thing*.[66] For this reason he conceives a spectacle with the purpose of seeing the truth put on stage. A spectacle that repeats in silence a reality ever less real the more it is repeated: the words no longer count. How to resolve the paradox of the word? If the crime does not refer, the crime will not be known. If it refers, it is no longer the same. Lyotard said it would be necessary to examine the means, which "are at least of two types: some proceed by annulment, others by representation. . . . To represent' Auschwitz' in images, in words, is a way of making it be forgotten."[67]

If for Borges "forgetting / is one of the forms of memory, [. . .] / the other secret face of the coin,"[68] the word is the best known face. Everything passes through the word, but in this way nothing really happens (*pasa*) either. The word is trance and transition. If one cannot speak, one must keep silent. It has been said already many times. But what does silence rescue? In Genesis, the interdiction of God is a command in contradiction: He who creates by way of the word does not enable a word to be named himself. As Lévinas said, "the marvel of a thought better than knowing. *Hors sujet.*"[69]

The narrator of the parable ends by saying:

> Such legends, it is clear, do not go beyond being literary fictions. The poet was a slave of the emperor and died as such; his composition fell into oblivion because it deserved oblivion, and his descendents still look for it, and they will not find the word of the universe.[70]

Until now, commentaries on "*UNDR*"[71] have not abounded, a story that not even Borges comments on when commenting on all the others in the epilogue to *The Book of Sand*. It is the story of a man who, realizing that the poetry of the *Urnos*[72] consists of one sole word, dedicates himself to search for it and, different from the descendents of the poet executed by the Emperor, finds it: "He said the word *Undr*, which means wonder."[73]

Like its reference, the word is strange, in a language that I do not understand. Its four letters maintain the mystery that the word signifies: *wonder* designates as much marvel as the bewilderment before the paradoxical event of *under*standing (*undr- under . . .*), which participates in an ambivalent way in both forms of amazement. The mystery is greater because the transcription suppresses the vowels, as if they were sacred characters that, read in Hebrew, invoke public prayers in memory of the dead.[74]

Today there is another word that is pronounced like a strange expression, but in Hebrew, which is a known language. Almost inarticulate, it claims silence as if exclaiming a cry. It disconcerts. It is said in Hebrew but it is already a universal word and is not even translated. It remains enigmatic and distant as if it assured via incomprehension its paradoxical universality: no one comprehends. A unique event, *inconceivable*. Destruction, extermination, annihilation. Even translated into all the languages it resists comprehension. Again because of a word made of four letters, reason remains in suspense; whatever reason fails.

CHAPTER TEN

Vox in Deserto:
Borges and the Story of Sand

> He told me his book was called the Book of Sand,
> because neither the book nor the sand have either begin-
> ning or end.
>
> —Borges, *Libro de Arena*

We would again have to allude to the writing of Borges, considering it a writing *avant la lettre*, insofar as it anticipates and prescribes the imagination and thought determining the historical, political, theoretical, and aesthetic tendencies that define ambivalently the culture of the second half of the last century, finalizing that century, that millennium, and other times. The revelations of his paradoxical vision, the aporias of his incertitudes, the disconcerts of suspended oppositions, the perfection of representations so precise that they obliterate what they represent, copies that surpass their originals, the vanishing of categories and genres, the undrawing of disciplinary limits, the fatality of a writing that does not distinguish although it is sustained by distinction, the progressive introduction of fiction into history, the omission that is another recourse of fiction, the totalitarian absurdity of inventories that impugn invention, the arbitrary enumerations, the incidences of possible worlds that displace known ones, the discontinuous parallelism of the encyclopedias that record or interpret them, the theoretical crises and the hermeneutic rescues of a truth, fragile and in flight, constitute some of the forms of those disparate definitions.

Observing these broken down gnosiological series, the meticulous clarity of rigorous cartographic registers, the iconic solidity of diagrams as valid as they are debatable, the measurable distances according to exact standards, the terminating borders between jurisdictions that tend to confront one another, the orientation of cardinal points as symmetrical as

they are arbitrary, the eventualities of a utopic geography could not cease
to be one of the favorite targets at which Borges would aim his negative
poetics.

"What are the Orient and the Occident? If they ask me, I do not
know. Let us look for an approximation,"[1] Borges replies, but in regional
terms, diffusely spatial, to the same question that Augustine formulated
about time, and, like the old professor of rhetoric who was a monk before
converting, responds by affirming that he knows space and does not know
it at the same time. Anterior and similar to the coincidences of the global-
ized present, Borges's epistemological fiction takes note of this planetary
reduction in which the confines, being conventional, do not count; where
distances, because of the immediacy of contexts and accelerated imagination, count less; where accidents are no more than accidental; where exotic
places appear juxtaposed—because they are neighbors or mythical—to
familiar im-mediations where Orient and Occident contract in a common
decline that brings them closer to one another. Preceded by the redundancies of *Der Untergang des Abendlandes* (*The Decline of the West*), a
title in which time and space are confounded in one and the same fall,[2] that
approximation constitutes a decline in two parts for two reasons: because
geographical reason declines (barely a primary topography); because conceptual reason declines (barely a discrete logic).

> And how to define the Orient, not the real Orient, which does
> not exist? I would say that the notions of Orient and Occident
> are generalizations but that no individual feels Oriental. I sup-
> pose that a man feels Persian, feels Hindu, feels Malay, but not
> Oriental. In the same way, no one feels Latin American: we feel
> Argentine, Chilean, Orientals (Uruguayans). It does not matter,
> the concept does not exist.[3]

Between prophecy or provocation, Borges's previsions were those of
an epoch in which countries vanish, regionalized into markets; in which
deterritorialization turns inside out the definitions of national statutes
submitted to the fluctuations of a conceptual stock market in which
notions of nation and narration are confounded, and not only because of
homophonic occurrences. Borges's imagination mocks borders because,
uncertain, they indistinctly unite or separate jurisdictions. They degrade
them, running through them by means of personal topology that explodes
into contiguities only conceived of in dreams, making of the whole world
a *common place, topoi koinoi*. More than sites, indisputable arguments,
they get by without fortuitous particularities, without the eventualities of
history, procuring to discover, beyond idiomatic, idiosyncratic contingen-

cies and the myths of identity that sustain them, the models of a knowledge capable of abstracting them. There the variants of being and knowing stand as instances of a movement, of a voyage that is directed beyond,
toward another reality, an *ultrareality* where the eventual does not count;
where the voyage is a disputable errancy of permanency in space, where
the vision of the whole Earth can be concentrated in a sacred place or
ciphered in an initial or initiatory letter that is not less so for spatializing
time in writing. Because if the world was made to finish in a beautiful
book, the book exists because it is beautiful—*cosmos*, a world—and
because it remains, it does not end. . .

It would not be excessive, then, to simplify a parallelism that would
implicate textual itineraries and recognize that—according to the genetic
analysis of Borges's manuscripts—if the *mihrab* is the place that "gives
place" to the *aleph*,[4] associated with an "Arabic geography,"[5] the desert is
the place that gives place to Borges's text, an imagination that tries to
comprehend in one expression, in one moment, eternity and infinity or, at
the same time, to claim them for itself.

This literary claim desires the desert. But, more than *vox in deserto*,
more than to speak in the desert or to desire to be heard, Borges speaks—
in Spanish—his desire for the desert: between *desire* and *desert*, *decirlos*
(to say them) in one sole word. It would be necessary to begin at the
beginning, but like the end, the beginning is neither one nor is it certain;
there are several, and perhaps for this reason one of the principal beginnings (*principios*)—which is the beginning of Writing—begins with *b* and
not with the first letter, as if presuming that something anterior had
already preceded it, one conjecture that the theologians have noted only
to have it refuted, as they must have noted and refuted a question no
longer of letters but of names (*nombres*), a word that means "numbers" in
French and "names" in Spanish, encompassing transidiomatically the
dualities of a common denominator or of a similar referent.

In this way is posed a brief philological discussion, a first question of
translation, of crossed languages, a question or a search for words that
Borges would not have avoided and that poetically engages the titles of
the books of the Torah with this allure of saying or of that desire of the
desert. Once again: instead of to speak (*decir*) in the desert, speak (*decir*)
the desert. The first title of the *Pentateuco*, *Genesis*, in Hebrew *Bereshit*,
which means "beginning," names the word with which the book of *Gen-*
esis begins. The second title, *Exodus*—from the Greek *exo*, "out of," and
hodos, "route, voyage, act of leaving"—is the distant translation of the
Hebrew *Shemot*, which means "Names," neither emigration nor exile, but
rather the Hebrew word with which *Exodus* begins: "These are the
names . . ." *Leviticus*, the third title of the Hebrew Bible, refers to the

priests, sons of Aaron, separating itself from the Hebrew *Ve ikra*, which means "and he called," another of Yahweh's ways of saying, with which the book begins. The fourth, *Numbers*—in Hebrew *Ba-midbar*—which is a title adopted by the Septuagint (the Seventy translators of the Torah, or Seventy two, in order to avoid sectarian misreadings). After it, the Vulgate passes over *Ba-midbar*, the title that anticipates the beginning of the book, making allusion to the census of the twelve tribes in place of referring to the place, the desert of Sinai, where Yahweh addresses Moses, speaks to him. *Midbar* claims its close relation with the word: *dibur*, "speech," *diburim*, "talks," "rumors, cheap talk," in modern Hebrew. Words and desert, both voices proceed from the same root, spoken voices rooted in the desert. On the one hand, the name of "words" is omitted to make reference to the voyage to the way of the one who leaves, to the route or path that is abandoned or the one that one tries to rescue (*Exodus*). On the other hand, the place is omitted, the desert, in order to make reference to numbers (*Numbers*). Intersection of voices and ways[6] in the desert: "The voice of him that crieth in the wilderness, Prepare ye the way of the Lord, make straight in the desert a highway for our God."[7]

The fifth book of the Hebrew Bible, *Deuteronomy*, adopted from the Greek and Latin meaning "second law," also does not translate the Hebrew *debarim*, "palabras": "These be the words that Moses spake . . . in the wilderness."[8] "In the beginning" of all the books of the Torah is found the word, speech, discourse, voices that are spoken in the desert. More than etymological, more than idiomatic, the profundity of the relation between "word" and "desert" sinks its roots in a mythology of the noth-ing, in a lettristic, consonant coincidence, *dbr*, originates as minimalist, as if in a previous language, a geography of the void, an empty space that is the origin of the world that, because of the word, remains to be made. Even by opposition, a semantic relation similar but contrary is to be ver-ified in Latin: *desertus*, adjectival past participle of *deserere*, "to separate oneself," "abandon," derives as does *sermo*, "speech, language," from the Latin *serere*: the desert depriving or deprived of the word. Signs cross one another in different languages, exchange signals, the semantic paths lead-ing to a common mystery. Thought in Spanish, in the "language of Borges," they are words that propitiate bilingual, multilingual interlac-ings, names for numbers and vice versa, words that reflect one another, confronting each other like mirrors, verbal mirages that attract infinite interpretations, dissimulated interior translations, transports, or meta-phors of a passing secularization.

When the narrator of "The Theologians"[9] recounts that Aureliano argues in favor of a thesis on circular time, he points out that in the sub-ject of theology there is no novelty without danger, but dealing with the idea that the thesis he defended was "too unlikely, too amazing for the risk to have been serious," he clarifies, in parenthesis, that "the heresies that we ought to fear are those which can be confused with orthodoxy."[10]

Years before writing this story, in "Circular Time,"[11] Borges had already foreseen its plot. In place of announcing it, he prefers to remit it to the past. The mis-ordered reversibility of this *work in progess*[12] justifies the prolongation of a quote:

(I imagined some time ago a fantastic story, in the style of León Bloy: a theologian consecrates all of his life to confuting a heretic, he vanquishes him in intricate polemics, he denounces him, he makes him burn; in Heaven he discovers that for God the heretic and he consisted of one and the same person.)[13]

This essay precedes, in the *History of Eternity*, "The Translators of the Thousand and One Nights."[14] An obstinate circularity, a regressive succession, series in cycles that repeat themselves *sub specie aeternitatis*, these are the foundations of a doctrine that affirms eternity in the multiplication of possible worlds, as conceived by Borges on the basis of and in the manner of Louis-Auguste Blanqui: like copies that repeat themselves eternally in infinite space. In *Eternity Through the Stars: An Astronomical Hypothesis*,[15] the plurality of facsimilar stars that Blanqui supposes and describes in the reclusion of prison, the slippages of some into others, the recurrence of his astronomical phantasmagorias, the desperate illusion of coincidences and differences, constitute the intellectual substance and constant aesthetic that Borges demands and dispenses in different versions[16]: "Of the three doctrines I have enumerated, the best-reasoned and most complex is that of Blanqui."[17]

Repetitions question continuity, refute succession if it is progressive, procure eternity, "whose shattered copy is time," and also space, since it is measured by time.[18] The coordinates being confused—to designate them somehow—they do not order, they enable melancholic references of a geometrical indefinition that the seller of Bibles and of The Book of Sand, in *The Book of Sand*,[19] utters in a low voice, as if he were thinking out loud: "If space is infinite, we are in whatever point of space. If time is infinite, we are in whatever point of time."[20] The pages of the book, like sand, are uncountable, "none is the first, none is the last."[21]

The sand, like "the water that in water is invisible,"[22] is lost in the desert, where neither the sand nor the desert is distinguished. In that indefinite or infinite space, similar but opposed to the rigorous precisions traced by the labyrinth, one makes out the primordial "topos," place and theme of a loss, the disorientation that justifies the search for the Borgesian writing. The Orient is the origin, or vice versa, since in the desert, like the word—let the redundancy stand—are in the beginning and everywhere, although he dedicates several texts to this ubiquity:

> "The desert": Some three or four hundred meters away from the Pyramid I bent over, took up a handful of sand, let it fall silently a little further on, and said in a low voice: *I am modifying the Sahara.* The deed was minimal, but the not ingenious words were exact and I thought that I had needed my entire life to be able to say them.[23]

Borges's "Thirteen Coins"[24] o "Quince monedas,"[25] as it appears in another edition, comprise a series of very short poems included in a discontinuous way in his different editions. Among these coins of fluctuating number, "The Desert" is the place where time does not count; present, it remains suspended or does not remain, canceled and potential, expectant, it is time in which eternity and the instant coincide, where differences vanish, soil, sun or moon, a battle or two:

> Space without time.
> The moon is the color of sand.
> Now, precisely now,
> Are dying the men of Metauro and Trafalgar.[26]

In another "The Desert," this one a longer poem, I transcribe here only a few verses:

> Before entering the desert
> the soldiers drank long of the water form the cistern.
> Hierocles spilt on the earth
> the water from his canteen and said:
> *If we must enter in the desert,*
> *I am already in the desert.*
> *If thirst is going to scorch me,*
> *Let it scorch me!*
> This is a parable.[27]

"The Book of Sand" is not an "Arabic story," like the *Vathek* of William Beckford, nor does it take place in the desert, although the desert, secretive, is absent and present at the same time. Even if "The Book of Sand" is a relatively brief tale, it refers to an infinite book, like the sand of the desert, without limits, or with invisible edges that extend it beyond the horizon. To reduce the excesses of that extravagant extension, before the impossibility of defining or of giving a reference to the indefinition, the narrator begins *ad absurdum*, making use of, *more geometrico*, all the recourses of exactitude. Contradictorily, he defines line, plane, volumes as forms of the infinite that are not those of the book, or not even its opposites. Recognizing the convention of all fantastic tales, the narrator affirms, from the beginning, that it is a true book. Given the literary verisimilitude, of that partial truth of writing, he prefers to occult—truth, the book—behind another book that is a fiction of fictions: "He opts for hiding them behind some uncompleted (*descabalados*) volumes of the *Thousand and One Nights*,"[28] a volume that is missing some parts, apparently "incomplete." Nor is "cabala" foreign to that disorder that the adjective qualifies, nor do the traditions of reading contradict that disperse "reception": "The Arabs say that no one can/ Read to the end of the Book of the Nights."[29] In addition to occulting the uncertain truth of other books, *The Thousand and One Nights* is one of his archetypal narratives, the spiral matrix where are produced the mirages of his abyssal imagination, anterior and interior to other books, or to the same book, that take place in the desert. More than the parable of the desert it is the voice in the desert, the word is lost in the word, they are not differentiated, just as the word is not differentiated from the book:

In the book is the Book. Without knowing it
The queen tells the king the already forgotten
Story of them both. . . .[30]

From the two books or from them both, the king and the queen? Consisting of its vigils, *The Thousand and One Nights* not only constitutes a book but also a temporal and nocturnal pretext of innumerable stories that figure the literary imagination of its bibliothecological rhetoric: figures of a talisman that protects or dispenses the luck of its erudition prolonged in fictions or in interminable histories that wager against time. Borges disperses in parts (*descabala*) the book: "takes out precise parts in order to construct another [book] which does not claim to be entire (*cabal*) or complete either."[31] Like a magical inscription that *circulates* in his texts, in more or less transparent quotes or in even more secret *rendezvous* (*cita* in Spanish brings together the two passions in one and the same word: the citation and the sentimental meeting), the book comes and goes in Borges's oeuvre, a literal and figurative "transport" of his metaphors. In the same way that the genie enclosed in the vessel is not the same one who escapes from Aladdin's lamp, he only appears "by enchantment," according to the French translation of *The Thousand and One*

Nights. Both play within the pages of Borges, weaving the plot and filtering, in bibliographical references, the autobiographical accidents that fiction reveals.

In "The South,"[32] Juan Dahlmann "had attained, that afternoon, an uncompleted copy of the *Thousand and one Nights*." It is the book with which he travels toward his destiny: the south, his fatality, the displacement in procurement of a double death. In that story, the ciphered and habitual reading postpones the duel, it serves "as if to cover reality,"[33] believing in this way to avoid the challenge and the fight. Like *The Book of Sand*, between whose pages "none is the first; none, the last,"[34] *The Thousand and One Nights* holds mysteries that hold other mysteries: occults the character or occults (from him) reality, like it occulted the Book of Sand on a shelf of the library, insinuating the rigor of an inexorable law: one book occults another, or more.

The Thousand and One Nights is, moreover, title and subject of a talk published in *Seven Nights*. The periodical brevity, to which the tutelary title of the book that compiles several other talks refers, appears in counterpoint to the millenary nocturnal fabulation, with the verbality preceding an enumeration that mocks, because of its scarcity, the enumeration of a series that does not end. "The idea of infinite is co-substantial with *The Thousand and One Nights*,"[35] the narration enables a universe where time and space are confused, where numerical precision makes fun, contradictorily, no longer of the limitations of enumeration but rather of its impossibility. The end in suspense, like in the stories of Sheherezade that suspend the ending, postpone the *sentence*, which is as much the verbal one as the condemnation, death, the end, always interrupted:

> I want to pause over the title. It is one of the most beautiful in the world, so beautiful [. . .] I believe that for us the word "thousand" is synonymous with "infinite." To say a thousand nights is to say infinite nights, the many nights, the innumerable nights. To say "a thousand and one nights" is to add one to the infinite.[36]

For this reason Borges prefers that title of numerous narration to the one that it presents in English, "The Arabian Nights," an Oriental, ethnic mention, which, like "the Arabic numerals," do not number the pages of the Book of Sand, which pass from 400,514, even, to 999, odd. Borges's story *The Book of Sand*—two times eponymous—presents the same title for the book that appears in the story and for the book wherein appears the story. Thus the book exists outside of the story and inside of the story, vanishing the limits from both sides, providing entrance or exit to the dualities of its ambiguous diegetic statute. It belongs to "a world that is made of correspondences, that is made of magic mirrors,"[37] which, facing one another, confuse reality with words, forging images that shed blinding light and are erased in the sand. In others of Borges's stories, the regions, the countries owe their existence to the mentions that figure in an Encyclopedia. This statute would not be unusual in a universe where Sheherezade's life depended on her word, the continuity of the story as well, narrator and narration exist equally with the word. An encyclopedic, literary, or verbal survival dissimulates the differences that no longer oppose life to anything that is not written.

From the beginning, the word is the commencement:

> I think we ought not renounce the word Orient, such a beautiful word, since in it, by happy coincidence, there is gold (*oro*) to be found. [and he insists] In the word Orient we hear the word gold (*oro*) because at dawn the heavens look like gold.[38]

Borges discovers affinities between words that, beyond phonetic coincidences, reveal a universe articulated by a different poetic logic: *arena* (sand), *A*rab, *a*rid, *a*rdent, *a*rcane, or more distant, "in the confines of the sand (*arena*) of *A*rizona,"[39] incipient rhymes, at the beginning, textual bonds are laid out like traps in unforeseen situations.

Although "its semantics has been restricted to places,"[40] for Borges the desert is not only infinite extension but also the place from which "one leaves" and, for this reason, a goal: an origin and a departure, the beginning and the leaving. Its desolation is, moreover, of another nature:

> I see that this theme is fecund in Borges since the desert—in any case as it is lived by the Arabs—is the sheer place of loss, of a virtual loss; and frequently, it is there where one loses and refinds oneself; and it is that disposition that brings about the paradigm of the footprint, of its inscription, of its fragility, of its blurring; of its furtive slippage toward the sign, in order to reveal in it the latency of its meaning; that is to say, the testimony of a presence in absence.[41]

Beyond tracing the roots of loss, Borges consecrates the sand as the original substance of space, deserted dust that remains in movement, since sand is not only the infinite sediment of the desert but also the shifting material of fiction in a book of which the narrator, like the mythical narrator, is a prisoner. If "the first metaphor is water," water becomes sand like "those rivers of sand with fish of gold" that, in the first place make us think of Islam.[42] That becoming would propitiate another experiencing of time by writing: if "the course of time and time are only one mystery and not two,"[43] discourse duplicates it. Emblematic, remote, *clepsydra* names the water and its disappearance, the water stolen by the discourse that is prolonged but, above all, by the word that designates and, at the same time, suppresses what it designates. Through the crystal of the clepsydra the water makes transparent twice over the secret order that the passage of time administers but, like a shaker that tosses the die, "the allegorical instrument"[44] turns around and chance returns. "Shakespeare—according to his own metaphor—put in the turn of an hourglass the works of the years,"[45] said Borges more than a half century ago.

If all history, like all story, is uncertain, Borges pushes that uncertainty to its extreme, prolonging it into a *History of Eternity* that tries to recount the impossible history of an eternity that has no time, or sets out to enumerate the moments of the instant, that also does not have it. He recounts, nevertheless, the history of the sand, he tells it two times, the history of the desert and the number, interminably, which is another incessant form of (re)counting. The voice is doubled in the desert or, the other way around, the desert is doubled in the voice, in one same voice or at the same time. It is doubled and comes back to itself, *vox in deserto*, like in a mirror, almost a mirage. In the image of *clepsydra*, Borges exhausts water into sand, exhausts time as its slips toward the end in order to return to the beginning. Fall, that is a symbol of other falls, of equally symbolic fractures, sand decants, meticulous, without pausing, without swerving, like a verse that returns by inversion, turning around itself, in a fragile orb or two, where are passing by, because they wander and disappear, the voices that do not count.

CHAPTER ELEVEN

The Mystery of the Name

Perhaps there was an error in the writing
Or in the articulation of the Sacred Name;
Despite such high sorcery
The apprentice of man did not learn to speak.
— Borges, "El Golem"

In one of Borges's best known stories, the one that continues to be—with reason—his most quoted story, resigning himself to the uselessness of all intellectual exercise, or demanding it, the narrator affirms: "A philosophical doctrine is at first a verisimilar description of the universe; the years go by and it is a mere chapter—when not a paragraph and a name—of the history of philosophy. In literature, that final caducity is even more notorious."[1] Thus, in trying to apply this prediction to the oeuvre of Borges's himself, in foreseeing, hypothetically and not without a certain irony, the reductions of a decadent epistemology or of a poetics on the path to extinction, it would not be unusual if we were to record the permanence, barely, of only one poem. In such case, if it had been left to him to decide, it would have mattered to him—Borges *dixit*—that "The Golem" remain; but even the entire poem seemed to him an excessive pretension, and that one stanza would be enough; in that case, he preferred that it be the first:

If (as the Greek affirmed in the Cratylus)
The name is the archetype of the thing,
In the letters of *rose* is the rose
And all of the Nile in the word *Nile*.[2]

If it were a name, it was not pronounced. But I did not ask. One would have to assume, because of it, the responsibility of maintaining that

133

relic. If it were thus so, perhaps he would have conserved "the Name which is the Key,"[3] and in such case, *that name would be the name*. Or a word, at the end, of negative resonances, almost nihilistic, a voice in the desert.

The apparent circular tautology of this presumption would not be more than apparent. Without revelations or occultations, far from any apocalyptic intonations, Borges's oeuvre abounds in diverse figurations of a paradoxical aesthetic insofar as it would consolidate *an aesthetics of disappearance*. If it were thus, the strange productions of this contradictory aesthetic would have vanished, like poetry, knowledge, and the disciplines that limit it: "there are no sciences in Tlön."[4]

Silent, literature would have been diffused in quotes; history, in eternity. Omitted or reiterated, the suppression of its monuments which that counterproductive creation propitiates is not distinguished from the disappearance of empires, of their extensions, or of their borders in space or in other dimensions: "One of the schools of Tlön goes so far as to negate time."[5] In Borges's literary imagination, even negation illuminates; progressive disappearance provoked and confirmed the history of the century. There is no despair or lamenting before collapse and harassment. Woven among his vast and various texts, it is not unusual that the forms of disappearance have found the most diverse figures in a poetics of silence, of nothingness, of annihilation. Because of that secret capacity that distinguishes literature, another poet would have already announced that the fatal vocation of the world would make him disappear in a book, like a book, in the same way that the novel about nothing to which another author aspired would succumb to the same fate. Neither words nor things, articulated in one and the same *davar*, in Hebrew, word, action, thing, suppressed at the same time.

Among his first writings, Borges had recognized in literature the debatable privilege of announcing its end and celebrating it. To invoke and revoke at the same time would be the double and ambiguous property of the name. If the world was created by the word, it should not surprise us if it were destroyed via the same expression. The variants of literary, literal, or graphic obliteration is a constant referential figure: the empire threatened by the minuteness of cartographic description, the palace of the emperor threatened by the perfection of the poem, the poet by the emperor, the world degraded, obliterated, literally.

The allusions to that minimal nominality are numerous: "There are famous poems composed of one, sole, enormous word."[6] The certitude of such an assertion could be as excessive as the word itself; nevertheless, the disconcerting reduction that his fiction proposes has not sufficiently caught the attention of the specialists. That specialized unscrupulousness could be explained, possibly, by the fact that the assertion is recorded within a fiction. Or, more than by that ambivalent statute, legitimated in part by invention, it could be explained by the fact that in the fiction in which it appears, which is "Tlön, Uqbar, Orbis Tertius," almost everything is surprising. As surprising as Tlön, a planet where "The metaphysicians do not search for truth or even verisimilitude: they search for amazement."[7]

From the perspective of that spectral aesthetic and the minimalist gnosiology it implicates, it seems valid to advance the mystery of a story in which, in reality, or in the allegories —as Kafka understood them[8]—the narrator takes on the search for a word, like one who takes on the search for a lost clue, a sacred relic, or a hidden treasure. Included in *The Book of Sand,* the story appears under the title *"UNDR,"*[9] in uppercase, an acronym. Less mysterious than the mystical tetragrammaton, doubtless less venerable, it does not claim to be less prodigious. It is not difficult to recall different titles of various poems of Borges or of other authors, of stories or novels that consist of four numbers, ciphering a particular year posterior to a millenium that enables them. Nevertheless, it does not seem that there has been formulated a title so succinct, literal, and at the same time enigmatic for any other story. Although in *Other Inquisitions* it could have already called attention that the essay "New Refutation of Time"[10] would be articulated in two chapters, the first has the letter capital *A* as title; the second chapter is titled, according to the same alphabetic subject matter, *B.* Although circumspect, the series assures a pertinent ordering, which the rationality of the essay propitiates.

Nevertheless, there are several titles in which the nominal precariousness gives cause for thought. A poem, "I," in *The Profound Rose* (1975),[11] or another, "You," in *The Gold of the Tigers* (1972),[12] a poem, "He," in *The Other, the Same* (1964),[13] might have anticipated a scarcity that, personal, pronominal, anterior, or posterior to the name, would alert us as to the recourses with which language counts, dramatically or grammatically, in order not to signify, to dissimulate an identity in debate. A pronoun, a word as theatrical as a mask, occults, almost anonymous, the *person* from which *person*, in Greek "mask," takes its name: "No one" is not distinguished from "Someone,"[14] *personne*, in French, the archetypal subterfuge that saved Ulysses. A long time after, without distancing himself from the itinerary of his odysseys and from the territories that Ulysses or Olisipo had founded according to the legend, giving the name to Lisbon, is the same mask: "Pessoa," the proper name of the poet, he who multiplies the occulting in patronyms or heteronyms that reveal the plurality of a life, in as many lives as masks, or more. As Pessoa says ". . . the mental origin of my heteronyms resides in a tendency, in myself, organic and constant, to depersonalization and simulation. [. . .] in this way everything ends up in silence and poetry."[16] Glimpsed among the poetic cracks, the mystery of the name haunts us, at the turn of roads wherein cross mythic, epic, tragic, religious tales, like the enigma of a sphinx willing to sacrifice him who does not provide the solution that is definitively only another enigma, the greatest, which is the human condition. In *Other Inquisitions* (1952), on more than one occasion, Borges transcribes a passage from Léon Bloy, whose combative conviction, a most militant faith deposited in the premeditations of a God who impedes him from doubting determinism—minute, secret, the most symbolic, which becomes Truth in the Sacred Scriptures—never ceases to amaze him. The admiration for one whom Borges once qualified as prophet or visionary is such that, in the same volume, with a difference of a couple of pages, he insists on transcribing the same reference, the same quote, textually, from which he omits barely a few words.[16] Transformed by its new contexts, Bloy's fragment radiates throughout all of Borges's thought, associating it with the method that the Jewish Kabbalists applied to the Scriptures, "a secret brother of Swedenborg and of Blake: heresiarcs."[17] The prolonged extension, infrequent, that he reserves for him in two brief essays, the importance of these two essays in his oeuvre, justify the transcription:

> Then, Léon Bloy wrote: "There is on earth no human being capable of declaring who he is. No one knows what he has come to do in this world, to what correspond his acts, his sentiments, his ideas, nor what his true *name* is, his imperishable Name in the register of Light . . . History is an immense liturgical text in which the iotas and the points are worth no less than entire verses or chapters, but the importance of the one or the other is indeterminable and is profoundly hidden. [*L'âme de Napoléon*, 1912][18]

A little further on, in "The Mirror of the Enigmas,"[19] Borges again makes reference to the same book of Bloy, assigning to it as its sole purpose that of deciphering the symbol *Napoléon*, in which he would recognize the precursor of another hero who would come in the future since for "this journalist of combat," as Bloy tends to be defined, every man is on earth in order to symbolize something he does not know and to contribute, in different measures, to building the City of God.

I am interested in pointing out the "hieroglyphic character—that character of divine writing, of cryptography of angels—in all instances and all beings of the world,"[20] which Borges attributes to the ponderous reflections of Bloy. The incomprehension of the meaning is only due to the ignorance of one's own condition, which is the human condition, to which he returns toward the end of "The Mirror of the Engimas": "No man knows who he is," asserted Léon Bloy, and for Borges, more than pointing out lack of knowledge, the very same Bloy illustrated "that intimate ignorance" of one who, despite believing himself a rigorous Catholic, "was a continuer of the Kabbalists, a secret brother of Swedenborg and Blake: heresiarcs."

Dealing with the impossibility of deciphering the mysteries of man that are hardly dissimulated beneath the mask of the name, letters count as meaningful footprints of an occult language that, in fragments, multiplies meanings. Combining them, in infinite acrostics and anagrams, the letters become articulating symbols of a signification that linguistics denies them. Before the rigor of a scriptural, spiritual practice where nothing is contingent, the incidence of chance is discarded. Among so much determination, one should not pass over an erratum that responds to a mechanism less trivial than mere carelessness, approximating the symptomatic lapsus of *shibboleth*; a *mot-de-passe*, a pass word reveals by mispronunciation, by defect, identity. In the first edition of the *Complete Works* (Buenos Aires: Emecé Editores, 1974), as in the second volume of the edition of 1989, in the last paragraph of that renowned essay that is "The Mirror of the Enigmas," there appears highlighted in italics the asseveration about which we are redunding, but where the typographic expert confuses "hombre" (man), with "nombre" (name). "No name knows who he is," and the reader, without hesitation, consents.

The confusion of both terms, in addition to being theoretically fair and discursively coherent, might turn out to be statistically valid. Without giving way to the quantitative temptation of the register, passing rapidly through the poetry of Borges, one observes that the association of *man and name* is all too frequent, almost constant, for the confusion to have been only accidental or fortuitous. Nevertheless, the tight association, which the similarity of sounds tightens in Spanish, overflows the coincidences of a paronomasia that tends to be restricted, abusively, to mere plays on words. It is a fault to elude them when it is those plays that discover, poetically, the most profound affinities that the useless or forced will to not repeat tends to avoid or renounce, failing to see that those coincidences contribute to rescuing from forgetting a history that frequently legitimates them.

> Gentil or Hebrew or simply a man
> Whose face has been lost in time;
> No longer will we rescue from forgetting
> The silent letters of his name.[21]

The alliterations, the rhymes, bring together both—man and name—in a distinct similarity, mystical, echoes of a sort of universal resonance that carelessness and silence make more mysterious.

> I thought that the poet was that man
> Who, like red Adam of Paradise,
> Imposed on each thing its precise
> And true and unknown name.[22]

Highlighted by the end of the verse, the terms rhyme within a greater harmony that the stanza articulates. But the same ones appear again in another stanza, with which they rhyme once again, from a distance, beyond the limits of a composition or a page, in whatever passage of the book or other books. If in the *Divine Comedy* the faith of the poet discards the possibility that the name of *Christ* can rhyme with another word that is not *Christ* and, being without equal beyond doctrine, only rhymes with itself, man has in the name an inextricable partner with which he agrees and is confounded. This total rhyme inhabits his "Arte poética" in which each final word coincides, complete, with another, from the first to the last letter.

The name is one of the dearest masks of man, which occults him and reveals him at the same time. But this figure is not the only double, similar to the drama within the drama, or "the water in the water"—"Comme l'air dans le ciel et la mer dans la mer" (like the air in the sky and the sea in the sea), as Baudelaire had said.[23] Like the dream within the dream of Verlaine, duality does not end there, but rather, doubled in folds, it is the origin and reserve of successive revelations and occultations. A name can hide another name and that recondite and—like semiosis—unlimited denomination displaces its secret in a deeper secret, so much so that from name to name, the true one becomes unknown:

> The one in mourning was not Perón and the blonde doll was not
> the woman Eva Duarte, but neither was Perón Perón nor was
> Eva Eva but rather they were unknown or anonymous people
> (whose secret name and whose true face we do not know).[24]

Metaphor of displacement, a symbol is like another symbol; ignorance, like knowledge, is complex and systematic. In the same way, it refers as much to the cosmos as to discourse, recurrent, ciphered by writing, calling them by their name, things and words are not distinguished:

I know that the moon or the word *moon*
Is a letter that was created for
The complex writing of that rare
Thing that we are, numerous and one.[25]

Different from the knowledge that is formulated, from the methods and theories that designate it, ignorance can do without disciplinary limits; such that the necessity to define, to give an end, a term, a name, is natural:

I imposed on myself, like all others, the secret
Obligation to define the moon.[26]

More than man, to the poet, that obligation engages an adamic, edenic language that, secret, anterior to knowledge and to the dispersion of Babel, anticipates a negative epistemology that, because unknown, does not pass through the particular dominance of a language, does not pass through knowledge, does not pass (occur).

I thought that the poet was that man
Who, like red Adam of Paradise,
Imposed on each thing its precise
And true and unknown name[27]

Through the name, the poet recalls vaguely a knowledge anterior to knowledge and to punishment; blurry memories, dark, of another space, of another species, of other times beyond time, shades that man barely evokes, shades of shades, he names them, indissociable, ancient, and ubiquitous:

Of dreams, which could well be reflections
Trunks of the treasures of the shade,
Of an intemporal orb that is not named.[28]

There is no need to say that, in his texts, Borges puts words into question; in the word is the secret the poet interrogates, and the answer is there too. It is a dilemma, a question, a fatal quest in which the secret is lost or the poet is lost, or both. Like in "The Parable of the Palace,"[29] where the poet who finds the perfect word makes the palace disappear, in the same way as the emperor makes the poet and the word (or the parable) disappear at the same time. A plural and sudden disappearance precipitates, by the perfection of the form, an aesthetic of disappearance that goes beyond the word. The narrator of the parable alludes that his descendents search in vain for the word of the universe.[30]

Ungraspable, like the horizon, in flight, the poet procures that unique voice, interior or anterior to language, to articulation, to definitions, "the etymologies, the synonyms of the secret dictionary of God."[31]

Secret or secretion of the word, it hides and is hidden at the same time, like the shade, required by light but illuminated, vanishes. Like in the parable, also in "*UNDR*" the poet tells how he no longer defines each deed, "we cipher it in a word that is the Word."[32] The poet realizes a setting in silence of the sound in order to "keep [the] silence," which is to maintain it and hide it at the same time.

He said the word *undr*, which means wonder.[33] What word might there be under that word?

CHAPTER TWELVE

The Imagination of Knowledge

Along with the words I dictate, there will be, I believe, the image of a great mediterranean lake with long, slow mountains, and the inverted reflection of these mountains in the great lake. That, of course, is my memory of Lugano, but there are also others.

One, that of a November morning, not too cold, in 1918, when my father and I read, on a blackboard, in an almost empty plaza, the letters in chalk that announced the capitulation of the Central Empires, in other words, the hoped-for peace. The two of us returned to the hotel and announced the good news (there was no radiophone then), and we did not toast with champagne but with Italian red wine.

—Borges, "Lugano"

I also managed to read Meyrink's novel *Der Golem*.

—Borges, "Autobiographical Essay"

It does not seem unlikely to presume that it was here, in Switzerland, in Lugano, that Borges read *Der Golem*, the novel by Gustav Meyrink. Next to the lake that submerges these mountains, inverting them in the water in the same way, his late reflections, less symmetrical, similarly slow, return from time. As Rodríguez Monegal affirms in the monumental literary biography he dedicates to Borges, the novel attracted his interest from the beginning due, among other reasons, to the fact that "Meyrink proved that the legend was another version of the theme of the double."[1] In a synthetic review, several years later, Borges recognizes: "I do not know if *The Golem* is an important book; I know that it is a unique book."[2] The brief mention that is transcribed in the epigraph above is the only allusion he makes in his succinct "Autobiographical Essay." He was also the author of the prologue to the translation of that fantastic narrative work,[3] a novel he not only includes among the foundational works of his personal library, but to whose priority he tends to allude with significant frequency.

In order to confirm the presumption that the reading of *The Golem* occurred in Lugano, and calling on the luck with which the *genii loci* tend to favor those who call upon them it behoves us to relate the indispensable literary particulars that Rodriguez Monegal formulates with the certainty of the chronologies that innumerable scholars, essayists, journalists, friends have put into order. The recurrent preference for his prolonged stay in Switzerland during World War I, in his remembrances, his choice there to learn the German language first, and the decisive recourses of his literary imagination come across one another in the reading of that fiction: "The first novel in German he managed to read in its entirety was a novel by the Viennese writer Gustav Meyrink. *The Golem* (1915) is loosely based on a Kabbalistic legend about a Prague rabbi who creates a creature out of clay and makes him his servant."[4]

From one of the many chronologies that try to introduce a dated inventory in his life, I transcribe the following: "1918. The maternal grandmother dies. The family moves to Lugano. He learns German with a volume by Heine and reads Schopenhauer, Meyrink, and the German expressionist poets. He earns his bachelors."[5] In one of his biographies, the same facts are confirmed: "The family remained in Switzerland until 1919; the last year was spent in Lugano, where Borges obtained his bachelor's degree."[6]

Beyond "fantastic causality,"[7] a notion Borges formulates to refer to a causality that, apparently, cannot be attributed to any situation or event, here there can not even be a suspicion of a relation between cause and effect. In order to illustrate the universality of this curious magic etiology, Borges alludes to examples from various cultures: the omnipotent genies of the *Thousand and One Arabian Nights*, the legends of hassidim,[8] as well as Chinese traditions. If on more than one occasion we have recurred to the protection of the *genii loci* and done so without attenuating their omnipotence, it would seem impossible in these circumstances not to call on their providential tutelage to attend to a theme that, in light of the precedent observations, acquires a further relevance.

❧

From the most ancient of myths to the reflections advanced in recent years, concerns about the nature of knowledge have adopted different forms that tend to oppose the recourses of reason to the revelations of the imagination, the rigor of disciplinary procedures, with their theories and methods, to the openness of aesthetic vision, its dreams and realizations. Semiotic plurality—and the variety of perspectives it tends to enable, as well as its incidence over related disciplines—continues to attend to the contemporary alternatives of this ancestral reflection on truth, observing the different arguments of a discussion that has been repeated throughout history. Still in force, its philosophical and religious, scientific and poetic theses constitute an inchoate subject that could be designated as an "epistemological matter"—in the same way one still speaks about the legends of a "Celtic matter" or *matière celtique* narrating the deeds associated with a hero and his mystic search for truth—in that it deals with a matter both substantial and elusive, a recurrent theme that procures the legitimization of a knowledge in which the inventions of the imagination do not discard the orderings of rational models.

At the end of the twentieth century, a century that proclaimed so many ends, and at the beginning of the twenty first, it is of interest to revise a poetic end, comprising, once again, the possible convergences between knowledges that, proceeding from truth or beauty, tend toward specific fields, searching, more than for a counter position or a complementarity, for a profound vision capable of attaining forms of universality ever more necessary.

Starting from the poetic imagination, I propose that we initiate, more than the mere revision of a lucid end, the instances of a *discourse of preterition*, that verbal aptitude, at once strange and specific, of a word that says and at the same time negates what it says. It is of interest to observe the transactions that precede a *poetics of disappearance*, as if the possibility of a performative action as well as abolition by the word, a faculty that also abolishes itself, were inherent to language. Surpassing the limits of conceptual segmentation, we would be reminded of the inclination of thought to recuperate aspects of a primordial unity, a set of learning that—without annulling its specificity—attempts to integrate the learning of different fields of knowledge, by way of a discourse that makes reference while at the same time suspending it.

It would not seem inopportune to consider, apropos of the "Golem effect"—to which the semiotic treatises tend to allude, especially in opposition to the "Pygmalion effect"[9]—some of the resonances in contemporary thought of this first myth, but from the perspective of poetry. Consequently, we would not attend, at this opportunity, to the associations that technology has multiplied around this notion, not to the meaning "embryo" that *golem* denotes in scientific, modern Hebrew, proper to the field of biology, nor to the doctrinal ambiguities that the term suggests in *Genesis*,[10] but rather to the myths that, between creation and disappearance, beginning and end, transmit the verbal condition of *truth* implied by the imagination as well as by knowledge.

Just as the word the rabbi inscribes in the forehead of the golem to give it life is "true," so is "truth" that which is at stake and at risk, like art, poetry, theory, ideology, the humanities, history, reality: culture devoted to progress and to technology is doomed, it will disappear one day and, perhaps, humanity will disappear with it. A theory of knowledge that does not discard imagination can also not ignore a theory of truth that analyzes the relation of coherence (representation) or of language games, social practices, the rules of language learning, which are involved in the discussions related to truth.

The "literal" destruction of the golem—its obliteration or disappearance consecutive to the elision of a letter—emblematizes a semiotic quarrel in which the tensions between epistemological scepticism, on the one hand, and metaphor as an instrument necessary for cognition, on the other, bring up a question that is closer to aporia than to the recourses of method. Wittgenstein claimed to find more philosophy in crime novels and in westerns than in the minds of his eminent colleagues, even more, "For the good of philosophy it should be written in the form of poetry."[11]

Like the sciences, or philosophy, or poetry, fiction tends to be concerned with the truth. Miguel de Cervantes in his *Don Quixote* (1605–1615)[12] and, after him "Pierre Menard, author of Don Quixote" (1941) in his, both affirm, word for word, "truth, whose mother is history, rival of time, deposit of actions, witness to the past, example and advice to the present, warning to the future."[13] In the parodic register of Cervantes, the quotation of the sentence of Cicero, altered, makes fun of the elegy of historical truth; in the literal repetition of Borges's story, "barefacedly pragmatic," the parody is more severe. Faced with a similar trick, Sherlock Holmes, for his part, is amazed and wonders—a semantic miracle that English does not usually distinguish: "It is, I admit, mere imagination; but how often is imagination the mother of truth?"[14] Such literary frequency makes us suspect that, from the ironies of narrative perspective, that truth affiliated with two mothers would be as disputable and probable as any paternity.

If it is the case that homonyms continue to tempt contemporary speculations, it is nevertheless not a question of becoming a "chasseur de homonymes,"[15] nor of failing to recognize that "*locus classicus* of signs in action, paronomasia,"[16] nor of attributing to pure coincidence—in order to avoid the luxuriant expedient of "coincidences"—the diversity of meanings united by one and the same word. It is of greater interest to observe how the words *reveal*, in their semasiological similarities, that ancestral disposition not to differentiate forms of knowledge that the traditional disciplines tended to oppose by way of the demarcation of limits. The transdisciplinary vocation demanded by semiotics, on the contrary, has contributed to making more flexible or even suspending disciplinary boundaries. Today's epistemological situation and the concomitant inadvertence of limits in different fields favors this suspension, as if there were a common cause that would force us to e-liminate them, or as if all *elimination* were "a question of limits," such as to suppress all unknowns in an equation in order to leave only one.[17] Almost annoyed by the insistence, Sherlock Holmes says: "How often have I said to you that when you have eliminated the impossible, whatever remains, *however improbable*, must be the truth?"[18] More than "revelation," since the term can perturb a tradition that still finds itself determined by the form of thinking of the "Lumières," it would be necessary to reason philologically, remembering that "the age of science is also the age of litterature."[19] In this case, perhaps one of the most significant examples of those homonymic coincidences would be that of the semantic alternatives of "theory." The history of the word itself constitutes an epistemological archive, the key to solving this question, since it partakes from its origins of the two poles that we are trying to superimpose. An entire shared semantic field implies the affinity in Spanish between unexpected pairs; *reflexión* and *reflejo* (mental reflection and reflection in a mirror), *especulación* and *espejo* (speculation and mirror), *teatro* and *teoría* (theater and theory), appealing to the same convergence from a sensorial function—that is confounded with an intellectual function[20]—to a conceptual knowledge that passes through imagination. John Ruskin pondered the appreciation of beauty by the "theoretic faculty,"[21] making the exultation of contemplation predominant in *theory*.

It catches our attention that the relation between zones common to the same knowledge are distinguished as distant or opposite. Some figures that are opposed on account of their meaning are shared paronomastically by geometry and rhetoric: ellipsis (an omission), hyperbole (an exaggeration) and between both, or comprising them, at two ends, the parabola. We must conclude that, either the denominative repertoire is limited—which would seem not to be the case—or rather that the homonym discovers profound affinities where persuasion (seduction) and abstract discernment are not opposed, as if this in indissociable duality were a deep foundation of the word, the fable, of something that is "another thing" (allegory) but at the same time negates that difference. That abstraction, nevertheless, requires rhetorical restitution, as if passing through language it were impossible to avoid figuration. In the same way that in speaking of the "truth" it would be impossible to avoid the *etumon* (Greek for "true") and discuss, as in Cratylus "truth as the exactitude of names."[22] Nevertheless, to return to Greek philosophy I would not leave aside the Jewish myth, thanks to an unexpected connection that unites two different and distant "characters" (Golem and Cratylus), associated in one poetic fusion.

In one of our last conversations,[23] Borges did not lament in the face of the forgetting into which, as he foresaw, his work would disappear. Although this certainty did not weigh on him, he wished that, among the thousands of pages, one poem could be conserved: "The Golem."[24] But then, repentant at having staked too excessive a claim, he reduced his wish to one stanza, the first:

> If (as the Greek affirmed in the Cratylus)
> The name is the archetype of the thing,
> In the letters of *rose* is the rose
> And all of the Nile in the word *Nile*.

Why preserve only "The Golem"? Why only one part? Why the first stanza? Why not all of it? Why not only a name? Many years earlier, in the famous "Pierre Menard, Author of the Quijote," already cited, the narrator, agreeing with the author, affirmed:

> There is no intellectual exercise that is not infinitely futile. A philosophical doctrine is at first a verisimilar description of the universe; the years turn and it is a mere chapter—if not a paragraph or a name—of the history of philosophy. In literature this caducity is even more notorious.[25]

If we were to recognize a predominant theme in Borges' story, that predominance would be the relation between *the truth and history* or *the truth and fiction*, but, above all, between *the truth and its versions*. For some time now, bibliometric techniques have quantified titles, themes, and authors cited. Without recurring to the techniques of that quantification, it would not be outrageous to affirm that Pierre Menard, an author who does not exist or, an author of a work that does not exist or, what is worse, that already existed under a different but proper name, is still, if not the most quoted author, the one who is most overquoted: "Unlikely, but true," exclaimed a character of that same story, putting himself more on the side of history than of fiction or poetry—according to Aristotle's opposition—stretching, once again, the tensions between the statute of truth and the forms of invention that reveal it.

It is not the first time that, anticipating by many years the alarming forecasts of a century split down the middle, Borges foretold the disappearance of literature, of poetry, of the word.[26] Given this *poetics of disappearance* from which he tends to rescue one word, what word would survive the first stanza? What would be the last word? *Nile*?

Nevertheless, in light of the biblical or Kabbalistic theme of the poetry and the Judaic context that nourished that aspiration, that Egyptian "survival" would be surprising.

There is no lack of surprises in that stanza: knowing the remote polarization of both cultures, to begin the Golem with the affirmation of the *Greek* would be the first. Nor is the vocative use of a philosophical reference so predictable in poetry. Nor does it fit the poetic tradition to begin by opening a parenthesis: if it begins by interrupting or suspending, what remains for the finale? The poet uses terms in italics, another unusual practice for poetic typography. That "In the letters of *rose* is the rose," is certainly the conviction of Plato's eponymous character. "All the Nile in the word *Nile*," said Borges, and in these italics he finishes. But if the conjectures are resplendent, the final word *Nile*, the last or only that remains after the elimination that the poet prophesied with less resignation than joy, would be the only relic. *Vernichtung*, in German: a destruction that erases even the traces of that annihilation, in English, *nil*. Its French homonym, *Nil*, returns to the name of the river.

In "*Le démon de l'analogie*," Mallarmé speculates about the painful enjoyment (*pénible jouissance*) that the words of sad nature produced in his mouth.[27] He did not avoid that same analogical perversity taking over his words in order to suppress the reference at the same time that he invoked it. "*The Penultimate is dead*," said Mallarmé, stressing the strange magic that torments the syllable *nul*, pen*ul*timate and *nul*, on the verge of disappearing in "that absurd sentence." He attributes that disquiet to a labor of linguistics that interrupts daily, as he says, his noble poetic faculty. If indeed it is not a question of a confirmation, it does not cease to be an interesting coincidence.

It is not strange that an aesthetics of annihilation swaddles a century that has made of sheer annihilation its shadow, of silence and sounds, its *danse macabre*. In the first letter to the Corinthians, Paul said: "Love never fails. But where there are prophecies, they will cease; where there are tongues, they will be stilled; where there is knowledge, it will pass away."[28] According to certain contemporary academic radicalisms, the prophecy has already been verified: if history disappeared again, if poetry was condemned and hermeneutics grew through the decline of theories— or the inverse, if the death of the author was announced more than once, confirming greater deaths that preceded it and those of them who announced it, if in this disappearance en masse, reality also fell, whom could it surprise that the work disappears and there only remains a word? *Nobody*, the negation gives name to a character, or is the name of a poet. Pessoa, Fernando Pessoa, who recalls in Lisbon the voyage of Odysseus, the name of a person, of a mask, which is its meaning in Greek. *Personne*, or *pessoa*, designates a person and nobody at the same time, semantic extremes between which the imagination swoons; nothing, one word, *in-none-dated*, covered by the waters, annihilated.

Like Cratylus, Borges believes in the truth of words, in the similarity they guard between themselves and with things, and this is why he would preserve a stanza, the first, and the final word, several times final: *Nile*, a variation of *nil* or of *nihil*, *res nata*, "nothing" is the contradictory redemption. In Genesis, *golem* designates the *man* created in the image and likeness, an embryo, a "larva," mask and specter, a being who still is not or is no longer. Similar is strange. He who prohibits imitation, does he imitate himself? That is why, observing the contradiction more than the interdiction, the rabbi of Prague does something further: he gives life to his semblant by way of the word, inscribing *emet*, Hebrew for "truth," in the same way as, in order to destroy it, he obliterates *aleph*, the first letter, leaving *met*, in Hebrew, and it remains transformed into a cadaver, or it does not remain at all.

Despite the aforesaid oppositions, one and the same cognitive passion associates the Jews with the Greeks. From the beginning, in Genesis, the Jews unite *knowledge* and *love* into the same term, and this ambivalent union precipitates the Fall. For its part, in *philosophy*, in one and the same term, the Greeks unite *knowledge* and *love*, in order to accede once again to the archetypes. As the poet has said: "Man kann auch in die Höhe fallen, so wie in die Tiefe" [One can fall into the heights, just as into the depths].[29]

CHAPTER THIRTEEN

The Place of the Library

To my mother

It is rather curious that "The Library of Babel"[1] is one of Borges's stories in which, if indeed literature is referred to, as in so many other of his writings, those references to books, stories, quotes, are less numerous and more trivial than one might have predicted. The library of a narration that lacks literary references continues to be a library? The narrator describes the place, the administration of space, aspects and details of the building's construction, the number of books, of pages, of lines, of letters. Those materials Borges's narrator proportions count more than the books it contains, than the stories told by the books, than the quotes, which count so much. However, when dealing with a library in an enigmatic story, contaminated by unreality, to reason according to a realist logic would be neither logical nor realist. Nor is the procedure unusual in a writing that, like Borges's, invents its own system. For example, one of his most recurrent, and most recognized, provocations consists of confirming the authenticity of the Koran by pointing out that in the Koran there are no camels. He understands that an imposter would abound in camels, caravans of camels on each page.[2] Coherent with this vision, he argues that if, in the story "The Garden of Forking Paths," the problem is time, the author "does not once use the word *time*."[3] Perhaps this significant literary lack in the library can be justified in a similar way.

For this reason, here, in the National Library of France and at the celebration of the centenary of the birth of Borges,[4] I am not interested in delving into the library, or the authors, or their books, or their readers, but rather into the tensions that are produced between a place and letters, a back and forth that makes of the library the common place par excellence, toward which all letters converge. I would run through the itinerary of an imagination that parts from a place, a sacred place, until arriving at a letter, a sacred letter, that displaces it. But, as all places and all letters exist in writing, I would like to legitimate, by way of the name, by way of the letter, a place.

∂

"Borges and the library": the theme seems excessive. By proposing it in these circumstances, the formulation implies something more and something less, since I could not well keep from referring to "Borges in the Library." Despite the monumental dimension, this location, in a determined space, is also a reduction. Be it *of* or *in* the library, it is a question of "Borges's universe," but this formula already exists as the title to a book that was dedicated to him here, in France, some years ago.[5] I presume that title alluded to the first words of one of Borges's stories that configures a "passage"[6] (*pasaje*) of today's literary landscape (*paisaje*).

"The universe (which others call the Library)," as is well known, are the first words of "The Library of Babel."[7] This story insinuates in turn "The caprice or imagination or utopia of the Total Library," the first words and the brief essay that Borges published years earlier in the journal *SUR*.[8] In dealing with Borges it would seem impossible, from the beginning, to elude the vinculum of the quotation, that is to say, to begin by evoking another book or one of his literary texts in order to protect, through the auspices of previous publications, the initiation of one's own discourse.

In recent decades, much has been said of quotations and ciphers, but even so, there has been perhaps insufficient emphasis placed on that anaphoric necessity of discourse that makes use of a quotation as a key and as an initiation. As if it were possible to make use of the word without realizing that the word had already been used before, as if the *B* that the commencement of the Bible introduces had been the model for all commencements to come; since even that first initiation, Genesis for some, "Heading" for others, which begins by describing the origins of the universe, does not begin with the first letter (*aleph*) but with the second letter (*beth*), whose traces are mimetically, mystically associated with a house, the universal dwelling, the universe.

On this occasion, despite my having tried to avoid them, it was not possible for me to dispense with the quotations that constitute a theme that, because it is too well-trodden, becomes more and more difficult to broach. It has attained a greater resonance above all on the basis of Borges as well as on the basis of Walter Benjamin, another bibliomaniac, impassioned by a "collection" that was of books first, of quotations later.[9] Nevertheless, and with the intention of attenuating that predominant meaning but without suspending it, I would not fail to recall the other meaning, stronger, more fortunate, in my view, which the word *quotation* has in Spanish (*cita*), a language in which it means "meeting," a sentimental "rendezvous" where amity and amorousness are confounded again in one and the same literary passion. It is both the idiomatic and foreign meanings that I would now try to keep in play.

It cannot be surprising that the meaning of *cita*, of a meeting of passions, is verified in a library. In this place privileged by the riches of the heritage and the archive, where the recording and conservation of knowledge enable the search (of what existed) or research (of what will exist), it is where, more than in any other place, Borges's *cita*, with Borges or with his readers, is imposed. It is the *differend* of this verbal, semantic disjunctive with which today's speaker is confronted almost despite herself: on the one hand she procures with anxiety a new meeting, a new conversation with Borges; she recalls Buenos Aires, Maipú Street, simulating, by way of the same words, a return to the first years of the decade of the eighties; and on the other, because they are excessive, she tries to abolish the *quotes*, to deny herself the discursive strategy of supporting herself abusively on the same strategies that Borges incomparably consecrated.

Although the futility of the effort would justify not making it, it would be difficult to adopt, without incurring parody, the literary recourse to which Borges gave a different scale, various scales, almost all of them. For that reason, it is impossible not to stay, in some way, on the margin of Borges: everything that is said, be it a commentary of his work or not, is inscribed on the margin of Borges. More difficult still would be not to recur to repetition. As in the troubles his imagination devised, like the sacred or more or less profane books that had already considered the problem: from *Ecclesiastics* to the theory of reading, their histories, their rhetorics, insist on the fact that it is impossible not to quote; moreover, if I say, "Nothing is left for us but quotations,"[10] I would be demonstrating that impossibility.

All of which goes to say that to negate the quotation—or one of its meanings—would only be another example of *preterition*, an "omission," which is what the word means in Latin, a confession that by being pronounced is thus repealed. Despite the fact that it would be risky to affirm, on the one hand, that Borges had never named this figure, since there can be no witness to all pronouncements, on the other hand, if fiction could guarantee convictions, we could recall one of his most explicit texts: "To *always* omit a word, to recur to inept metaphors and obvious paraphrases, is perhaps the most emphatic way of indicating it."[11] Although the metaphor was the recurrent figure, invoked, inventoried, theorized by Borges, poeticized in writings and conferences, he was, without a doubt, the greatest craftsman of preterition, who unfolded, on the basis of this figure of negation, his aesthetic. From irony to paradox, passing through the different forms of contradiction, more than to persuade as to his reasons, preterition serves him to think his fiction, or to imagine his hypotheses, in the conjectural and brilliant sense of abduction.

Just as there exists a negative theology, or a negative dialectics,[12] one could conjecture, as well, that this figure constitutes the rhetorical archetype of his "negative poetics": a figure that is permitted to negate itself and, by way of this very negation, instead of making the negated expression disappear, is brought unexpectedly into relief. It would even be the specific figure, inherent to language, which for Borges—close to mention, to the mendacious—tends to be synonymous with fraud. Obliteration, that is to say, the literal negation of an entity by writing, does not exclude another obliteration at a second level: a negation of a negation, that becomes a superlative negation, an epic of writing itself, if not a representation of its tragedy.

The elaborations of his negative poetics in which preterition is a rhetorical display are numerous. The literary variations of the Yellow Emperor, for example—one of his mythical, infamous characters—who, in order to assure his presence beyond the accidents of geography or history, either commands walls to be built and books to be burnt, or commands a proud palace to be built for the greater praise of the poet. The ode being perfect, its exactitude rivals the palace, which disappears, provoking the annihilation of the poet and the poem at the same time. In "The Parable of the Palace,"[13] the epic of disappearance is poetic and geometric at the same time, like word (*palabra*) and palace (*palacio*) in Spanish, both figures begin by coinciding, and by way of that coincidence come to disappear into one another, equally.

The genius of the poem and of the poet bring the palace into *relief* (in the sense of the German *aufheben* [normally translated in English as *sublate*, in Spanish, *relevar*. W.E.]). In the same way that in "Of Rigor in Science"[14] the description of the empire is not distinguished from the diagrammatic tracing or from the prestidigitations of a cartography that suppresses, because it is analogous, meticulous, perfect, the territories that it represents as well as the representation of those territories. Perhaps his text is more concise; in a few lines he proposes the thesis that consolidates—contradictorily—his fiction: the more rigorous the knowledge, as is said of the climate, the intemperances of weather, the more scientific the descriptions that formulate it, the more devastating, at least within literary limits.

Fulminating, the poetic brevity of the parable precipitates a series of disappearances: of the palace, of the poet, of the poem, that "afforded him immortality and death."[15] "The Maker,"[16] which is Borges, questions as much the creation by the word as the fact that disappearance occurs along the same path. The authority of the author like the authority of the emperor are confounded in the same command, as if, having sentenced poetry, in those same years of the twentieth century, theory, history, geography, ideology, words, and things had all been sentenced at the same time. The bit of reality that remains perishes among the exacting precisions of the sciences and technologies, among the words that discuss it, and there is no leftover, because it has already been said . . . it is silence or it is literature.

The evidence of annihilation should not surprise us too much, neither the usurpation of the landscape by the word, nor the desolation it affords. In the beginning, the word designates the *desert, desertion*, it is the same, in its origin, as the one that designates *discourse*, or *sermon*. Things disappear, like in the desert, when faced with discourse. As it is said: "It's in the Bible," but it is there that the word in the desert is the double of the desert. More than etymological, more than idiomatic, the profundity of the relation between "word" (*palabra*) and "desert" (*desierto*) sinks its roots into a mythology of nothingness, in a letristic, consonantic, minimalist coincidence: *dbr*. The mystery of affinity originates, like in a previous, anterior language, in an aesthetics of the void that is a vision of the beginning and the end. A similar semantic relation, but contrary, is verified in Latin: *desertus*, adjectival past participle of *deserere*, "to separate," "to abandon," derives, like *sermo*, "tongue, language," from the Latin, *serere*: the desert, privative or deprived of the word, as was said before.

But let us return to the library that is the theme of this talk and, above all, the place of this meeting, where the library is put into question, or where we pose the question of the library. In whichever of the two cases, the question does not cease to be a quest, a "question" and, according to Borges, the greatest, so much so that the objective is assimilated to the question of the Universe. As has been said of other questions, it supposes a problem. But, above all, it supposes the incursion of various redundancies that do not seem deplorable, hardly avoidable, necessary, even desirable.

To speak of a library in a library would be one of the first redundancies. Given the previous considerations, to what extent is it prudent to represent what is present? The prefix *re-* is an ambiguous prefix, it duplicates the reference that it precedes at the same time that it rescinds it. To represent, it seems like a dream; confusing or vanishing: it *revokes*, which is to say, it names two voices, two times. It would not be the first time that duplication rescinds. And if the risk of the Yellow Emperor is to see his magnificent lodgings, patios, libraries, the hexagonal room, the paradise or garden disappear, would it not only be an artifice of paronomasias, but also one of the contradictory fatalities that posterity dangles over the palace exposed to poetry and to history? Why, according to "The Garden of Forking Paths,"[17] is the problem of time, which is the greatest problem, the only one that does not figure in the pages of the book that has the same name as the story: *The Garden of Forking Paths*? It is the title of the chaotic novel by Ts'ui Pên—that monk who is the author of the eponymous book in which "he does not even use the word that means time."[18] The story deals with a garden, and there—as in another Garden that is longed for—time disappears in "that lost labyrinth" that the narrator imagines under the species of paradise: "I thought in a labyrinth of labyrinths, in a sinuous growing labyrinth that would embrace the past and the future and that would in some way implicate the stars. Absorbed in those illusory images, I forgot my persecuted destiny."[19]

Since reason is only part, one sole reason is never enough. Nor is speaking of the library in a library the only redundancy. In relation with Borges, the library is an allegory, emblem, and synonym of his literature, of his *persona*, which confounds mask and identity in the same word. In "The *Garden* of Forking Paths" is confounded the title of a story with the title of a book, between both of which a parabola could be formed, because of its allusion to Paradise, to a space without time or to the time of all times, that totality which fulfills and annuls it. Proximate or similar to eternity, the foresight of Borges, which figured Paradise under the species of library,[20] alludes to the felicity of comprehending, to the happiness afforded by talmudic or theological readings that cipher the *pardes*, a garden, an orangery in modern Hebrew but, before anything else an acronym that doctrinally, etymologically, is formed by the initials, in Hebrew, of those four readings propitiated by orthodoxy: *pshat* (simple meaning), *remez* (the complete allusion to the void formed on the basis of something expressed in the text), *drash* (a second-grade void, concerning not the text but the unsaid context), and *sod* (the hidden meaning, totally absent from the text).[21]

The futures are various, the times numerous, all options possible. Different from the story that speak of the forking paths—"it is an incomplete, but not false image"[22]—in which a possibility is opted for that excludes the others, in that other dimension *all* possibilities are encompassed. A *réponse normande*?[23] "I chose all"? Absurd or a joke, to conceive of the total choice is semantically impossible, is an aspiration that logic rejects. To choose within the totality of the library, within that collection, is the function of *homo legens*—lector, elector, who cannot read without e-lecting. The plurality of times that brings with it a plurality of worlds, serves to console the persecuted, condemned character, it is a cosmic variation that proceeds from France, a "hypothesis" of the story's character that remits us to Louis-Auguste Blanqui.

Although the controversial "Communard," "the bronze voice that shook the previous century"[24] may be no expert in astronomy, or in astrology—as indeed the author of *The Garden* was not either—his book, *Eternity Through the Stars: An Astronomical Hypothesis*,[25] constitutes an obligatory starting point for understanding one of the most traveled itineraries of Borges's imagination. It determines and configures his will to fiction, as a philosopher could have proposed the will to truth.

Given the differences between them, given the apparently contrary political, historical, and biographical coordinates that oppose them, although it seems unlikely, the cosmogonic vision of Blanqui; the hope for a revolution that, more than political, is literally astral in virtue of the repeated and different worlds that he imagines, the events that are repeated until infinity in the spaces that are multiplied like copies, like exemplars of the same books; the multitudinous lookalikes that people Blanqui's fiction; justify the surprising alternatives of the greater part of Borges's texts. Speaking of facsimilar worlds and dissimilar words, and also of interminable space, Borges reveres him: "His book is beautifully titled *L'éternité par les astres*; it is from 1872."[26]

In the story, "The Total Library"—it is one of the anticipations of the better known "The Library of Babel"—the narrator affirms: "I would add that it is a typographical avatar of that doctrine of the Eternal Return that, adopted by the stoics or by Blanqui, by the Pythagoreans or by Nietzsche, eternally returns."[27] These are not the only times he cites Blanqui. Nor is it necessary that he do so. Both hold that each individual exists equally in an infinite number of exemplars, with and without variations. In "The Garden of Forking Paths":

> I felt again that pullulation of which I spoke. It seemed as if the humid garden that surrounded the garden was saturated to infinity with invisible persons. Those persons were Albert and I, secret, kept busy and multiform in the other dimensions of time.[28]

If, for the writer as for the poet, the world does not exist except in order to end in a book, this belief is symmetrical with that of the legions of believers who do not doubt that it began there. The thousands of exemplars of that total book assure a vastness and variety of possible words, of times and spaces in which the eventuality of events is always repeated, although in different forms. Like Blanqui, like Bioy Casares—but that is another story—the reader finds in the French terrorist's astronomical hypothesis an escape from the cloister of the numerous prisons in which Blanqui suffered, an exit from the cloister of the libraries in which Borges lived, from the felicity of the paternal library from which he never wanted to part to the vicissitudes he suffered in the Miguel Cané branch of the Municipal Library, where he resisted nine years of sadness, monotony, ignorance, of which he only recalls numerous heartaches in his "Autobiographical Essay"[29] and in some interviews.

No less than the world, the library is that "prisonhouse of language" from which every poet suffers and which Nietzsche pointed out, an author who appears cited several times along with Blanqui, although Borges considers the German philosopher's theories on the eternal return to be less interesting than those of "that phantasm of the bourgeoisie"— as Marx calls him—who consoles himself in astronomical fiction.

The narrator of "The Garden of Forking Paths" refers to the Chinese writer, but the interpellation to the addressee could be applied in these circumstances:

> Different from Newton and Schopenhauer, his ancestor did not believe in uniform, absolute time. He believed in infinite series of times, in a growing and vertiginous network of divergent, convergent, and parallel times. This weave of times that bifurcate, split, or are secularly ignored, comprise *all* possibilities. We do not exist in the majority of those times; in some you exist but I do not; in others, I and not you; in others, both of us. In this one, to which a favorable chance brings me, you have arrived at my house; in another, when crossing the garden you found me dead; in another, I say these same words, but I am an error, a phantasm.[30]

Although the narrative intrigue may restrict laying out the articulation of the thematic incidents, the voice, its tone, the ironic insinuation, the register between philosophical and essayistic specific to his fiction, the mystical emphasis of a certain epistolary style in "The Library of Babel," its conceptual foundations do not differ too much from the lines of Blanqui quoted by Borges, by Bioy Casares, on more than one occasion. The three are obsessed with the "bifurcations" of this "eternalized present" of which Blanqui speaks, completed by infinite worlds, identical.[31]

> What I am writing at this moment in a dungeon of the fort of Taureau, I wrote and will write throughout eternity, at a table, with a pen, beneath these garments, in similar circumstances. Just so, all of them. (. . .) The number of our lookalikes is infi-

nite in time and in space. (. . .) there is not here either revelation or prophet, but a simple deduction of spectral analysis and of the cosmogony of Laplace. These two discoveries make us eternal. Is it a godsend? Let's take advantage of it. Is it a mystification? Let us resign ourselves.[32]

And so Blanqui continues with his cloistered and methodical quests, bumping into, among books and stars, the pullulating multitude of his lookalikes. All those individuals who, similar to him, exist in infinite numbers of exemplars, with and without variations, with his melancholy optimism, with his stars that multiply, bifurcate, perpetually, because "The universe repeats without end and marches in place. Eternity interprets, imperturbably, in the infinite, the same representations."[33]

Bioy, Blanqui, Walter Benjamin, Borges or his characters, are seduced by the hypothesis of plural exit through the multiplication of times. Their hope is rooted in that plurality. I cite a few lines from an article he dedicates to Blanqui in the magazine *SUR*: "Blanqui crams, with infinite repetitions, not only time, but also infinite space. Imagine that there is in the universe an infinite number of facsimiles of the planet and of all its possible variants. Each individual exists equally in an infinite number of exemplars, with and without variations."[34]

We would have to recall one of Borges's first books—which he himself submitted to the most severe censorship to the end of his days—but posthumously reedited, *The Size of My Hope*,[35] which replicates the title *The Size of Space*, the small volume that Leopoldo Lugones (1921) had written a few years earlier on mathematical questions, but which is not often remembered.[36] The author discovers in the writings of Blanqui a buttress for an aesthetic vision that goes beyond mathematical disquisitions or political or police injustices, engaging, in a literary way, a species of eternity *sub specie* of the library: "the universe brusquely usurped the unlimited dimensions of hope," he said in "The Library of Babel."[37]

"To speak is to incur tautologies,"[38] says the narrator, who confesses to be the author of "This useless and wordy epistle [that] already exists in one of the thirty volumes of the five shelves of one of the uncountable hexagons—and also its refutation."[39] It would not be unusual, then, for one of Borges's poems to speak of a poem or of poetry, its own or another's, just as if in a book one spoke of a book or of literature. They are foreseeable redundancies, in the same way that it is also foreseeable that in a library one would speak of libraries, or of Borges, as the *Quijote* is already in the *Quijote*, and the Koran in the Koran.

More than any other author, Borges appears as a prosopopoeia that personifies the library, not only because he makes of the library his narrative, poetic, autobiographical *topos* par excellence, but equally because, if there exists an emblematic image of Borges's thought—more than the well-trodden labyrinths, the reiteratedly ambiguous mirrors, the gestures of a tiger, more fixed than ferocious—this image would be that of the library, the place wherein are crossed and reconciled the visions and divisions of reading. Or rather, those lost labyrinths (a hypallage in this case, since it is the individual who is lost there), similar to lost paradises, among those self-facing and ambivalent mirrors, where is reflected, several times, the image of a reader inclined over a page. Mirrors in the desert or in discourse that are also mirages or a miracle of reflection. Wondered, his eyes half closed, inclined over the indistinct open pages of a book of sand, the reader does not notice that time is slipping way into the clepsydra, which "steals water" or life or time itself, busy as he is with the word. Among these waters being lost is blurreed the face of Narcissus who, while repeating himself annuls himself. Similar to the stubborn stripes of the obsessive tiger, his lines are confused through the bars, like replete shelves or through crystals, suggested by Kurd Lasswitz's *Traumkristalle*, in which are aligned the books of the total library.[40] Identical to "The Other Tiger," literary, rhetorical, equally mysterious:

> It is a tiger of symbols and shades,
> A series of literary tropes.[41]

They are nothing but variations on a theme: the literalness of the library, just as Borges concludes in "Pascal's Sphere" as regards universal history, which is nothing other than "the history of the different intonations of some metaphors."[42] Even when a character who is tired, wonders, in one of his "Utopias": "There are still museums and libraries?",[43] the library does not cease to be the archetype of the symbolic modulation of his poetic and intellectual imagination.

From one story to the next, the "imperfect writers" of "Examination of the Work of Herbert Quain,"[44] or the "imperfect librarian" in "The Library of Babel,"[45] or in the previous "The Total Library," "of astronomic size," in which "Everything will be in its blind volumes. Everything: the meticulous history of the future, (. . .) Everything, but for each reasonable line or each correct notice there will be millions of senseless cacophonies, of verbal ramblings, and of incoherencies. Everything, but generations of men can pass by without the vertiginous shelves—the shelves that obliterate the day and that chaos inhabits—having granted them one tolerable page."[46]

Everything that occurs, occurs in the library. There everything is repeated, a totality that, in French, facilitates the alliteration—another paronomasia—with tautology: repetition as totality, in Latin, *in toto* is not audibly distinguished from its own repetition. *Tautology*, repetition, identical proposition, from *tauto*: "the same," contraction of *to auto*: "the same thing," a term of rhetoric. Frequently used with a pejorative value, it becomes a term of logic in the twentieth century. The word designates a complex proposition that can only be true, that is to say, a proposition in which the predicate says nothing that the subject does not say. The redundancies had already been anticipated, although on this occasion they are not totally superfluous, they would be, in addition to abundant, inevitable.

Although it is of Babel, the library is total: "everything is in Everything,"[47] is also a quote, but this time from Jules Laforgue, one of Borges's favorite poets. The sentence, especially tautological, is the watchword of Pan, the character of "Pan and the Syrinx or the invention of the seven reed flute," from his *Moralités légendaires*: "It is for something that Everything is in Everything!"[48] The circularity of tautology describes and confirms the totality to which it remits, an affirmation that cannot *not* be true, since the predicate does not differ from the subject. In virtue of that specular revelation that reflects everything in everything, Borges repeats other authors, the reader repeats Borges, other authors repeat Borges, turns and returns of rings formed by two serpents that never stop mutually devouring each other: "I affirm that the Library is interminable."[49]

It is notable that, when passing from "The Total Library" to "The Library of Babel," Borges obsessively ciphered his imagination into a geometric figure: the hexagon. The galleries are hexagonal in the same way that the rooms are hexagonal, "For four centuries already men have worn out hexagons."[50] The narrator does not stop insisting on the figure of the hexagon, of the term or of its derivations. The author of the epistle says that someone proposes to conquer the books of the Carmesí Hexagon, "In some shelf of some hexagon (reasoned the men) there must exist a book that is the cipher and perfect compendium of *all the rest*."[51] Without a doubt, beyond the mystical interpretations that the geometric figure evokes, its allusion to the number six that, Kabbalistically, alludes to the six days of the creation of the Universe, the alchemical unfoldings and limitations through which one arrives at the mysterious figure,[52] it makes sense to insinuate a historical reading that would add another redundancy to the series of inevitable redundancies.

To speak of hexagons in a hexagon . . . Beyond the banality of repetition and of cartographic diagramming that gives place to the obvious association, it would be pertinent to recall that the French reference does not seem far off: "It is enough for me, for now, to repeat the classical saying: The Library is a sphere whose complete center is whatever hexagon, whose circumference is inaccessible."53

Borges recalls, in another text, that is it in the *Timeus* where Plato says that the sphere is the most perfect and uniform figure, considering that all points on the surface are found equidistant from the center. He observes as well that the circumference is one of the mystical constants about which alchemical reflection has most meditated.54 He distances himself from Pascal's affirmation in order to adequate, to his geometric vision of the Library, the mysterious and reiterated reference, but he approaches it when he shudders before the terror that distance, silence, space, eternity, the infinite; the spheres inspire in him. ("The eternal silence of these infinite spaces frightens me."55 [. . .] What then will man become? Will he be equal to God or to the beasts? What frightening distance!"56):

> He felt the incessant weight of the physical world, he felt vertigo, fear, and solitude, and he put them in other words: "Nature is an infinite sphere, whose center is everywhere and circumference is nowhere." Thus Brunschvig publishes the text, but the critical edition by Tourneur (Paris, 1941), which reproduces the erasures and variations of the manuscript, reveals that Pascal began to write *effroyable*: "A frightening sphere, whose center is everywhere and circumference is nowhere."57

He pauses to register the variations of the famous affirmation of Fragment 72. He speaks in *Other Inquisitions* of "Pascal's Sphere" and of "Pascal," in another text. In his lucubrations, however, more than in Pascal's *Pensées* he is interested in Pascal himself. Curiously, he does not register that Blanqui, accustomed to the melancholic meditation of the numerous dungeons in which he had been recluded, also initiated the first chapter: "L'Univers-L'Infini," alluding to the same "magnificence of language" of Pascal: *"L'Univers est un cercle, don't le centre est partout et la surface nulle part."*58 It is possible, on the other hand, that he had at hand Laforgue's carnivalization, which reads:

> Art is everything, from the divine right of the Unconscious;
> After it, the deluge! And its slightest look
> Is the infinite circle whose circumference
> Is everywhere, and immoral center nowhere.59

As is noted in the La Pléiade volume, the publication of "Examination of the work of Herbert Quain"—the story that precedes "The

Library of Babel"—appears in *SUR*, both in the same year (*SUR*, n. 79, 1941), between "India," the text by Fernán Silva Valdés, a translation into Spanish by Rafael Alberti of the *Farce de Maitre Pathelin*, and an article by Roger Callois titled "Exámenes de conciencia," similar to the title of his story; an article that comments on three contemporary stories— *Tragédie en France* by André Maurois, *Sept mystères du destin de l'Europe* by Jules Romains, and *A travers le désastre* by Jacques Maritain. According to Jean Pierre Bernès, this contextualization ably banalizes the text of Borges's fction, which has all the appearances of a chronological note.[60] I would even say that he begins in a mocking way by giving the text the funereal character of a necrological note: "Herbert Quain dies in Roscommon,"[61] but in neither case should the homogeneity of the cultural context, it implicates, be disregarded.

If we take into account that only infrequently, in his writings, did Borges describe the space in which the actions of his stories took place, the meticulous detail of the place, of the locale, of the ambiance that "The Library of Babel" presents is surprising: "Vast ventilation shafts in the middle, surrounded by very low banisters,"[62] and on it goes. If we also recall that one of his recourses of universalization consists of the decircumstantialization of episodes, opting, precisely, not to mention the places that are no more than accidents of universal space or, with similar purposes, to ironize the precise procedure of descriptive mention by way of oneiric juxtapositions, their meticulousness is unusual. He alludes to the streets he mentions in the nightmare that is "Death and the Compass": "a nightmare in which figure elements of Buenos Aires deformed by the horror of nightmare"[63] similar to mythical localization (Heliopolis or the garden of Thebes), extravagant clarifications like "El Cairo, Illinois," couplings that, like the Parisian metro station called "Sèvres-Babylone," do not end up any less eccentric than "Illiers-Combray." The attention to the literary and municipal construction of place is suggestive, or curious.

Among many other procedures, another example of decircumstantialization—a globalization *avant la lettre*—he begins by misleading the reader, as in "Theme of the Traitor and the Hero":[64] "The action occurs in an oppressed and tenacious country: Poland, Ireland, the Republic of Venice, some South American or Balkan state . . . Let us say (for narrative comfort) Ireland."[65]

Or, in the conclusion to another story, he opts, with the same purpose, for mixing up or erasing particular footprints: "The story was in fact incredible, but it imposed itself on everyone, because substantially it was true. The tone of Emma Zunz was true, the modesty true, the hatred true. True as well was the outrage she had suffered; only the circumstances were false, the time and one or two proper names."[66]

Nevertheless, he is the author of a book that orders the itineraries of its voyages according to country, place. An *Atlas*? [67] Borges? It would seem unlikely, however, and without giving greater concessions to geographical circumstances, his atlas is to be denominated like he denominates a *History of Eternity*,[68] or *of Infamy*,[69] as discontinuously historical. As a consequence, more than forced it would be contrived not to make the association of the hexagon with France. Among such contexts, that insistence on hexagons cannot not be associated with the colloquial metonymy that schematizes or identifies metropolitan France with the hexagon. A common denomination, affective, a certain discretion of nationalist modesty avoids the name of the country and, in order to abstract it, *more geometrico*. I do not believe that it would have occurred to General de Gaulle to say in those years that "Thousands of the covetous men abandoned the sweet natal hexagon,"[70] although he could certainly have referred to "the venerated secret hexagon that sheltered him,"[71] as the geometric and rhetorical figure occurred to him after 1934. Since then it has become a stereotype, a domestic appellation, a common place, which competes with the more nostalgic *"douce France"*: "Like all men of the Library, I have traveled in my youth; I have been a pilgrim in search of a book, maybe a catalogue of catalogues; now that my eyes can almost not decipher what I write, I prepare myself to die a few leagues away from the hexagon in which I was born."[72]

One could affirm that for Borges, in general terms, the *place* is, like the *common place* for Aristotle, more than a site, an argument, a rhetorical topic, convincing, cognized, cohabited, common. The space of the library legitimates the localization of the *common place*, an abundant reserve or quarry of redundancies where it would be, more than infrequent, incoherent to find something new: "Clearly, nobody hopes to discover anything."[73] Nevertheless, the new is not necessarily the unheard of: "The new is new if it is unexpected."[74] Such that the library, in addition to propitiating the common place, propitiates the effective recourse of surprise: "Serendipity."[75]

In order to discard any suspicion of pejorative insinuation in the argument of the *common place*, we could have to confirm the strategic arguments of a logic that would facilitate, because it is known, the invention of reasonings necessary for the case at hand.[76] A fourth axiom, which the narrator does not formulate, could be that all which exists there, like in an Arabic legend, exists because it has already been written: "The certainty that all is written annuls us or phantasms us."[77] The two anterior axioms: "The Library exists ab aeterno," and "The number of orthographic signs is twenty five,"[78] are affirmations that allude explicitly to "The Total Library," to Kurd Lasswitz, whom he does not name in this story but to whom he attributes the complete inventory that only comprises, to elaborate its totality, out of the twenty five letters of the alphabet, the period, the comma, and the space, the motif of greatest attention in the previous story. He does not present the affirmation as a third axiom but rather as "the fundamental law of the library": "*There are not, in the vast Library, two identical books.*"[79]

This identification between place and common place would not be alien to Borges's poetics. As if words *gave place*, literally, to a portion of space, narrowing conventional place and conventional language in one and the same contraction. To verify the substitutions of a place for a word or the contrary are constant mechanisms of his textual magic. We had begun with the letter *beth*, which is both things, the space man inhabits and the second letter of the Hebrew alphabet, following with the map that displaces the Empire, with the poem that displaces the palace, with the library that displaces the Universe. Walls and books[80] have maintained an intimate and adverse association of mutual conservation and reciprocal substitution, a movement, a literal metaphor: displacement.

The place where this *displacement* is observed most clearly, to the letter, is in one of his most quoted stories: "The Aleph."[81] For Borges, the Hebrew term designates a point, a letter, a word, a title, a story, a book, an anticipatory allegory of the mediatic universe: everything. Everything: what existed and will exist, including what will not exist. The narrator clarifies: "He clarified that an Aleph is one of the points of space that contain all points."[82] That the letter cannot do without spatialization is clear. What is also clear is the confusion—notwithstanding the contradiction—between letter and space, or their partial reciprocal necessity. As the letter needs to be inscribed against time in a place, Carlos Argentino Daneri, the vulgar poet of the story, needs this aleph that exists in the basement of his house in order to write his poems: "he said that to finish the poem his house was indispensable, since in a corner of the basement there was an Aleph."[83]

But it is not the only displacement to illustrate narratively the substitution of the place by the word. It is necessary to have recourse to genetic research and to compare to it the manuscript of "The Aleph," one of the few that are conserved from Borges's oeuvre. In a previous version of the text to the published one, the name of the initial letter of the Hebrew alphabet, the aleph is not mentioned, but instead he writes "mirhâb," that sacred space dedicated to worship, from where the imam addresses the prayer. It constitutes, in Muslim religious architecture, the most important space of the mosque, to which the wealth of the decoration adds an even greater dimension. Important for the history of art and theology, object of historical, artistic, sociological, philological and, to a lesser degree liturgical reflection, [84] it is "a refuge, the most secret place of the temple, which symbolizes the essence of the dogma."[85]

At a conference on the *Thousands and One Nights*, Borges wonders: "What are Orient and Occident? If you ask me, I do not know. Let us look for an approximation.[86]

In cardinal, hemispherical terms, Borges poses himself in relation to space the same question that Augustine formulated in relation to time and, like the ancient African bishop, he responds by rejecting the question and formulating it again. In Borges's epistemological fiction—anterior and similar—like in the computerized present, planetary distances and differences are no more than accidents of space, which only counts eventually. The mirhâb is the sacred place, the place of all places, it becomes the aleph, a letter that is the mysterious unity from which all letters spring. In the epistemological fiction of Borges, space is literalized to the same extent that the letter is spatialized. That movement replicates the back and forth of the first letters of the Hebrew alphabet: the beginning begins with *beth*, a house, a tower, a library, in order to insinuate that before this letter began, space had already begun. Perhaps so that the letter could exist and displace it.

Notes

THE INTERPRETIVE FIX
AND THE FIXATIONS OF FICTION

1. Martin Heidegger, "Letter on Humanism," trans, Frank M. Capuzzi, in *Pathmarks* (Cambridge: Cambridge University Press, 1998), 239–276.

2. Block de Behar, *Una palabra propiamente dicha* (Argentina: Siglo XXI Editores, 1994).

3. Block de Behar, *Borges ou les gestes d'un voyant aveugle*, traduit de l'espagnol par Patrice Toulouse (Paris: Honoré Champion Éditeur, 1998).

4. Block de Behar, *Una retórica del silencio. Funciones del lector y los procedimientos de la lectura literaria* (México: Siglo XXI Editores, 1984); *A Rhetoric of Silence and Other Selected Writings* (Berlin/New York: Mouton de Gruyter, 1995).

5. *Hamlet*, II.ii.

6. Jorge Luis Borges, "Pierre Menard, autor del quijote," in *Obras Completas* (Buenos Aires: Emecé, 1974), 444–450.

7. Jacques Derrida, *Of Grammatology, Corrected Edition*, trans. Gayatri Chakravorty Spivak (Baltimore/London: The Johns Hopkins University Press, 1998), 37.

8. Gilles Deleuze and Félix Guattari, *A Thousand Plateaus: Capitalism and Schizophrenia*, trans. Brian Massumi (Minneapolis: University of Minnesota Press, 1987), 154.

9. Sigmund Freud, "Beyond the Pleasure Principle," in *The Essentials of Psychoanalysis*, ed. Anna Freud, trans. James Strachey (London: The Hogarth Press, 1986), 218–268.

10. Jacques Lacan, *The Seminar of Jacques Lacan. Book I: Freud's papers on Technique. 1953–1954*, trans. John Forrester (New York & London: W. W. Norton & Co., 1991), 42.

11. Although the actual German adds a letter, again the omnipresent *n*, the unknown of pure change, to the *nth* degree: *redner;* a *reder* is rather one who builds ships.

12. *Wörter und Zahlen, Das Alphabet als Code* (Vienna/New York: Springer, 2000).

13. Ibid., 7.

14. His whole thought deals with this problem, but was first expounded in *Philosophy and the Mirror of Nature* (Princeton: Princeton University Press, 1979)

15. Gilles Deleuze and Félix Guattari, *What is Philosophy?*, trans. Hugh Tomlinson and Graham Burchell (New York: Columbia University Press, 1994), 5.

16. And yet Kabbalah, as Bloom has said, is not mysticism, but interpretation, "a theory of writing." Harold Bloom, *Kabbalah and Criticism* (New York: Continuum, 1975), 52.

17. Chapter 6 of this book.

18. Etymology, what Deleuze and Guattari call "a specifically philosophical athleticism" (ibid., 8), is one of Block de Behar's cherished tools. Her analysis of the relation between *chance* and *fall* appears in chapter 8.

1. FIRST WORDS

1. Jorges Luis Borges, *Obras Completas* (Buenos Aires: Emecé Editores, 1974), 522–544.

2. Ibid., 444–450.

3. Ralph Waldo Emerson, *Essays and Lectures* (NY: Literary Classics of the United States, 1983), 455.

4. August of 1999 marked the centennial of Borges's birth. Beyond the chronological precision of commemorations, the intention of this book was to contribute to his constant celebration.

5. *Perlas de la sabiduría judía (Antología de los hagiógrafos y de Pirké Avot),* 2ª edición bilingüe ampliada (Buenos Aires: Editorial Yehuda), 317.

6. There is a connotation of the phrase *cita sin fin* that "Endless quotation" does not capture, namely, that of a *cinta sin fin*, or tape recorder on auto-reverse, a metaphor of audio reproduction that resonates with Lisa Block de Behar's notion of the quotation. [W.E.]

2. VARIATIONS ON A LETTER AVANT-LA-LETTRE

1. Blanqui, *L'éternité par les astres. Hypothèse astronomique*, ed. L. B. de Behar (Genève: Fleuron-Slatkine, 1996), 149.

2. English in the original.

3. Borges, *Obras Completas* (Buenos Aires: Emecé Editores, 1974), 712.

4. Rodríguez Monegal, "Borges y la nouvelle critique," *Revista Iberoamericana* (July–Sept., 1972): 367–390; *Borges par lui-même* (Paris: Seuil, 1981).

5. Gregory Ulmer, "The Puncept in Grammatology," in Jonathan Culler, ed., *On Puns. The Foundation of Letters* (New York: Blackwell, 1988), 164–189.

6. *Obras*, 173.

7. Ibid., 773.

8. See Lisa Block de Behar, "El milagro de la rosa o el ultrarrealismo de Borges," in *Al margen de Borges* (Buenos Aires: Siglo XXI Editores, 1987), 193–210, and "Le seuil d'autres mondes: l'ultraréalisme de Borges et Bioy Casares en regard de Walter Bejamin et Louis Auguste Blanqui," in *Nouveau monde autres mondes* (Paris: Pleine Marge 5, 1995), 75–92.

9. *Obras*, 847.

10. Ibid., 801–802.

11. Ibid., 802.

12. The following depends on the double meaning of the Spanish word *parábola*: parable and parabola [W.E].

13. Ibid., 441.

14. Ibid., 440.

15. Ibid., 773.

16. Roland Barthes, "Le bruissement de la langue," in *Essais critques IV* (Paris: Seuil, 1984, original from 1968), 93–96.

17. Michel Foucault, "What Is an Author?" in *Critical Theory Since 1965*, eds., Hazard Adams and Leroy Searle (Gainsville: University Press of Florida, 1986, original essay, 1969), 140.

18. Jacques Derrida, "La différance," in *Marges de la philosophie* (Paris: Minuit, 1972), 3–29.

19. Derrida, *Glas. Que reste-t-il du savoir absolut?* (Paris: Denoël/Gonthier, 1981).

20. Gianni Vattimo and Aldo Rovatti, *Il pensiero debole* (Milan: Felitrinelli, 1983).

21. Borges, *El libro de arena. Obras Completas*, III (Buenos Aires: Emecé Editores, 1989), 52.

22. *Encyclopedia Universalis*. CD-Rom (France: Encyclopedia Universalis France S.A., 1995).

23. Ibid., 124.

24. Ibid., 124.

25. Gershom Scholem, *La kabbale et sa symbolique* (Paris: Payot, 1975), 40.

26. "Entendre" in French means both *to hear* and *to understand* [W.E.].

27. Borges, *Oeuvres Complètes*, édition établie, présentée et annotée par Jean-Pierre Bernès (Paris: Gallimard, 1993), 1602–1603.

28. English in the original.

29. English in the original.

30. Borges, *Obras Completas*, 627.

31. *Obras*, 885.

32. "Larve Lat. larva, Gespenst, quälender Geist eines Verstorbenen, Maske der Schauspieler, Larve." Bertelsmann, *Wahrig Deutsches Wörterbuch*, 1997.

33. Paul Virilio, *Esthétique de la disparition* (Paris: Balland, 1980).

34. Adolfo Bioy Casares, *La invención de Morel* (Madrid: Alianza Editorial/Emecé Editores, 1972).

35. Ibid., 12.

36. Agamben, *Means without Ends*, trans.Vincenzo Binetti and Cesare Casarino (Minneapolis: University of Minnesota Press, 2000).

37. Lyotard, *Le différend* (Paris: Minuit, 1983).

38. Adorno, *Negative Dialectics*, trans. E. B. Ashton (New York: Continuum, 1983).

39. Harold Bloom, *Kabbalah and Criticism* (New York: Continuum, 1983), 90.

40. Borges, *El tamaño de mi esperanza* (Buenos Aires: Proa, 1926).

41. Lugones, *El tamaño del espacio: Ensayo de psicología matemática* (Buenos Aires: Ateneo, 1921).

42. From the Greek *idioma*, own or particular language.

43. *Obras*, 772.

44. Walter Benjamin, "The Task of the Translator/Die Aufgabe des Übersetzers," trans. James Hynd and E. M. Valk, *Delos: A Journal on & of Translation* 2 (1968): 76–99.

45. *Obras*, 772.

46. English in the original.

47. English in the original.

48. Ibid., 867–868.

49. English in the original.

50. As Borges says in an issue of *La Maga* (issue in homage to Borges, Buenos Aires, February 1996).

51. That union that according to the concepts of Isaac Luria, taken up again by later currents, "portrays the Messiah as cleaving to the divine power in order to restore the divine system to its harmonious status." Moshe Idel, *Kabbalah. New Perspectives* (New Haven: Yale University Press, 1988), 57.

52. The word means "lay," while maintaining an etymological association with "reading" or "lecture" through the latin verb *legere*.

53. Adorno, 76.

54. Lyotard, *Un trait d'union* (Grenoble: Le Griffon d'argile, 1993), 5.

55. English in the original.

56. Emmanuel Lévinas, *Hors sujet* (Paris: Fata Morgana, 1987), 217.

3. *PARADOXA ORTODOXA*

1. Jorge Luis Borges, *Obras completas* (Buenos Aires: Emecé Editores, 1974), 259–262.

2. Ibid., 1068–1073.

3. Ibid., 259.

4. Ibid.

5. In the original: "(a)copiar," a play on words between "to copy" and "to gather or store." [W.E.]

6. Ibid., 1068.

7. Jakobson, "Du réalisme en art," in *Questions de Poétique* (Paris: Seuil, 1973), 34.

8. Borges, *Obras completas*, 491–495.

9. Borges, "Milonga del infiel," *Los conjurados, Obras completas*, 90.

10. Friedrich Nietzsche, *Genealogy of Morals*, trans. Walter Kaufman and R. J. Hollingdale (New York: Vintage Books, 1989), 25.

11. Emmanuel Lévinas, *Sur Maurice Blanchot* (Paris: Fata Morgana, 1975), 47.

12. Eco, *Semiotics and the Philosophy of Language* (Bloomington: Indiana University Press, 1984), 26.

13. Derrida, "La pharmacie de Plato," in *La dissémination* (Paris: Seuil, 1972), 120.

14. Paul de Man, *Allegories of Reading* (New Haven: Yale University Press, 1979), 58.

15. Bloom, *A Map of Misreading* (New York: Oxford University Press, 1980).

16. Charles Baudelaire, "L'Héautontimorouménos," *Fleurs du mal, Œuvres complétes,* I (Paris: Gallimard, 1975), 78.

17. Ibid., 78.

18. Derrida, "La différance," *Marges de la philosophie* (Paris: Minuit, 1972), 3.

19. Exodus 20.18, in *Young's Literal Translation.*

20. "Revelations," 1:12.

21. Paul, "Corinthians," I: 21, in *The Holy Bible,* King James version (Chicago: Good Counsel Publishers, 1965), 140.

22. Paoli, *Borges: Percorsi di significato* (Florence: Casa Editrice D'Anna, 1977), 95.

23. A popular magazine devoted to rural themes.

24. Borges, *Obras completas,* 1070.

25. Roland Barthes, "Proust et les noms," in *Les critiques de notre temps et Proust* présentation par Jacques Bersani (Paris: Garnier, 1971), 160.

26. The eponymous character of a dialogue of Plato that often carries the subtitle "On the Precision and Property of Names."

27. Barthes, "Proust et les noms," 160.

28. The action of calling, as much in the religious sense in which God calls, attracts to Himself a person, a people, as in that of the action and result of an installing voice; although similar, that *vocation* does not correspond completely with what linguistics considers performative utterances.

29. Ibid., 163.

30. In this case we would have to understand *motivation* in two of its senses: (1) in general, as movement or that which puts into movement (from Latin: *motor, movere:* to move); (2) specifically, linguistically, as a principle opposed to the arbitrariness of the sign, a natural reason of being or the (onomatopoetic) possibility that the sign is imitating the thing.

31. Roger Dragonetti, *La vie de la lettre au Moyen Âge* (Paris: Seuil, 1980), 22.

32. *Propio,* which also means "own" [W.E.].

33. Lugones, *Obras poéticas completas* (Madrid: Aguilar, 1974), 197.

34. Hartman, *Saving the Text, Literature/Derrida/Philosophy* (Baltimore: The Johns Hopkins University Press, 1982), 111.

35. Reading Dante, Luce Fabbri de Cressatti observed that some Italian nouns carry two meanings: one subjective and the other objective. "The distinction is found in the Latin grammars apropos of the specifying complements that carry out a subjective as well as an objective function, when the idea of an action or a sentiment is included in the respective noun. There are still today nouns that can have a specifying complement

of both kinds. Typical example: 'The love of God' (*of God* is ambiguous. According to the context it could be 'the love of God for the world' or 'the love of the world for God')." From *Informe sobre sustantivos italianos susceptibles de dos significados, uno subjetivo y otro objetivo*, by Luce Fabbri de Cassetti, whom I asked and now I thank.

36. Rodríguez Monegal, "Borges and Derrida: Boticarios," 123.

37. Block de Behar, "A manera de prólogo," in *El texto según Genette, Maldoror* 20 (1985): 17–29.

38. Scholem, *La kabbale et sa symbolique* (Paris: Payot, 1975), 40.

39. What follows depends on words *clave* and *llave* in Spanish, both of which are translated by the English "key," the former denoting the musical key and connoting the more figurative meanings of "key," the latter the literal, physical object [W.E.].

40. Jabès, *Ça suit son cours*, 58.

41. Block de Behar, *Una retórica del silencio* (México: Siglo XXI Editores, 1984).

42. *Lectarios*—The term I use for those characters who, in the text, appear as listeners of an out-loud reading realized by another character: neither proper listeners nor proper readers (the Gutres, little Marcel of the *Recherche*, little Jean of *Les mots*, and so on); they are included in a literary species whose complexity requires an attention that I will give it in another work.

43. Borges, *Obras completas*, 1071.

44. Ibid., 1072.

45. Hartman, *Saving the Text*, 109.

46. Borges, "Del rigor de la ciencia," *Obras completas*, 847.

47. Derrida, *La dissemination*, 182.

48. Baltasar Gracián, *El criticón* (Barcelona: Fama, 1950), 375.

49. Jakobson, *Essais de linguistique générale* (Paris: Minuit, 1963), 238–239.

50. de Man, *Allegories of Reading*, 77.

51. Borges, *Obras completas*, 259.

52. Ibid., 718.

53. 2 Corinthians, 3.6.

54. I analyzed the detailed development of this thesis with reference to Woody Allen's film *The Purple Rose of Cairo* (1985) where, in the same way as in "The Gospel According to Mark," the narrative action implies more than a narrative action and, between them, the characters move from one to another diegetic space. This ironic transit is verified, as in "The Gospel According to Mark," in a cinematographic narrative that has cinematic narrative as its theme, a transit enabled in turn by the conviction that legitimates credulity, seduction, literalness, a conviction shared by the

characters of these narratives in which "I am in heaven" is heard intoned at the beginning and the end, in heaven or in eternity. On the basis of T. S. Coleridge and beyond the quote from Borges transcribed in the epigraph, the transit is conceived and consolidated in a most Borgesian way.

55. Gérard Genette, *Figures III* (Paris: Seuil, 1972), 243–251: *diégesis* (equivalent to history). In normal usage diegesis constitutes the spatio-temporal universe referred to by the tale or in which the story plays itself out. Genette uses the term in the sense that E. Souriau gave it when he opposed diagetic universe, as the place of the signified, to universe of the screen, as place of the filmic signifier. *Metalepsis*: a transgression that consists of the reference to the intrusion of a narrator or the extra-diegetic narratee into the diegetic universe (or of diegetic characters into an extra-diegetic universe). The effect produced is one of strangeness, humoristic or fantastic, and insinuates the impossibility of remaining outside of the narrative. (Definitions formulated on the basis of Genette's texts and assembled in *Maldoror* 20 (1985): 142–150.)

56. Julio Cortázar, "Axolotl", *Final de juego* (Buenos Aires: Sudamericana, 1964), 161–168.

57. Ever since the *Divine Comedy*, in Italian the name Galehaut (Galeotto), character of the Breton Cycle, has been used antonomastically to designate whichever character, object, or situation provokes an amorous relation: "Galeotto fu il libro e chi lo scrisse!" (Galeotto was the book and he who wrote it.) Dante, *Inferno*, v, 137.

58. Derrida, *Carte postale* (Paris: Flammarion, 1980), 210.

59. Borges, *Obras completas*, 1025–1028.

60. Ibid., 1025.

61. Ibid., 462.

62. Jung, *Mysterium Conjunctionis*, 13.

63. *Dictionnaire de la foi chrétienne, I*, publié sous la direction de O. de La Brosse, A.-M. Henry and Ph. Rouillard (Paris: Les éditions du cerf, 1968), 52.

64. Hans von Campenhausen, *Les Pères Grecs* (Paris: Edition L'Orante, 1963), 51.

65. Browne, *Religio Medici and Other Writings* (Oxford: Oxford University Press, 1964), 9.

66. Nicolas of Cusa, *De la Docta Ignorantia* (Paris: La Maisnie, 1979).

67. Colie, *Paradoxia Epidemica* (Princeton: Princeton University Press, 1966), 23.

68. Victor-José Herrero Llorente, *Diccionario de expresiones y frases latinas* (Madrid: Gredos, 1985), 77.

69. Wilde, *The Artist as Critic. Writings of Oscar Wilde*, edited by Richard Ellman (Chicago: The University of Chicago Press), 307.

70. Personal conversation with Borges, Buenos Aires, 1983.

4. ON "ULTRAREALISM"

1. Both the cabaret and the magazine were founded by Rodolphe Salis. The first issue appeared on January 14, 1982. Allais did not publish anything in *Le Chat Noir* until 1883. The biography of François Caradec is in *Alphonse Allais. Oeuvres anthumes* (Paris: R. Laffont, 1989).

2. Breton, *Anthologie de l'humour noir* (Paris: J. J. Pauvert, 1966), 122.

3. Ibid., 221–226.

4. This painting of Malevitch was presented in a vanguard exposition in Saint Petersburg in 1915.

5. Arthur Rimbaud: "Square où tout est correct, les arbres et les fleurs." "À la musique," *Poésies complètes* (Paris: Gallimard, 1963), 34.

6. Roger Penrose, *The Emperor's New Mind. Concerning Computers, Minds and Laws of Physics* (New York: Penguin Books, 1991), 329.

7. Breton, *Anthologie de l'humour noir*, 11. "*Nantissement*": a real contract on guarantee (*Petit Robert*).

8. Eco, "Possible Worlds and Text Pragmatics: 'Un drame bien parisien,'" *VS* 19/20 (1978): 6–72.

9. Eco, *Lector in fabula. La cooperazione interpretativa nei testi narrativi* (Milan: Bompiani, 1979).

10. Eco, *The Limits of Interpretation* (Bloomington: Indiana University Press, 1990).

11. This fragment from the letter to Arnaud (7/14/1686) is cited with frequency: "If in someone's life or in the entire universe each thing had gone a different way than has actually occurred, nothing could stop us from saying that it was another person or universe that God had chosen." Quoted from "Mondi possibili, logica, semiotica," *VS* 19/20, ibid., 125.

12. Metz, *Essais sur la signification au cinéma*, II: "Pour une phénoménologie du narratif" (Paris: Klincksieck, 1968), 28.

13. Breton, *Dictionnaire abrégé du surréalisme*, en collaboration avec Paul Eluard, *Œuvres complètes* (Paris: Gallimard, 1988), 801.

14. Metz: ". . . 'the open-ended' stories of which cultural modernity is so fond are closed sequences of non-closed events. The closure of the recounted (*raconté*) is a variable one, the closure of the story (*récit*) is a constant" (Ibid., 32).

15. Eco, "Possible Worlds and Text Pragmatics: 'Un drame bien parisien,'" 5.

16. The term derives from *fumiste* (French): "people who install or repair chimneys." In the figurative sense, *fumiste*, that of a person lacking gravity, seems to come from the expression, "c'est une farce de fumiste," "an expression repeated by the hero of a vaudeville (*La famille du fumiste*, 1840) in which a suddenly wealthy *fumiste* boasts of his good turns." *Dictionnaire historique de la langue française* (Paris: Robert, 1992).

17. In the issue from May 15, 1880.

18. Daniel Grojnowski and Bernard Sarrazin, "Présentation," *L'esprit fumiste et les rires fin de siècle. Anthologie* (Paris: José Corti, 1990), 20; "E. Goudeau defined Fumism as a kind of interior madness, expressed on the outside as imperturbable buffooneries." *Dix ans de bohème* (Paris: 1888), 100.

19. Breton, 222.

20. Douglas Hofstadter, *Metamagical Themas: Questing for the Essence of Mind and Pattern* (New York: Bantom Books, 1985), 456. The reference is also, of course, to Heisenberg's uncertainty principle.

21. Eco, *Limits*, 64.

22. Lodge, *Small World* (New York: Warner Books, 1984).

23. Borges, "El otro Whitman," *Discusión, Obras completas*, 296.

24. Benjamin, *Das Passagenwerke* (Frankfurt, Suhrkamp, 1982).

25. Benjamin, *Paris, capitale du XIXe siècle. Le livre des passages* (Paris: Cerf, 1989), 48.

26. "While, because of my occupations and interests, I feel here in Germany completely isolated from the men of my generation, there are in France some manifestations (writers like Giraudoux and especially Aragon, like the surrealist movement), in whose work I see that which also preoccupies me." *Briefe*, 446, following the translation of Ricardo Ibarlucía, "Benjamin y el surrealismo," in *Sobre Walter Benjamin. Vanguardias, historia, estética y literatura. Una visión latinoamericana* (Buenos Aires: Alianza Editorial/Goethe Institut,1993), 153.

27. Blanqui, Louis-Auguste, *L'éternité par les astres. Hypothèse astronomique*, ed. L. B. de Behar, (Genève: Fleuron-Slatkine, 1996), 149.

28. "The object of Marx, among others, [in the Communist Manifesto] is to confront the 'legend of the specter' with the manifesto of a party." Miguel Abensour, "Walter Benjamin entre mélancolie et révolution. Passages Blanqui," in *Passages. Walter Benjamin et Paris*, ed. Heinz Wismann (Paris: Cerf, 1986), 228.

29. *Spectres de Marx. L'état de la dette, le travail du deuil at la nouvelle Internationale* (Paris: Galilée, 1993).

30. Pierre Missac, "Walter Benjamin: de la rupture au naufrage," *Critique* 395 (1980): 380.

31. Gustave Geffroy, *L'enfermé* (Paris, 1897).

32. Abensour, "Walter Benjamin entre mélancolie et révolution. Passages Blanqui," in *Passages*. *Walter Benjamin et Paris*, 221.

33. Benjamin, quoted in Fabrizio Desideri, "Le vrai n'a pas de fenêtres," in *Passages*. *Walter Benjamin et Paris*, 201–215, 209.

34. Graciela Wamba Gaviña, "La recepción de Walter Benjamin en Argentina," ibid., 202.

35. Borges comments, in *Sur* 3 (Winter, 1931), on the German film *Der Mörder Dimitri Karamasoff* (1931), directed by Fedor Ozep. Reprinted in Edgardo Cozarinsky, *Borges y el cine* (Buenos Aires: Sur, 1974), 27.

36. Benjamin, *Escritos escogidos de Walter Benjamin*, trans. H. A. Murena (Buenos Aires: Sur, 1967).

37. Honorio Bustos Domecq, *Seis problemas para don Isidro Parodi* (Buenos Aires: Sur, 1942).

38. Borges, *Obras completas* (Buenos Aires: Emencé, 1974), 431–443.

39. Adolfo Bioy Casares, *La invención de Morel* (Madrid: Alianza Editorial/Emecé Editores, 1972).

40. Metz, 30.

41. "Everything is full of sense, he said, I reveal much of it to you but I will not show you all of it, I allow a shadow of suspicion or even of skepticism to glide over my purpose, because I do not want you to congeal in code what I am showing you, nor to make resurge, by your interpretations, a phantom, the phantom of the referent." Eco, "La maitrise de Barthes," *Magazine Littéraire* 314 (October, 1993): 45.

42. Borges, *Obras completas*, 431.

43. The 1910 edition of the Encyclopedia Britannica includes the following entry: "America. I. *Physical Geography*. The accidental use of a single name, America, for the pair of continents that has a greater extension from north to south than any other continuous land area in the globe, has had some recent justification, since the small of the geological opinion has turned in favour of the theory of tetrahedral deformation of the earth's crust [. . .] roughly represents the triangular outline that is to be expected from tetrahedral warping; and although greatly broken in the middle, is nevertheless the best witness among the continents of today to the tetrahedral theory. There seems to be, however, not a unity but a duality in its plan of construction, for the two parts."

44. *Obras completas*, 802.

45. Ibid., 847.

46. Benjamin, *Gesammelte Schriften* (Frankfurt/Main: Suhrkamp, 1972) I, 9, 1071. Quoted in Missac, 374.

47. Paul Virilio, *Esthétique de la disparition* (Paris: Balland, 1980).

48. Ibid., 89.

49. Adolfo Bioy Casares, "La trama celeste," *Sur* 116 (June 1944). Revised edition by Centro Editor de América Latina (Buenos Aires, 1987).

50. ". . . the curious thesis of Dunne, "according to which each man, at each instant of his life, disposes of an infinite number of futures, all foreseeable and all real." Borges, *Obras completas*, IV (Buenos Aires: Emecé Editores, 1996), 331.

51. Adolfo Bioy Casares, *La trama celeste y otros relatos. Antología* (Buenos Aires: Centro Editor de América Latina, 1987), 37.

52. Ibid., 48.

53. Ibid., 57.

54. Ibid., 58.

55. Ibid., 60.

56. Blanqui, *L'éternité par les astres*, 148.

57. Bioy Casares, *La trama celeste y otros relatos. Antología*, 60.

58. Borges, *Obras completas*, 434.

59. Ibid., 472–480. "Different from Newton and Schopenhauer, his ancestor did not believe in uniform, absolute time. He believed in infinite series of times, in a growing and vertiginous network of divergent, convergent, and parallel times. This weave of times that bifurcate, split, or are secularly ignored, comprise *all* possibilities. We do not exist in the majority of those times; in some you exist but I do not; in others, I and not you; in others, both of us. In this one, to which a favorable chance brings me, you have arrived at my house; in another, when crossing the garden you found me dead; in another, I say these same words, but am an error, a phantasm." Ibid., 479.

60. Ibid.

61. Ibid., 499–507.

62. Ibid., 507.

63. Ibid., 571–575.

64. Ibid., 525–530.

65. Ibid., 550–556.

66. Blanqui, 152.

67. "The palimpsests and codices burned, but in the heart of the fire, among the ashes, there perdured, almost intact, the twelfth book of *Civitas Dei*, which narrates how Plato taught in Athens that, at the end of time, all things would recuperate their previous status, and that he, in Athens, before the same audience, would again teach this doctrine. . . . In

Frigia they called them *simulacra*, and also in Dardania." The Theologians, *Obras completas*, 550–552.

68. Borges: "I believe that common places are most necessary. If not, one is simply extravagant and ephemeral." Roger Callois: "Yes, and one becomes a *outrist.*" *Diálogo fugaz*, trans. Alberto Ruy Sánchez, *Revista de Cultura* no. 7 (Fortaleza, octubre de 2000), http://www.secret.com.br/jpoesia/agcaillois/.htm.

69. Jakobson: "We call realist the works that seem verisimilar to us, that most closely reflect reality." "Du réalisme en art," *Questions de poétique* (Paris: Seuil, 1973), 31–39, 32. Original in Czech in 1932.

70. "Perhaps contaminated by the monotonies, they imagined that each man is two men and that the true is the other, the one who is in the sky. They also imagined that our acts project an inverted reflection, such that if we stay awake, the other sleeps, if we fornicate, the other is chaste, if we steal, the other is generous. Dead, we will be united with him and will be him. . . . Other histrions reasoned that the world would conclude when the cipher of its possibilities was exhausted." Borges, "Los Téologos," *Obras completas*, 553.

71. Block de Behar, *Al margen de Borges* (Bueno Aires: Siglo XXI, 1987), 193–210.

72. Paul Virilio, *La machine de vision* (Paris: Galilée, 1988).

73. Blanqui, 151.

5. A COMPLEXLY WOVEN PLOT

1. "Objective chance is that stroke of luck through which is manifested to man, still most mysteriously, a necessity that escapes him although he experiences it vitally as a necessity. [. . .] it is the place of manifestations so exalting for the spirit that they let filter though a light that could pass for that of a revelation." André Breton, "Conferencia de México," *Oeuvres Complètes II* (Paris: Gallimard, La Pléiade, 1988), 1280.

2. Born in Puguet-Théniers on February 8, 1805, died in Paris the first of January 1881.

3. Paris: Librairie Germet-Baillière, 1872. 8 chapters, 76 pages.

4. Blanqui, *L'éternité par les astres* (Paris/Genève: Slatkine), 121.

5. Ibid., 142.

6. Bioy Casares, *La invención de Morel* (Madrid: Alianza/Emecé, 1972).

7. Bioy Casares, *Historias desaforadas* (Buenos Aires: Emecé, 1986) 11–23.

8. Ibid., 27–53.

9. Ibid., 57–73.

10. Ibid., 201–211.

11. Blanqui, *L'éternité par les astres*, 101.

12. Borges, *Obras completas* (Buenos Aires: Emecé, 1974), 431–443.

13. Ibid., 525–530.

14. Ibid., 550–560.

15. Ibid., 571–575.

16. Ibid., 465–471.

17. Ibid., 472–480.

18. Ibid., 499–507.

19. Ibid., 465 and 466.

20. Blanqui, Blanqui, *L'éternité par les astres*, 37. Originally formulated by Nicholas of Cusa, *Of Learned Ignorance*, tr. Germain Heron (London, 1954), cited in: Giorgio de Santillana, *The Age of Adventure: The Renaissance Philosophers, Selected, with Introduction and Interpretative Commentary* (New York: New American library, 1956), 53; also cited and discussed in Lisa Gorton, "The Paradox Topos," *Journal of the History of Ideas* 61.2 (2000): 343–346.

21. Ibid., 37.

22. Borges, *Obras completas*, 467.

23. Blanqui, *L'éternité par les astres*, 104.

24. Borges, *Obras completas*, 470–471.

25. Bioy Casares, "El cuarto sin ventanas," *Historias desaforadas* (Buenos Aires, 1986), 203.

26. Blanqui, *L'éternité par les astres*, 103.

27. Ibid., 100.

28. Baudelaire, *Œuvres complètes*, II , texte établi, présenté et annoté par Claude Pichois (Paris: Gallimard, 1976), 59.

29. Ibid., I, 357.

30. Marcel Proust, *La recherche du temps perdu*, édition établie et annotée par Pierre Clarac et André Ferré, III (Paris: Gallimard, 1978), 895.

31. Blanqui, *L'éternité par les astres*, 39.

32. Borges, *La cifra* (Buenos Aires: Emecé 1981), 71.

33. Borges, "La creación y P. H. Gosse," in *Otras inquisiciones, Obras completas* (Buenos Aires: Emecé, 1974), 650–652, 650–651.

34. Borges, "El tiempo circular," *Historia de la eternidad, Obras completas* (Buenos Aires: Emecé, 1974), 393–394.

35. Hippolyte Castille, *L.-A. Blanqui. Autour de la Seconde République (1848 à 1852)* (Paris: Ferdinand Sartorious éd., 1857), 53.

36. Bioy, *La trama celeste y otros relatos*, 65.

37. Ibid., 65.

38. Ibid., 37.

39. Ibid., 57–58.

40. Ibid., 60 and Blanqui, *L'éternité par les astres*, 148.

41. Blanqui, *L'éternité par les astres*, 151–152.

6. THEORETICAL INVENTION IN FICTION

1. Baudelaire, "Les phares" *Œuvres complètes*, I (Paris: Gallimard, 1975), 13.

2. de Campos, *Galáxias* (São Paulo, Editora Ex Libris, 1984).

3. Salvador de Madariaga, *Cuadro histórico de las Indias* (Buenos Aires: Ed. Sudamericana), 238.

4. W. Reyes Abadie and A. Vázquez Romero, *Crónica general del Uruguay. Vol I: "El nuevo mundo"* (Montevideo: Ediciones de la Banda Oriental), 245.

5. Salvador de Madariaga, Ibid., 949.

6. Ibid., 238.

7. Ibid., 237.

8. Ibid., 239.

9. Maurice Blanchot, *L'entretien infini* (Paris: Gallimard, 1969), 35.

10. Metz, "Le perçu et le nommé," *Essais sémiotiques* (Paris: Klincksieck, 1977), 132.

11. Borges, *Inquisiciones* (Buenos Aires: Proa, 1925), 160.

12. Gregory Ulmer, "The Puncept in Grammatology," in Jonathan Culler (ed.), *On Puns. The Foundation of Letters* (Nueva York: Blackwell, 1988), 164–189.

13. H. Parret, "Semiotica de la similitud ficcional," *Lienzo* 16 (Lima: Universidad de Lima, 1994).

14. Alain de Libera, *La querelle des universaux. De Platon à la fin du Moyen Âge* (Paris: Seuil, 1996), 25.

15. Eco, *Interprétation et surinterprétation* (Paris: PUF, 1996), 4.

16. "Writing is the destruction of every voice, of every origin. [. . .] the black and write wherein all identity comes to be lost, to begin with that very one of the body that writes." Barthes, "La mort de l'auteur," *Le bruissement de la langue. Essais critiques IV* (Paris: Seuil, 1984), 61.

17. Foucault, "What Is an Author?," *Bulletin de la Société Française de Philosophie* (Paris, 1969). I quote from the English translation published by Adams and Searle in *Critical Theory Since 1965* (Gainsville: University Press of Florida, 1986): "We find the link between writing and death manifested in the total effacement of individual characteristics of the writer [. . .] his link to death, which has transformed him into a victim of

his own disappearance. [. . .] Another thesis detained us from taking full measure of the author's disappearance. [. . .] This is the notion of *écriture*" (140).

18. It is not the first time I insist on this idea. After its death sentence had been pronounced, the author has more than once failed to resign itself to its own disappearance; its phantasm (a *revenant*) returns, continues to haunt us from the very writings of those who condemned it.

19. *Encyclopedia Universalis*: "mondialisation." Paul Valéry, *Regards sur le monde actuel* (Paris: Stock, Delamain et Boutelleau), 1931.

20. Borges, "El soborno," *El libro de arena. Obras Completas* (Buenos Aires: Emecé, 1989), 57–61, 61.

21. Immanuel Kant, *Critique of Judgement* (New York: Hafner Press, 1951), 13. "Of the critique of Judgement as a means of combining the two parts of philosophy into a whole."

22. Paul de Man, *The Resistance to Theory* (Minneapolis: University of Minnesota Press, 1986).

23. Jacques Derrida, Gianni Vattimo, *La religion* (Paris: Seuil, 1996), 21.

24. Giorgio Agamben, quoted in an epigraph by Michel Stanesco, "Du démon du midi à l'Éros mélancholique," *Poétique* 106 (1996): 131.

25. Vattimo, *Credere di credere* (Milan: Garzanti, 1996), 12.

26. Ibid., 43.

27. Ibid., 57.

28. Thomas A. Sebeok, *The Play of Musement* (Bloomington: Indiana University Press, 1981), 3.

29. Alfred J. MacAdam, "The Boom: A Retrospective," interview with Emir Rodríguez Monegal, *Review* 33 (Summer 1984): 30–36, 36.

30. English in the original, from "shooting" on.

31. ". . . for some mysterious reason" was in English in the original, as were the film title and MGM slogan [W.E.]. The original of the letter that Puig writes to Monegal from Buenos Aires, on February 6, 1969, figures among the copious correspondence conserved and classified in the Firestone Library of Manuscripts and Rare Books, of Princeton University.

32. Peter Greenaway, *Prospero's Books* (New York: Four Walls Eight Windows, 1991), 17.

33. *Jacques Derrida: Mémoirs d'aveugle*, video directed by Jean Paul Fargier, Paris, 1992.

34. Ernest Renan, *Caliban* (1878) and *L'Eau de Jouvence: Suite de Caliban* (1880), in *Drames philosophiques* (Paris: Calmann-Lévy Éditeurs, 1888). Paul Groussac gives a talk on May 2, 1898 (partially published in the daily *La Razón*, Montevideo, May 6, 1898). Rubén Dario writes a

review of that talk in the weekly, *El Tiempo* (Buenos Aires, May 20, 1898). José Enrique Rodó, *Ariel* (Montevideo: Dornaleche y Reyes, 1900); *El mirador de Próspero* in *Obras completas* (Madrid: Aguilar, 1967). Dominique O. Mannoni, *Prospero and Caliban: the Psychology of Colonization*, trans. Pamela Powesland (London: Metheun, 1956); Franz Fanon, *Peaux noires, masques blancs* (Paris: Editions du Seuil, 1952). Aimé Césaire, *Une tempête* (Paris: Editions du Seuil, 1969). Roberto Fernández Retamar, *Calibán* (Caracas: Rocinante, 1972). Emir Rodríguez Monegal, "Las metamorfosis de Calibán" (en revista Vuelta, III, No. 25, México, pp. 23–26, Dec. 1978). Richard Morse, *El espejo de Calibán* (México: Siglo XXI, 1982). Harold Bloom, *Caliban* (New York/Philadelphia, Chelsea House Publishers, 1992).

35. English in the original.

36. *Thea*: "action of looking, sight, spectacle, contemplation," is related to "*theoros*: spectator, oracle, religious spectacle, contemplation, abstract vision, and to "*thauma*: marvel, object of surprise or admiration."

37. Block de Behar, "La mirada del ángel: *After the Tempest*," in *Una palabra propriamente dicha* (Buenos Aires: Siglo XXI Editores, 1994).

38. William Shakespeare, "The Tempest," Act V, in *The Illustrated Stratford Shakespeare* (London: Chancellor Press, 1982), 28

39. J. Bessière, *Énigmaticité de la littérature* (Paris: PUF, 1993), 186.

40. English in the original. Sebeok, *The Play of Musement*, ibid., 2.

41. Gadamer, *La philosophie herméneutique* (Paris: PUF, 1996), 73; original may be found in Gadamer, "Vom Zirkel des Verstehens," *Gesammelte Werke*, 2, 57–65.

42.Friederich Daniel Ernest Schleiermacher, *Herméneutique. Pour une logique du discours individuel*, traduit de l'allemand par Christian Berner (Alençon: Les Éditions du Cerf/P.U.L., 1987).

43. Paz, *Árbol adentro* (Barcelona: Seix Barral, 1987), 13.

44. Interview with Octavio Paz in *Marca registrada*, Sergio Marras, Buenos Aires, 1992.

45. Meddeb, "Le palimpseste du bilingue," in Bennani, Boukous, Bounfour, Cheng, Formentelli, Hassoun, Khatibi, Kilito, Meddeb, and Todorov, *Du bilinguisme* (Paris: Éditions Denoël, 1985), 125–140.

7. THE IRONIES OF A BLIND SEER

1. Borges, *Obras completas* (Buenos Aires: Emecé, 1974), 1098.

2. Borges, *Inquisiciones* (Buenos Aires: Ediciones Proa, 1925).

3. Umberto Eco, "La abducción en Uqbar," en *Homenaje a J. L. Borges*, ed. Lisa Block de Behar, Montevideo, *Jaque* 9 (November 1984).

4. de Man, "A Modern Master" in *New York Review of Books*, 3:7 (November 19, 1964), 8–10.

5. de Man, *The Resistance to Theory* (Minneapolis: University of Minnesota Press, 1986).

6. de Man, *Critical Writings 1953–1978* (Minneapolis, University of Minnesota Press, 1989).

7. de Man, *The Resistance to Theory*, 120.

8. *Critical Writings*, 125.

9. Denis Donoghue, "The Strange Case of Paul de Man," *New York Review of Books*, 6/29/89.

10. Borges, *Obras completas*, 472–480.

11. Ibid., 479.

12. English in original.

13. de Man, *Blindness and Insight. Essays in the Rhetoric of Contemporary Criticism* (Minneapolis: University of Minnesota Press, 1983), 104.

14. Borges, *Obras completas*, 496–498.

15. Yeats, "Nineteen hundred and nineteen," *The Tower* in *The Collected Poems of W. B. Yeats*, edited by Richard J. Finneran (New York: MacMillan Publishing Company, 1989), 208. "So the Platonic year / Whirls out new right and wrong, / Whirls in the old instead; / All men are dancers and their tread / Goes to the barbarous clangour of a gong."

16. Borges, *Obras completas*, 496.

17. Ibid., 498.

18. I am referring to Oscar Wilde, with whom Borges shares, in addition to numerous narrative and poetic coincidences, epigrammatic formulations, ironies and paradoxes, substantial aesthetic convictions, common references, and the same address in Paris.

19. Borges, *Obras completas*, 497.

20. de Man, *Blindness and Insight*, 110.

21. Harold Bloom, *The Anxiety of Influence* (Oxford: Oxford University Press, 1966). The pathways continue to cross. Emir was the one responsible for this book being translated and published in Spanish (Caracas, Monte Ávila, 1972).

22. Borges, "Kafka y sus precursores," *Otras inquisiciones* (Buenos Aires: Emecé, 1952).

23. *Les mots et les choses* (Paris: Gallimard,1966), 1.

24. Borges, *Obras completas*, 706–709.

25. Jean Bessière, *Énigmaticité de la littérature. Pour une anatomie de la fiction au XXe siècle* (Paris: PUF, 1993).

26. Douglas R. Hofstadter and Daniel Dennet, *The Mind's I* (New York: Bantam Books, 1982).

27. Borges, "Góngora," *Los conjurados*, 83.

28. Borges, "Prólogo," *La rosa profunda* in *Obra poética 1923–1977* (Buenos Aires: Emecé, 1977), 413.

29. Borges, "G. A. Bürger," *Historia de la noche* in *Obra poética 1923–1977*, 535.

30. Willis Barnstone, *Borges at Eighty, Conversations* (Indiana University Press, 1982).

31. Barnstone, *Conversations avec J. L. Borges à l'occasion de son 80e anniversaire* (Paris: Éditions Ramsey, 1984).

32. Barnstone, Jorge Luis Borges, *Conversazione americane* (Roma: Editori Riuniti, 1984).

33. Borges, *Elogio de la sombra* in *Obras completas*, 1016.

34. Borges, *La rosa profunda* in *Obra poética 1923–1977*, 443.

35. "Insight" in English in the original.

36. Sebeok, *A Sign Is Just a Sign* (Bloomington: Indiana University Press, 1991), 152. Quotes Peirce, *Collected Papers*, 1935–1966: 5, 484.

37. Borges, *El informe de Brodie* in *Obras completas*, 1073–1078.

38. English in the original.

39. Borges, ibid., 1077.

40. Borges, Buenos Aires, 1921. Published in *Cosmópolis de Madrid*, and in Hugo J. Verani, *Las vanguardias literarias en Hispanoamérica. Manifiestos, proclamas y otros escritos* (Roma: Bulzoni Editore, 1986), 279–280.

41. Borges, *Obras completas*, 890.

42. Ibid., 890.

43. Borges, *Siete noches* (Argentina: Fondo de Cultura Económica, 1980), 153.

44. Borges, "An Autobiographical Essay," in *The Aleph and Other Stories, 1933–1969* (New York: Dutton, (1970), 250.

45. *Jacques Derrida: Mémoires d'aveugle*, videofilm directed by Jean Paul Fargier, Paris, 1992.

46. Jean Bessière, *Énigmaticité de la littérature*, XI.

47. Borges, "Prólogo," *La moneda de hierro* (Buenos Aires: Emecé, 1976), 10.

48. English in the original.

49. English in the original; Borges, *Obras completas*, 868.

50. English in the original.

51. Borges, *Obras completas*, 211.

52. Borges, *Obra poética*, 127, 274, 332.

53. Ibid., 425.

54. Borges, *Obras completas*, 737.

55. In Webster's Third International Dictionary, under the entry for "scot," is written: "Middle English Scottes (pl.). Scotchmen. Old English:

Scottas Irishmen, Scotchmen. Scotus-scottus-Irishmen. 1. One of a Gaelic people of Northern Ireland settling in Scottland about A.D. 500."

56. The evocation of Gilles Deleuze's *Difference and Repetition*, trans. Paul Patton (New York: Columbia University Press, 1994), is not without justification.

57. Borges, *Obras completas*, 499–507.

58. J. Hillis Miller worked on this transidiomatic synonym in "Red Scharlach, Hermeneutica," in *Diseminario. La desconstrucción, otro descubrimiento de América*, ed. Lisa Block de Behar (Montevideo: XYZ Editores, 1987), 163–173.

59. Joan Corominas, *Diccionario crítico etimológico castellano e hispano* (Madrid: Gredos, 1961), 321.

60. Borges, *La cifra* (Buenos Aires: Emecé, 1981), 79.

61. Block de Behar, talk given in Porto Alegre: "Jules Laforgue, una figura uruguaya," 6/4/88. Included in *Dos medios entre dos medios* (Buenos Aires: Siglo XXI, 1990), 62–82.

62. Jules Laforgue, "Complainte du pauvre-chevalier errant," *Les complaintes* (Paris: 1880), 119.

63. Borges, lecture, "La ceguera," *Siete Noches*, 143–160 .

64. Barnstone, *Borges at Eighty, Conversations*, 12.

65. Borges, *Obra poética*, 113.

66. Ibid., 353–354.

67. Ibid., 353.

68. Ibid., 353.

69. Ibid., 463.

70. Jacques Derrida, *Mémoires d'aveugle. L'autoportrait et autres ruines* (Paris: Éditions de la Réunion des musées nationaux, 1990), 18.

71. Borges, *Obra poética*, 200–202.

72. Scholem, *Major Trends in Jewish Mysticism* (Jerusalem: Schocken Publishing House, 1941).

73. Helmut Hatzfeld, *Estudios sobre el barroco* (Madrid: Gredos, 1973), 190.

74. Borges, "La Divina Comedia," *Siete Noches*, 9–32.

75. See *La Bible*, traduite et présentée par André Chouraqui (Desclée de Brouwer, 1989), 1225; and *La Bible, Ancien Testament*, II, introduction par Édouard Dhorme, traduction et notes para Édouard Dhorme, Jean Kœnig, Franck Michaéli, Jean Hadot et Antoine Guillaumont (Paris: Gallimard, 1959), 1202.

76. *The Holy Bible*, King James version (Chicago: Good Counsel Publishers, 1965), 483.

77. *La Santa Biblia, Antiguo y Nuevo Testamento*, antigua versión de Casiodoro de Reina, revisada por Cipriano de Valera y cotejada posteri-

ormente con diversas traducciones y con los textos hebreo y griego (Miami: Editorial Vida, 1981), 633.

78. On many occasions Borges has busied himself with the Golem. In "La vindicación de la Cabalá" (*Discusión*, 1931), in the prologue to *El otro, el mismo* (1958), in his poem "El golem" (ibid.), in his talk "La cabalá" (*Siete Noches*), he gives it a most important place in his memories in *An Autobiographical Essay* and, above all, he defines it minutely in his *Libro de los seres imaginarios*, above all relating it with *Der Golem* by Gustav Meyrink (1915), perhaps the first book he read in German. In "Guayaquil," a story from *El informe de Brodie*, the narrator tells this to Zimmerman.

79. Borges, *Obras completas*, 451–455.

80. Borges, *Obra poética*, 202.

81. Eco, "La abducción en Uqbar" in *De los espejos y otros ensayos* (Barcelona: Editorial Lumen, 1988).

82. Ibid.,178.

83. Quoted by Sebeok, *A Sign Is Just a Sign*, 19.

84. Borges, *La cifra*, 71.

85. Borges, *Obras completas*, 626.

86. Ibid., 623.

87. Borges, "Una mañana," *La rosa profunda*, in *Obra poética*, 439.

88. Sebeok, *A Sign Is Just a Sign*, 19

89. Borges, *Obra poética*, 201.

90. Borges, *La cifra*, 11.

91. Borges, *Siete noches*, 149.

92. Borges, "On His Blindness," *Los conjurados*, 59. The title is in English in the original.

93. Miguel de Cervantes Saavedra, *El ingenioso hidalgo don Quijote de la Mancha*, edición y notas de Francisco Rodríguez Marín (Madrid: Ediciones La Lectura, 1911)

94. Borges, *Obra poética*, 201.

95. "Signos," *Moneda de hierro*, ibid., 500.

96. Ibid., 500.

97. Borges, *Obra poética*, 459. The title is in English in the original.

98. Ibid., 459.

99. Ibid., 167.

8. SYMBOLS AND THE SEARCH FOR UNITY

1. This text corresponds to a presentation given at University of California Berkeley, in the plenary session of the Fifth Congress of the

IASS/AISS (June 12, 1994): "Semiotics around the World: Synthesis in Diversity."

2. Michel Serres (*La légende des anges*, Paris: Flammarion, 1993), Massimo Cacciari (*L'angelo neccesario*, Milano: Adelphi Edizioni, 1986), and others.

3. Wim Wenders and Jean-Luc Godard follow a path not too different from a century that did not skimp on them cinematographically: Josef von Sternberg, Luis Buñuel, of various angels, both colorful and exterminating.

4. Peirce, "*Frasier's*. The Works of George Berkeley," in *Writings of Charles S. Peirce. A Chronological Edition, vol. 2, 1867–1871* (Bloomington: Indiana University Press, 1984), 465.

5. Borges quotes Berkeley in "Nueva refutación del tiempo. B," in *Otras inquisiciones* in *Obras completas* (Buenos Aires: Emecé, 1974), 766.

6. *Diaballein* is composed of *dia*, "through," and *ballein*, from *ballo*, throw, shoot, hit, fall, or drop.

7. "'The first comprises all mere Ideas, those airy nothings to which the mind of the poet, pure mathematician, or another *might* give local habitation and a name within that mind' . . . The second Universe is 'that of the Brute Actuality of things and facts'" (quoted by Sebeok in *The Play of Musement* [Bloomington: Indiana University Press, 1981]), 2.

8. The normal use of the Spanish word is that of "meeting" [W.E.].

9. Quoted by Idel, *Kabbalah. New Perspectives*, 137.

10. Jean Baudrillard, *La guerre du Golfe n'a pas eu lieu* (Paris: Galilée, 1993).

11. English in the original.

12. Roger Penrose, *The Emperor's New Mind. Concerning Computers, Minds and Laws of Physics* (New York: Penguin Books, 1991), 329.

13. André Breton, *Anthologie de l'humour noir* (Paris: J. J. Pauvert, 1966), 222.

14. "Congressus 'action of meeting' from which 'sexual union,' derived from Lat. *congredi* 'to meet,' from *cum*-(co) and *gradi* (walk). The word was introduced to the meaning 'sexual union,' proper to the XVI and XVII centuries and at the origin of ancient juridical specialization of 'the legal proof destined to establish the impotence of a husband (with the testimony of a matron or wise woman), case invoked to annul a marriage" (Alain Rey, *Le Robert. Dictionnaire historique de la langue française* (Paris, 1992).

15. Peirce, "Lowell Lecture XI, 1866," *Writings of Charles S. Peirce. A Chronological Edition, vol. 1, 1857–1866* (Bloomington: Indiana University Press, 1982), 495.

16. Sebeok, *Contributions to the Doctrine of Signs* (Lanham: University Press of America, 1985), 134–135.

17. John Barth, *The Friday Book. Essays and Other Nonfiction* (New York: Perigee Books/Putnam, 1984).

18. Peirce, "Lowell Lecture XI, 1866," 502–503.

19. Peirce, "Design and Chance," 222.

20. "Chance came from the evolution of the Latin *cadere* 'fall' - (*choir*) taken as feminine, properly 'action of falling,' especially used in Latin in the game of knucklebones" (Alain Rey, ibid.).

21. Borges, "El ingenuo," in *Obra poética* (Buenos Aires: Emecé, 1977), 480.

22. Borges, "El informe de Brodie," *Obras completas*, 1077.

23. In the initial paragraph, the narrator, before transcribing and translating Brodie's report, notes that he will omit some verse of the Bible and a "curious passage about the sexual practices of the Yahoos that the good Presbyterian confined to Latin." Ibid.

24. English in the original.

25. Quote from Peirce, in "Introduction" to Nathan Houser, Christian Kloesel, *The Essential Peirce. Selected Philosophical Writings*, xxii.

26. *The Dialogues of Plato,* trans R. E. Allen (New Haven: Yale University Press, 1991), II, 190 a, 130.

27. Ibid., 190 d, 131.

28. Ibid. 191 e, 132.

29. I take the title from Peirce's review of Royce's *Religious Aspects of Philosophy* (1885), in N. Houser and Charles Kloesel, ibid.

30. Peirce, "Lowell Lecture XI, 1866," 494.

31. Borges, *Obras completas*, III, 31.

32. Borges, *Obras completas*, 522–524.

33. Roland Barthes, *Le plaisir du texte* (Paris, 1973).

34. 1 Genesis 4.1: "The man knew Eve, his wife . . ." The note clarifies that "The verb *yâdá*, 'to know,' is regularly used to signify sexual relations, speaking as much of man as of woman. [. . .] The same expression as in other Semitic languages, with the verbs meaning 'to know.' The initiation to an act covered in mystery seems to us the origin of this use of the verb 'to know.'" *La Bible. Ancient Testament,* trans. and notes by Édouard Dhorme (Paris: Gallimard, 1956).

35. Gershom Scholem, *La kabbale et sa symbolique* (Paris: Payot, 1975), 130.

36. Shakespeare, "The Tempest," in *The Illustrated Stratford Shakespeare* (London: Chancellor Press, 1982), Act I, Scene II, 10.

37. *Dialogues*, 193 a, 133–134.

38. Platon, "Le Banquet," *Oeuvres complètes* (Paris: Les Belles Lettres, 1929), IV, 191d, 33–34.

39. *Dupin, Holmes, Peirce. The Sign of Three* (Bloomington: Indiana University Press, 1983), preface.

40. Quoted by Sebeok in "One, Two Three, Spell UBERTY. (In lieu of an introduction)," ibid., 3.

41. Peirce, "A Guess at the Riddle," in Houser and Kloesel, ibid., 255.

42. Paz, *Árbol adentro* (Barcelona: Editorial Seix Barral, 1987), 34.

43. Umberto Eco, *La ricerca della lingua perfetta* (Roma-Bari: Editore Laterza, 1993), 6.

44. Borges, *Obras completas*, III, 28.

45. Douglas R. Hofstadter, *Metamagical Themas. Questing for the Essence of Mind and Pattern. An Interlocked Collection of Literary, Scientific, and Artistic Studies* (New York: Bantam Books, 1986).

46. Ibid. He comments on David Knuth´s article on pages 260 to 295.

47. Ibid., 272.

48. Ibid., 264. He is alluding to Scott Kim´s book *Inversions* (Peterborough, N.H.: Byte Books, 1981), "in which a single written specimen, or 'gram,' has more than one reading, depending on the observer's point of view." 274.

49. Ibid., 279.

50. Ibid., 279.

51. Ibid., 264.

52. Ibid., 261.

53. At the Xth Congress of the Association of Academies of the Spanish Language, Madrid, May 24–28, two letters of the Spanish alphabet were eliminated and there were rumors of a third elimination.

54. Eco, *La ricerca della lingua perfetta*, 358.

55. Borges, *Obras completas*, III, 31.

56. Ibid., 31.

57. Eco, *La ricerca della lingua perfetta*, 90.

58. Peirce, "Lowell Lecture XI, 1866," 503. "In many respects, this trinity agrees with the Christian trinity: indeed I am not aware that there are many points of disagreement. The interpretant is evidently the Divine Logos or word; and if our former guess that a Reference to an interpretant is Paternity be right, this would also be the *Son of God*. The *ground*, being that partaking of which is requisite to any communication with the Symbol, corresponds in its function to the Holy Spirit." Ibid.

59. Stéphane Mallarmé, "Un coup de dés jamais n'abolira le hasard. Poéme" in *Œuvres complètes*. Édition établie et anotée par Henri Mondor et G. Jean-Aubry (Paris: Gallimard, 1945), 457–477.

60. In Hebrew, earth is *Adama*, red is *Adom*, and blood is *Dam*.

61. Jules Laforgue, "Complainte du pauvre-chevalier errant," *Les complaintes* (Paris: 1880), 118–120, 119.

62. *Continente*, both continent and container. This is one of the philosophical definitions of space: the container where materials objects come together.

63. Sebeok, *Semiotics in the United States* (Bloomington: Indiana University Press, 1991), 1.

9. THE PARADOXES OF PARADOXES

1. Borges, *Libro de prólogos. Con un prólogo de prólogos* (Buenos Aires: Torres Agüero Editor, 1975), 7–9.

2. Borges, "El escritor Argentino y la tradición," *Discusión* in *Obras completas* (Buenos Aires: Emecé, 1974), 270.

3. A valid antecedent to this affinity would be the doctrine of *cassatio*. According to Nicholas Falleta, the scholastics were the first to develop completely the doctrine of the *cassatio* and to examine attentively such utterances as "I am not speaking" or "I am silent." Nicholas Falleta, *Le livre des paradoxes*, trans. J. F. Hamel (Paris: Belfond, 1985), 140.

4. Jean Hyppolite, *Hegel. Préface à la phénoménologie de l'esprit* (Paris: Gallimard 1966), 54.

5. Block de Behar, *Una retórica del silencio* (México: Siglo XXI Editores, 1984), 97.

6. Borges, "Poema de los dones," *El hacedor* in *Obra poética* (Buenos Aires: Emecé Editores 1977), 113.

7. "Let others boast of the pages they have written; / what makes me proud are the one I have read." Borges, "Un lector," *Elogio de la sombra* in *Obra poética* , 353.

8. Haroldo de Campos, "Leitura de Novalis/1977," in *Transideraciones/Transiderações*, recopilación y traducción de Eduardo Milán y Manuel Ulacia (México: Ediciones El Tucán de Virginia, 1987), 76.

9. Borges, "La ceguera," in *Siete noches* (Argentina: Fondo de Cultura Económica, 1980), 153.

10. Octavio Paz, "Decir: Hacer," *Árbol adentro* (Barcelona: Editorial Seix Barral, 1987), 12.

11. Hartman, *Saving the Text* (Baltimore: Johns Hopkins University Press, 1982), 111. "The subject can also appear as being the slave of language, as if it were in addition part of the discourse of a universal movement, in which place would already appear inscribed when it was born, as if it were only by virtue of its proper name." Ibid.

12. Barthes, *Les critiques de notre temps et Proust* (Paris: Éditions Garnier, 1971), 160.

13. "Between what I see and say, / between what I say and do not say, / between what I do not say and dream, / between what I dream and forget, / poetry. It slips / between the yes and the no." Paz, *Árbol adentro*, 11.

14. *Sir Francis Drake and the Age of Discovery*, documents exhibited at the Pierpoint Morgan Library, New York, January to May 1998.

15. *Magazine Littéraire*, 259 (Paris, November, 1988).

16. Pierre Fontanier, *Les figures du discours* (Paris: Flammarion, 1968), 137.

17. Block de Behar, "Paradoxa Ortodoxa," chapter 3 in this volume.

18. Derrida, "La pharmacie de Platon," in *La Dissémination* (Paris: Seuil, 1972), 182.

19. Alain Robbe-Grillet's title for his film based on two of Borges's stories (Paris, 1968).

20. Borges, "Tlön, Uqbar, Orbis Tertius," *Ficciones*, in *Obras completas*, 436.

21. Borges, "La parábola del palacio," in *Obras completas*, 801.

22. Borges, *Obras completas*, 351–423.

23. Ibid., 856–949.

24. Derrida, *Schibboleth, pour Paul Celan* (Paris: Galilée, 1986), 45.

25. Borges, "Tema del traidor y del héroe," in *Obras completas*, 498.

26. Borges, *Obras completas*, 491–495.

27. "Your mind must leap from a third-person perspective—'he' or 'she'—to a first person perspective—'I.' Comedians have long known how to exaggerate this leap . . . To see ourselves as others see us. . . . This dramatic shift is a discovery." Douglas R, Hofstadter and Daniel C. Dennett, *The Mind's I. Fantasies and Reflections on Self and Soul* (New York: Bantam Books, 1988), 20–21. The text with which the book begins is "Borges and I." It would have been interesting to observe that dramatic chance—in the strong sense of the term, as well—on the basis of the story we are analyzing here.

28. Derrida, *La Dissémination*, 120.

29. Borges, *Obras completas*, 496–498.

30. Ibid., 514–518.

31. Ibid., 550–556.

32. Ibid., 556.

33. Bloom, *A Map of Misreading* (New York: Oxford University Press, 1980), 3.

34. Peirce, *Collected Papers* (Cambridge: Harvard University Press, 1931–1958), 332.

35. Umberto Eco, *Semiotics and the Philosophy of Language* (Bloomington: Indiana University Press, 1984), 26.

36. Rosalie Colie, *Paradoxia Epidemica. The Renaissance Tradition of Paradox* (Princeton: Princeton University Press, 1976), 517–518.

37. Borges, *Obras completas*, 508–513.

38. Ibid., 508.

39. Heraclitus, fragment 70, quoted in Abel Jeannière, *Héraclite*, traduction et commentaire des *Fragments* (Paris: Aubier, 1985), 114.

40. Borges, "De las alegorías a las novelas" and "El ruiseñor de Keats," *Otras inquisiciones* in *Obras completas*, 718 and 745.

41. I here adopt both literary notions of the two famous essays of John Barth that appear, respectively, under those titles in *The Friday Book* (New York: Perigee Book/Putnam, 1984), 62–76 and 193–206.

42. Derrida, "'Psyche' o la invención del otro," in *Diseminario. La deconstrucción, otro descubrimiento de América*, ed. Lisa Block de Behar (Montevideo: XYZ Editores, 1987), 49–106, 57.

43. Borges, "Tema del traidor y del héroe," in *Obras completas*, 496. Borges combines the disjunctive gesture (an excluding alternative) with equivalence (a copulative union).

44. Although Borges does not explicitly consider this semantic and numeric aspect of the term, he titles one of his last collections of poems *The Cipher* (*La cifra*, Buenos Aires: Emecé Editores, 1981).

45. Heraclitus, fragment 51, quoted in Abel Jeannière, *Héraclite*, 111.

46. Borges, in *Ficciones*, in *Obras completas*, 485–490.

47. Borges, *Obra poética*, 353–354.

48. Ibid., 353.

49. Borges, *Obras completas*, 488.

50. Ibid., 490.

51. Ibid., 490.

52. Ibid., 718.

53. Martin Heidegger, *Phénoménologie de l'esprit de Hegel*, sec. II, trans. Francoise d'Emmanuel Martineau (Paris: Gallimard, 1984), 112.

54. Octavio Paz, *Árbol adentro*, 179.

55. Borges, *Obras completas*, 801–802.

56. The Venerable Bede (672–735) recounts in his *Ecclesiastical History* the double poetic revelation that illuminated Caedmon, an illiterate shepherd who receives in a dream his first poem and his poetic vocation at the same time. Both, poem and poet, are begun by "The Beginning of the Created Things." *Ecclesiastical History of the English People*, trans. Leo Sherley-Price (London: Penguin, 1955).

57. Borges, *Obras completas*, 802.

58. Borges, "Utopía de un hombre que está cansado," in *Obras completas*, III, 53.

59. Borges, *La cifra*, 12.

60. Lyotard, *Le différend* (Paris: Les Éditions de Minuit, 1983), 29.

61. "One day, a crocodile trapped a baby who was playing by the back of the Nile. The mother begged the animal to return to her child. — So be it, said the crocodile. If you guess exactly what I am going to do, I will give you the child. But, if you are wrong, I will eat it. —You are going to eat it! —screamed the mother. —I cannot give it to you. Because if I give it to you, you would have been wrong and I had already warned you that in that case your child would be eaten. —On the contrary! You cannot eat it because if you do so, I would have said the truth and you had promised me that, in that case, you would return him to me. And I know you are an honorable crocodile, respectful of the given word. —Who is right? What will happen?" Falleta, *Livre des paradoxes*, 149.

62. Lyotard, *Le différend* , 24.

63. Ibid., 18.

64. This is an expression from Georges Braque. Jean Beaufret quotes it in his prologue to *Le poème* by Parmenides (Paris: PUF, 1955), 10.

65. English in the original.

66. English in the original.

67. Lyotard, *Heidegger et "les juifs"* (Paris: Galilée, 1988), 50.

68. Borges, *Obra poética*, 353.

69. Lévinas, *Hors sujet* (Paris: Fata Morgana, 1987), 11.

70. Borges, "Parábola del palacio," *Obras completas*, 802.

71. Borges, *Obras completas*, III, 48–51.

72. Borges attributed to Adam de Bremen the description of a town called Urnos.

73. Ibid., 51.

74. This is the meaning of the Spanish verb *meldar*: "To study," "to teach," "to read Hebrew." Joan Corominas and José A. Pascual, *Diccionario crítico etimológico castellano e hispano* (Madrid: Gredos, 1985). *Webster's Third New International Dictionary, Unabridged* gives for "to meld," "to show or announce (a card or combinations of cards . . .)."

10. *VOX IN DESERTO*

1. Borges, "Las mil y una noches," in *Siete noches* (México: Fondo de Cultura Económica, 1980), 58.

2. If we attend to the meaning of fall that is designated by both *Untergang* (decline) and *Abendland* (Occident), the title of the book by

Oswald Spengler duplicates the crepuscular condition. Oswald Spengler, *Der Untergang des Abendlandes; Umrisse einer Morphologie der Weltgeschichte* (Munich: Beck, 1922).

3. Borges, "Las mil y una noches," 67. Those of us born in Uruguay—whose official denomination is "The Oriental Republic of Uruguay," because the country is located, seen from Argentina, to the east of the Uruguay river—are "Orientals." Borges himself, born in Buenos Aires, identified himself as "Oriental" because of having been conceived in the hacienda of the Haedos, in Rio Negro, a province of Uruguay.

4. I am thankful to Salvio Martínez and Jorge Panesi for the information about the manuscript of the story "The Aleph," which Borges had dedicated to Estela Canto, where in place of *aleph* appears *mirhab*, crossed out in all cases.

5. It is the only specific entry that the CD-Rom of the *Encyclopedia Universalis* presents in its extensive reference for "Geography."

6. A homofrancophonic coincidence (*voix*) that I owe to Alfons Knauth, although he refers it to the sea and not the desert. In "Transport poétique par voix maritime. Laforgue entre l'Amérique et l'Europe," in *Lautréamont et Laforgue. La cuestión de los orígenes / La quête des origines* (Montevideo: Academia Nacional de Letras/Embajada de Francia en el Uruguay, 1993), 21–39.

7. Isaias, 40:3, *The Holy Bible*, containing the Old and New Testaments in the authorized King James version (Chicago: Good Counsel Pulishers, 1965), 540.

8. Deuteronomy, ibid., 145.

9. Borges, *Obras completas* (Buenos Aires: Emecé Editores, 1974), 550–556.

10. Ibid., 550.

11. This text appeared under the title "Three Forms of the Eternal Return," in *La Nación* of Buenos Aires, 12/14/1041. The story "The Theologians" was published in 1947 in *Anales de Nuevos Aires*.

12. English in the original.

13. Borges, *Obras completas*, 395.

14. Ibid., 397–413.

15. Louis-Auguste Blanqui, *L'éternité par les astres. Hypothèse astronomique*, ed. L. B. de Behar. (Genève: Fleuron-Slatkine, 1996).

16. Block de Behar, "Conjonctions et conjectures à la limite des mondes parallèles. Une lecture de L.-A. Blanqui," *Pleine Marge* 25 (Paris, 1995).

17. Borges, "El tiempo circular," *Historia de la eternidad,* in *Obras completas*, 393.

18. Borges, "Las mil y una noches," 57.

19. Borges, *Obras completas*, III, 10–73.

20. Ibid., 69.

21. Ibid., 69.

22. Borges, "Otra versión de Proteo," in *Obra poética* (Buenos Aires: Emecé Editores, 1977), 438.

23. Borges, *Atlas*, with colaboration by María Kodama (Buenos Aires: Editorial Sudamericana 1984), 82.

24. Borges, *Obras completas*, 1090.

25. Borges, *Obra poética*, 429.

26. Borges, *Ibid.*, 429.

27. Borges, *La cifra* (Buenos Aires: Emecé Editores, 1981), 85.

28. Borges, *Obras completas*, III, 70.

29. Borges, *Obra poética*, 512.

30. Ibid., 512.

31. This is the definition of the verb *descabalar* given by the *Diccionario de la Real Academia Española*.

32. Borges, *Obras completas*, 525.

33. Ibid., 529.

34. Borges, *Obras completas*, III, 69.

35. Borges, "Las mil y una noches," 61.

36. Ibid., 61.

37. Ibid., 73.

38. Ibid., 63.

39. Borges, "Al coyote," in *Obra poética*, 408.

40. "Désert." Alain Rey, *Le Robert: Dictionnaire historique de la langue française* (Paris: Dictionnaires Le Robert, 1992).

41. Abdelwahab Meddeb, letter to the author of August 28, 1997.

42. Borges, "Las mil y una noches," 64.

43. Borges, "El tiempo y J. W. Dunne," in *Obras completas*, 648.

44. Borges, "El reloj de arena," in ibid., 811.

45. Borges, "Time and the Conways, de J. B. Priestly" (journal *El Hogar*, 10/15/1937), reimpreso in *Textos cautivos. Ensayos y reseñas en "El Hogar" (1936–1939)*, ed. Enrique Sacerio-Garí and Emir Rodríguez Monegal (Buenos Aires: Tusquets Editores, 1986) and in *Obras completas*, IV (Buenos Aires: Emecé Editores, 1996), 324.

11. THE MYSTERY OF THE NAME

1. Borges, "Pierre Menard, autor del Quijote," in *Obras completas* (Buenos Aires: Emecé Editores, 1974), 449–450.

2. Borges, "El Golem," 200.

3. Ibid., 201.

4. Borges, *Obras completas*, 436.

5. Ibid., 436.

6. Ibid., 436.

7. Ibid., 436.

8. Franz Kafka, *Amerika: Roman* (Frankfurt am Main: Fischer, 1956).

9. Borges, *Obras completas*, III (Buenos Aires: Emecé Editores, 1989), 48–51.

10. Borges, *Obras completas*, 757–771.

11. Borges, *Obra poética*, 415.

12. Ibid., 381–382.

13. Ibid., 214.

14. Borges, "De alguien a nadie," *Obras completas*, 737–739.

15. Fernando Pessoa, *Sur les hétéronymes*, trans. Rémy Hourcade (Trans-en-Provence : Éditions Unes, 1985), 22.

16. "There is no human being capable of saying [with certitude] what he is. No one knows what he has come to this world to do, to what correspond his acts, his sentiments, his thoughts; [who are the closest to him among men], nor what his true name is, his imperishable Name in the register of light. [Emperor or docker, no one known his burden or his crown.] History is like an immense liturgical text in which the iotas and the points are worth the same as entire verses or chapters, but the importance of the one or the other is indeterminable or profoundly hidden" (I transcribe the quote extracted from *L'âme de Napoléon*, as it figures in the "Notes et variantes," established by Jean Pierre Bernès for the French edition, Borges, *Œuvres complètes*, I (Paris: Gallimard, 1993), 1693.

17. Borges, *Obras completas*, 722.

18. Ibid., 716.

19. Ibid., 720–722.

20. Ibid., 722.

21. Borges, *Obra poética*, 151.

22. Ibid., 127.

23. Charles Baudelaire, "Les phares," in *Œuvres complètes*, texte établi, présenté et annoté par Claude Pichois (Paris: Gallimard, 1975), 13.

24. Borges, *Obra completas*, 789.

25. Borges, *Obra poética*, 128.

26. Ibid., 127.

27. Ibid., 127.

28. Ibid., 266.

29. Borges, *Obras completas*, 802.

30. Ibid., 802.

31. Ibid., 708.

32. Borges, *Obras completas*, III, 50.

33. Ibid., 51.

12. THE IMAGINATION OF KNOWLEDGE

1. Rodríguez Monegal, *Jorge Luis Borges. A Literary Biography* (New York: E. P. Dutton, 1978), 137.

2. "Gustav Meyrink," *Revista El Hogar* (April 29, 1938). Reedited in *Textos cautivos. Ensayos y reseñas en "El Hogar" (1936–1939)*, eds. Enrique Sacerio-Garí and Emir Rodríguez Monegal (Buenos Aires: Tusquets Editores, 1986), 230–231.

3. Prologue to Gustave Meyrink, *El Golem*, 1985. Reprinted in *Biblioteca personal. Prólogos. Obras completas*, IV (Buenos Aires: Emecé Editores, 1996), 492.

4. Rodríguez Monegal, *Jorge Luis Borges. A Literary Biography* , 136.

5. María Esther Vázquez, "Cronología," in *Borges. Sus días y su tiempo* (Buenos Aires: Javier Vergara, 1984), 328.

6. Horacio Salas, *Borges. Una biografía* (Buenos Aires: Planeta, 1994), 69.

7. Borges, in Vázquez, *Borges. Sus días y su tiempo*, 143.

8. He mentions (in Vázquez, ibid., 143) the "work of the German Jew Martin Buber, *History of Hassidim.*"

9. I recall in passing that it was Umberto Eco who founded an Italian journal "on line" under this name, coedited with Gianni Riotta, director of *La Stampa* in Turin.

10. *The Holy Bible, New International Version* (Colorado Springs, CO: International Bible Society, 1973), 26; http://www.gospelcom.net/ibs/bibles/use.html.

11. Christiane Chauviré, *Ludwig Wittgenstein* (Paris: Éditions du Seuil, 1989), 234.

12. Miguel de Cervantes Saavedra, *El Ingenioso Hidalgo Don Quijote de la Mancha*, 9 vols, ed., Francisco Rodríguez Marín (Madrid: Ediciones "La Lectura," 1911).

13. "Pierre Menard, autor del Quijote," in *Obras completas* (Buenos Aires: Emecé Editores, 1989), I, 444–450.

14. Arthur Conan Doyle *The Valley of Fear* (1915), *The Penguin Complete Sherlock Holmes* (England: Penguin Books, 1981), 802.

15. Jacques Rancière, *Les noms de l'histoire. Essai de poétique du savoir* (Paris: Éditions du Seuil, 1992), 98.

16. Thomas A. Sebeok, *A Sign Is Just a Sign* (Bloomington: Indiana University Press, 1991), 20.

17. From Lat. *eliminare*, "faire sortir, mettre dehors," of *ex-limen*, *liminis*, "seuil." (. . .) 1777; "[the term] is resurrected in algebra in the sense of 'to make disappear' (one or more unknowns) of a group of equations such as to obtain one equations with only one unknown. Alain Rey, *Dictionnaire historique de la langue française* (Paris: Le Robert, 1992), 673.

18. Arthur Conan Doyle, *The Sign of Four* (1890), *The Penguin Complete Sherlock Holmes* (England: Penguin Books, 1981), 111.

19. Rancière, *Les noms de l'histoire*, 22.

20. *Idea*—from Gr. v. *idein*, aorist of *horan* = to see.

21. Robert Hewison, *John Ruskin. The Argument of the Eye* (Princeton: Princeton University Press, 1976), 57.

22. Plato, *Kratylos. Crátilo. Diálogos*, trans., foreword and notes by J. L. Calvo (Madrid: Editorial Gredos, 1983), II, 365.

23. Buenos Aires, October 1985.

24. "El Golem," in Borges, *Obras completas*, II, 263–265.

25. "Pierre Menard," in Borges, *Obras completas*, 449–450.

26. "La supersticiosa ética del lector" (1932), *Discusión, Obras completas*, I, 202–205, "Parábola del palacio" (1960), *El hacedor, Obras completas*, II; 179–180; "Del rigor en las ciencias" (1960), *El hacedor, Obras completas*, 225.

27. Stéphane Mallarmé, "Le démon de l'analogie" (1874), in *Oeuvres complètes*, eds. Henri Mondor et G. Jean-Aubry (Paris: Gallimard, 1945), 272–273.

28. 1 Cor., 13, 8–10.

29. Quoted in Philippe Lacoue-Labarthe, *La poésie comme expérience* (Paris: Christian Bourgois, 1986), 54.

13. THE PLACE OF THE LIBRARY

1. Borges, *Obras completas* (Buenos Aires: Emecé, 1974), 465–471.

2. Ibid., 270.

3. Ibid., 479.

4. This text corresponds to an address given at the *Biblioteque nationale* on December 4, 1999.

5. *L'univers de Borges* (Paris: BPI/Éditions du Centre Pompidou, 1992).

6. I prefer to remit the term to the French "Pan," where it signifies a fragment, recalling, however, at the same time, that in Greek it alludes to the totality that the prefix pan- continues to signify.

7. *Obras completas,* 465.

8. Borges en *SUR.* 1931–1980, eds. Sara Luisa del Carril and Mercedes Rubio de Socchi (Buenos Aires: Emecé, 1999), 24–27.

9. Hannah Arendt, "Walter Benjamin": "Le pêcheur de perles," *Vies politiques* (Paris: Gallimard, 1974), 292.

10. Borges, "Utopía de un hombre que está cansado," *El libro de arena,* in *Obras completas,* III (Buenos Aires: Emecé, 1989), 55.

11. *Obras completas,* 479.

12. "The concept—the organon of thinking, and yet the wall between thinking and the thought—negates that yearning. Philosophy can neither circumvent such negation nor submit to it. It must strive, by way of the concept, to transcend the concept." Theodor W. Adorno, *Negative Dialectics,* trans. E. B. Ashton (New York: Continuum, 1983), 15.

13. *Obras completas,* 801–802.

14. Ibid., 847.

15. Ibid., 801.

16. Ibid., 779–854.

17. Ibid., 472–480.

18. Ibid., 479.

19. Ibid., 475.

20. Borges, "Poema de los dones," in *Obra Poética* (Buenos Aires: Emecé, 1977), 114.

21. Henri Atlan, "Niveaux de significations et athéisme de l'écriture," in *La Bible au présent, donées et debats. Actes du XXIIè colloque des intellectuels juifs de langue française* (Paris: Gallimard, 1982), 69.

22. Borges, *Obras completas,* 479.

23. The French phrase alludes to responses that are as astute as they are ambiguous.

24. Walter Benjamin, "Theses on the Philosophy of History," in *Illuminations,* trans. Harry Zohn (New York: Schocken Books, 1969), 260; translation modified.

25. Louis-Auguste Blanqui, *L'éternité par les astres: hypothèse astronomique* (Paris/Gèneve: Édition Slatkine, 1996).

26. Borges, *Obras completas,* 394.

27. The narrator is referring to Theodor Wolff, *Der Wettlauf mit der schildkröte; gelöste und ungelöste probleme* (Berlin: A. Scherl g.m.b.h., 1929), which he mentions in the same story. *Borges en SUR. 1931–1980,* 24.

28. Borges, *Obras completas,* 479.

29. Borges, with Norman Thomas Di Giovanni, "An Autobiographical Essay," in *The Aleph and Other Stories,* 1933–1969 (New York: Dutton, 1970), 203–260.

30. Borges, *Obras completas,* 479.

31. Lisa Block de Behar, *Borges ou les gestes d'un voyant aveugle* (Paris: Champion, 1998).

32. Blanqui, *L'éternité par les astres*, 148.

33. Ibid., 152.

34. *Borges en SUR*, 227–228.

35. *El tamaño de mi esperanza* (Buenos Aires: Proa, 1926).

36. Lugones, *El tamaño del espacio. Ensayo de psicología matemática* (Buenos Aires: El Ateneo, 1921).

37. *Obras completas*, 468.

38. Ibid., 470.

39. Ibid., 470.

40. *Borges en SUR*, 26.

41. *Obra poética*, 133.

42. *Obras completas*, 638.

43. Ibid., 55.

44. Ibid., 461–464.

45. Ibid., 465–471.

46. *Borges en SUR*, 26–27.

47. Laforgue, *Moralités légendaires, Oeuvres complètes, III* (Genève: Slatkine Reprints, 1979), 191.

48. Ibid., 204.

49. *Obras completas*, 465.

50. Ibid., 468.

51. Ibid., 469.

52. In Ph. O. Runge, *Écrits posthumes*, 1810, quoted in Alexander Roob, *Alquimia y mística: el museo hermético* (Köln: Taschen, 1997), 686.

53. *Obras completas*, 466.

54. Ibid., 636.

55. Blaise Pascal, *Pensées*, texte établi par Louis Lafuma (Paris: Garnier-Flammarion, 1973), fragment 392, 145.

56. Ibid., fragment 394, 145.

57. Borges, *Obras completas*, 638.

58. Blanqui, 37.

59. Laforgue, "La lune est stérile," *Imitation de Notre-Dame-la-Lune, Oeuvres complètes, I* (Genève: Slatkine Reprints, 1979), 259.

60. Borges, *Oeuvres complètes, I* édition établie, présenteee et annotée par J.-P. Bernès (Paris: Gallimard, YEAR), 1578.

61. Borges, *Obras completas*, 461.

62. Ibid., 465.

63. Borges, ibid., 270. *El paseo Colón* becomes "la rue de Toulon"; *las quintas de Adrogué* becomes "Triste-le-roy."

64. Ibid., 496–498.

65. Ibid., 496.

66. Ibid., 568.

67. Borges, *Atlas*, with the collaboration of María Kodoma (Buenos Aires: Editorial Sudamericana, 1984).

68. Borges, Obras completas, 347–423.

69. Ibid., 289–345.

70. Ibid., 468.

71. Ibid., 465.

72. Ibid.

73. Ibid., 468.

74. Octavio Paz, *Los hijos del limo. Del romanticismo a la vanguardia* (Barcelona: Editorial Seix Barral, 1974), 17.

75. That natural talent that some people have thanks to which they come upon interesting and valuable things by chance. The word was created by Horace Walpole who, in a letter of January 1, 1754, addressed to Horace Mann, claimed to have invented the term on the basis of a fairy tale, "The Three Princesses of Serendip." (Serendip is the old name of Ceylan, or Sri Lanka.)

76. Aristotle, *On Rhetoric*, trans. George A. Kennedy (New York: Oxford University Press, 1991), book 1.

77. Borges, *Obras completas*, 470.

78. Ibid., 466.

79. Ibid., 467.

80. Ibid., 633–635.

81. Ibid., 617–628.

82. Ibid., 623.

83. Ibid.

84. Alexandre Papadopoulo. *Le Mihrâb dans l'architecture et la religion musulmanes*, Actes du Colloque International, Paris, May 1980 (Leiden: E. J. Brill, 1988), 49.

85. Ibid., 18.

86. Borges, "Las mil y una noches," in *Siete noches* (México: Fondo de cultura Económica, 1980), 58.

Index